Date Due

APR 2 9 1988	OCT 2 1 1998
APR 1 9 1988	OCT 1 9 1998
MAR 3 1 1993	
MAR 2 2 1993	NOV 2 2 2000
JUL 1 4 1993	NOV 1 3 2000
JUL 2 2 1993	SEP 1 9 2002
AUG 1 9 1994	SEP 0 6 2002
AUG 0 8 1994	NOV 1 5 2002
OCT 2 7 1994	NOV 1 4 2002
OCT 1 9 1994	
OCT 2 1994	OCT 0 1 2004
FEB 2 0 1995	OCT 0 1 2004
FEB 2 4 1995	

Job Evaluation

Wage and Salary Administration

Douglas L. Bartley
Pan American University

ADDISON-WESLEY PUBLISHING COMPANY
Reading, Massachusetts • Menlo Park, California
London • Amsterdam • Don Mills, Ontario • Sydney

Library of Congress Cataloging in Publication Data

Bartley, Douglas L   1919-
  Job evaluation.

  Bibliography: p.
  Includes index.
  1. Job evaluation.   2. Compensation management.
I. Title.
HF5549.5.J62B37   658.3'2   80-21099
ISBN 0-201-00095-4

ISBN 0-201-00095-4
ABCDEFGHIJ-AL-8987654321

Preface

In today's society, the compensation of all employees is a varied, complex, and ever-changing problem. Because of this, it is important that everyone in business have some idea of how their own individual pay is computed. Wage and salary administration is a management function that goes on in all companies, whether there is a formal or informal approach, and whether the company or agency is large or small, private or public, or a profit or non-profit type of business.

Employment practices and policies do change over a period of time, but it is certain that people must receive monetary compensation and that the compensation, if the employees are to be motivated, must be just. Justice, from the employee's point of view, is based on two assumptions:

1. Are his wages comparable to those of other employees working within the company?
2. Are his wages comparable to the area rates for a similar job?

In attempting to answer these questions, this text has been written and subdivided into the following three general areas.

Part I   The field of job evaluation and the non-analytical methods of job evaluation primarily used in small companies

Part II   Quantitative systems of job evaluation used by intermediate and large companies

Part III   Basic wage and salary administration

Each of these sections discusses vital aspects of the process of establishing the proper payment of the employee.

It is true that many employees are dissatisfied because they feel there is some real or fancied internal discrimination between their rate and the wages or salaries paid to other employees within the organization. To overcome this problem, aggressive companies of all sizes have installed a formal job evaluation program. One of the basic aims of sections I and II is to present to the wage and salary administrator the principles that are important and/or essential in selecting the correct job evaluation program for a particular part of the work force of a company (blue-collar, non-exempt office employees, professional employees, or management).

Once the proper program has been selected, a detailed step-by-step procedure is outlined on how the proper evaluation program may be implemented. The advantages and disadvantages of each of the four methods of evaluation are explained.

The analytical approach and thorough presentation of the four main approaches to job evaluation make this book readily adaptable for use in senior courses in universities. It should be equally adaptable for management, in that it will allow them to choose the proper program for their company and to implement the program without the use of outside consultants.

The text repeatedly stresses that each job evaluation program should be specifically designed to fit the particular needs of the group of employees that are being evaluated. Portions of the book, such as job questionnaires, job descriptions, factor definitions, etc., may be adapted to a company's program, but each plan should be tailor-made to fit the particular work group requirements.

The analytical approach has several important advantages. It gives a sound, logical, and easily understood presentation. It makes possible the comparison and selection of the proper program for a group of employees within a company, and the right program for a company whether it is small or large.

One of the main reasons for job evaluation is to arrange the jobs into a hierarchy of importance so that monetary values may be assigned to the respective jobs. Part III of the text does just that; it explains how the wage structure for a program should be established and maintained. As explained in the text, job evaluation, including wage and salary administration, is not an exact science; but it is a logical and systematic approach to the proper payment of employees. By seeing examples of items that are presently in use, the reader may readily grasp the information being presented. In all four sections many examples are cited to show how to put to use the information being given. Part III is an attempt to provide a set of principles and policies that will assist management to design, build, and administer a rational pay structure.

A sound wage and salary program is designed to attract, retain, motivate, and reward employees according to their contribution toward the success of the operation. The various parts of the text are intended to show how these objectives are carried out. It is recognized that the total compensation of employees in a company involves more than the application of a single technique. Total compensation for an employee involves many different items. The text is designed to establish and maintain the basic wage or salary structure. Additional compensation benefits such as incentive rates, commission, profit sharing, premium rates, shift differentials, hazard pay, pension programs, and insurance programs that apply to all or part of a work force are all part of the total picture. However, since each of these subjects has its own unique problems and requirements, they are not covered in this text. Many articles and other publications concerning each of these subjects are available.

Part III of the text also deals with the personal evaluation of how an employee is performing at work. Although this is not part of establishing a wage structure, it is a vital part of seeing that employees do an acceptable job and that they are compensated in a fair and reasonable manner.

To assist in better understanding the problems being discussed each chapter contains review questions that tend to focus on the important points of the chapter. In addition, some chapters, whenever applicable, also have specific work assignments that require the student to complete a work project concerning the material in the chapter.

I am grateful to the companies and publishers that were responsive to my requests for permission to quote and/or reprint some of their material. I stand indebted to many people for their help in making this book possible: To my wife Ruth, for her patience and for her help with editing during the writing of the book. To K. Peel, E. Villar, Y. Chapa, C. Garner, C. Lackey, R. Cowley, L. H. Stover, L. Hobbs, C. Ellard, and W. Platzer for having either typed, reviewed, or offered constructive criticism.

January 1981   D.L.B.
Edinburg, Texas

Contents

PART I The Field of Job Evaluation and Job Evaluation for Small Companies

1 The Field of Job Evaluation and Wage Administration 3

2 Job Evaluation Methods 9

3 Non-Analytical Method—Ranking 13

4 Non-Analytical Method—Job Classification 31

PART II Quantitative Systems of Evaluation

5 Quantitative Systems—Factor Comparison 57

6 Quantitative Systems—Weighted in Points 77

7 Notifying All Employees of the Pending Program 85

8 Updating the Organization's Structure and Assigning Duties to Employees 91

9 Preparing a Job Questionnaire and Job Analysis 95

10 Preparing Job Descriptions 115

11 Selecting Factors 139

12 Weighting of Factors 145

13 Establishing Rules for Evaluation   183

14 Evaluating Jobs, Assigning Point Values, and Writing
    Job-Rating Specifications   189

15 Establishing and Slotting Jobs in Pay Grades   203

PART III Wage and Salary Administration

16 Conducting an Area Survey   215

17 Establishing a Wage Structure   231

18 Adjustments to the Wage Structure, Individual Adjustments
    within the Rate Range, and Salary Management   259

19 Reevaluating Present Jobs, Slotting New Jobs, and
    Red Circle Rates   289

20 How Employee Performance Appraisal Programs Blend
    with the Program   295

21 Conclusion   323

    Glossary   327
    Bibliography   333
    Index   335

PART I

The Field of Job Evaluation and Job Evaluation Programs for Small Companies

PART 1

The Field of Job Evaluation and Wage Administration

Questions relating to the amount and type of work an individual should perform and the amount of wages that should be received reflect the source of most employees' gripes and grievances [1]. One of the primary responsibilities of management is to see that all employees are properly compensated for their contribution to fulfilling the objectives of the company. This wage should also have parity with the general wage level of neighboring companies. To accomplish this, a planned approach of wage management should be used.

At any given time, hundreds of compensation decisions are being made in the United States. How much an employee should make is a delicate question. Just as important is the way the company arrives at the answer. The procedure must be understood and accepted by the employee. To the workers, such decisions are important because they affect their incomes and thus, indirectly, their standards of living. These decisions often influence the employee's ability to meet status, esteem, and self-fulfillment needs [2]. They also affect the approach to work. Although money is not considered a true motivation factor, it is the number one extrinsic reward, and the employee will certainly be dissatisfied if reasonable compensation is not forthcoming.

1. Lytle, C. W. *Job Evaluation Methods.* New York: The Ronald Press Company, 1954.
2. Dunn, J. D. and F. M. Rachel. *Wage and Salary Administration.* New York: McGraw-Hill, 1971.

If this happens, several things can occur: the employee may (1) quit, (2) fight back at the company by submitting many gripes and grievances; (3) turn to unionism; or (4) deteriorate on the job, doing just enough to get by. This last happens in too many cases, and is the very thing a company wants to avoid.

To the employer, the compensation decision is also crucial because labor costs represent a large percentage of the total cost of operating the business. Compensation decisions may have a substantial impact on profits, which is a major objective of most businesses [3].

The amount of compensation earned by an employee is determined primarily by what is done (the job). It is not necessary for all employees to be compensated equally; i.e., employees will accept the fact that some jobs receive greater or lesser compensation than others. Employees must, however, perceive some type of justifiable or equitable relationship between what they contribute to the organization and what they receive in the form of compensation.

The relative involvement or importance of skill, effort, responsibility, and working conditions inherent in a particular job is presented in the job description. The act of determining the relative involvement of those factors for a particular job, and of comparing, for compensation purposes, the results with those obtained from other jobs is called **job evaluation.**

The purpose, therefore, of a job evaluation program is to determine the relative involvment of skill, effort, responsibility, and working conditions for the jobs within an organization, and to provide corresponding wage or salary levels reflective of this determination.

What, then, is the best approach for a compensation program that the employee will understand and accept? Such a program *should be custom made* to evaluate the group of jobs involved. One of the cardinal principles of evaluation is that the same evaluation program should not be used for both the hourly paid and management positions. If more than one type of work in a company is to be evaluated, there should be more than one program. The reason that several programs should be used within a company is that no one job evaluation program adequately evaluates all types of work assignments such as production, management, sales, office, etc. For example, there is very little basis for comparison between the jobs of a janitor and a supervisor; consequently very few job evaluation programs try to evaluate different

3. *Ibid.*

types of work assignments within the same program. Usually, two programs are involved using different sets of factors for comparison (see Chapter 11) or, in some cases, two different systems of job evaluation tie two or more programs together into the total compensation program for the company. This is covered in Chapter 17.

THE VALUE TO MANAGEMENT OF INSTALLING A JOB EVALUATION SYSTEM

There are many advantages for management when a job evaluation system is installed. They are outlined here.

A job evaluation program shows relationships between jobs in the company and establishes correct differentials between these jobs. An understanding of this fact is extremely important in getting the employee to accept his position on the wage scale.

Such a program establishes a system whereby new jobs may be properly "slotted" or placed into the system, thus establishing a sound and understandable basis of how the new job relates to the jobs already in the system.

The program is established on facts and principles that can be readily explained and accepted by the employee, the union, and management. These principles and impartial techniques help the supervisory force to be more objective and prove to the employee that the company is fair in its approach to compensation [4].

It takes the personal approach out of paying employees. As the title suggests, the job is evaluated, not the employee who is performing the job. The job ultimately will have a wage assigned to it, and anyone assigned to work on this job will receive the predetermined amount of pay.

Wages are assigned to the various jobs in a systematic manner, but occasionally, because of supply and demand of a certain skill, a particular job may be classified as a "red circle" rate and receive more money than its relative worth to that particular company. (This out-of-line rate will be discussed in Chapter 19.)

It helps to establish a clear understanding of what tasks or activities an employee should perform.

4. Lytle, *loc. cit.*

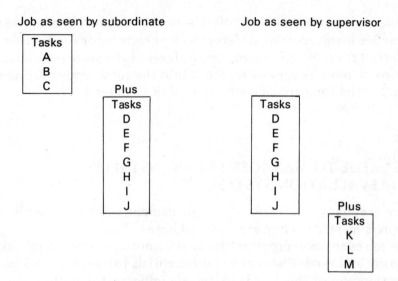

The employee is performing tasks A, B, and C, which the supervisor does not want by this particular employee, and is not performing tasks K, L, and M, which the supervisor feels are parts of the job [5]. Through completing the job questionnaire and writing the job description this misunderstanding will be clarified.

As an outgrowth of the above advantage, better communications between the supervisor and the subordinate are established.

There is a better understanding by management of the functions of all departments, of relations between departments, and of relations between sections within a department. It also clarifies authority and responsibility between departments.

There can be uniformity in job titles. Revision of job titles, based on realistic job descriptions, makes possible the comparison of rates of pay for jobs having the same title and content as those in other departments, in other business firms in the area, and in other cities.

Overlapping of jobs and unnecessary activities performed by the employees can be reduced. The rearrangement of the work situation and reallocation of duties among jobs in the department will result in improved efficiency.

5. Deegan, Arthur X. II and Roger J. Fritz. *MBO Goes to College.* Boulder, Colorado: University of Colorado, 1975.

By use of job specifications derived from the job analyses, minimum qualifications for hiring and placement standards can be established. This will improve recruiting, selection, and placement of the new employee.

Job indoctrination, orientation, and training are facilitated. New employees can readily be oriented and training programs can be developed by use of job descriptions.

By assisting with, and becoming involved in, the preparation of a job description, the supervisor develops a more objective point of view and an improved knowledge of the job duties of his employees; this new point of view usually means improved supervision.

Improved supervisory–employee relations result from the increased understanding by the supervisor of the problems inherent in the jobs of his employees. The supervisor becomes more aware of the need for the appropriate counseling relationship with the workers.

Performance-rating procedures for the employee are developed. Although performance rating of an employee is not a part of a job evaluation program, it is essential that a review is made on how an employee actually is performing the job. By having a job evaluation system, a supervisor now has criteria against which the employee can be compared. The job description enumerates the tasks each employee should perform and the supervisor can now review how well the employee is performing.

The program clarifies the distinctions between performance evaluation and job evaluation. Supervisors learn that rate ranges are best arrived at by job evaluation and that an employee's position within the rate range is best arrived at by merit rating.

There is improved employee motivation and morale. A systematic approach to why a person's pay is at a certain level and what the pay level is on other jobs in the department helps the employee to be motivated to do a better job, with the hope of being promoted to various potential jobs in the department or business [6].

In order to understand fully the job evaluation procedure it is important for the reader to understand the author's definition of terms. For this purpose, a glossary of terms specifically used in job evaluation programs is included at the end of the book.

6. Rush, Carl and R. M. Bellows. Job evaluation for a small business. *Personnel Psychology Journal* 2(3):301–310, 1949.

2

Job Evaluation Methods

This book will explain the four most-used approaches to job evaluation:

ranking
job classification
factor comparison
weighted in points

Of the above-listed methods of job evaluation, ranking and job classification are generally used if the company is small. Of these two, ranking seems to be more common, especially for very small companies.

These approaches, however, are not very satisfactory when large numbers of jobs (25 or more different jobs) are involved. So, for any size company, but particularly for large ones, the weighted-in-points method is preferred.

This book will explain four methods of evaluation as well as give a step-by-step approach for installing one. Since the weighted-in-points is the preferred method of the four, a more detailed outline explaining it starts with Chapter 11. If you wish to use one of the other three methods and would like more insight into a particular area of it, you may refer to the corresponding step in the weighted-in-points section to see if this would help clarify your inquiry.

Since it is the responsibility of job evaluation to arrange the jobs in a hierarchy of importance (from the least important to the most important), and then to slot the jobs into pay grades, there is only one section written on wage administration. Consequently, when using one of the first three methods, as soon as the job evaluation part is completed, turn to Part III—Wage and Salary Administration, and continue there.

Ranking and job classification (grading) are non-analytical approaches to evaluation, while the other two methods use quantitative methods in establishing a numerical differential between the various jobs.

All four methods approach the task in a similar way. The approach generally is:

1. To review the organization of the work group and to make sure that the *proper tasks are assigned* to the logical or *right employees* in the department.

2. To *analyze* each job and to prepare a written *job description*. The major part of the description shows the function and scope of the job and the tasks, duties, and accountabilities for the job. This is explained in detail in Chapter 10.

3. To *assess systematically* and *compare each job* with the other jobs in the department and/or company.

4. To *produce a rank order of jobs,* from the one that is the least important in the group to the one that is the most important.

5. To *assign jobs* with similar demands or importance into *pay grades*.

6. To *determine* how much *money* each pay grade is to receive.

7. To *keep the system up to date* by:
   a. *re-evaluating a job* if the job content changes, to ascertain if it should be promoted or demoted to a different pay grade,
   b. "*slotting*" or inserting new jobs into the program,
   c. periodically *updating the monetary value* of the pay grades.

A job evaluation program shows relationships between jobs in the company. The job is analyzed, not the employee performing the work. This approach reduces any bias that might occur if the evaluation were based on how the individual performed the jobs. Since most evaluations are the work of a committee, this also helps to reduce any bias. A system is established whereby, if an existing job changes or if a new job is started, the proper level of pay for the job may be systematically established. Although the program, when compared to an exact science such as mathematics or chemistry, is not as scientific, it does establish a logical, systematic approach in determining a pay structure for a group of jobs. The program is established on facts that can be readily explained and accepted by the employee, by management, and by a union, if one is present. Although there is some subjectivity involved when using the ranking or job classification method, this feature is greatly reduced when either the factor-comparison or weighted-in-points method is used.

Many companies want to be able to reward an employee for performing well on a particular job. Various types of wage levels may be assigned to each job, but the base rate for all jobs is established in an unbiased job evaluation program. Personal evaluation and merit raises may be established in the wage structure, but the level of the base rate is established by the evaluation program.

Total compensation for an employee is a varied and complex program. Table 2.1 illustrates how complex it can be.

Because of the many varied items and the complexity of most of them, this text will address only the problems of establishing a job evaluation system with a resulting wage structure and the granting of

Table 2.1
Possible Payroll Costs for Employing an Employee

Productive Hours	Non-productive Hours	Fringe Benefits
Wages*	Vacation	Pension programs
Incentive pay	Holiday pay	Severance pay
Bonus	Sick leave pay	Uniform allowance
Overtime pay	Funeral leave pay	Discount purchases
Premium pay	Jury duty pay	Hospitalization
Shift differential	Supplemental unemployment benefits	Surgical insurance
Hazard pay		Medical insurance
Merit raises*		Life insurance

*The subjects of this book.

increases to employees who are performing well on their job (the two items marked with the asterisk). However, each company, if it is going to be competitive in the labor market, must establish a reasonable level of fringe benefits as well as a fair base wage rate.

3

Non-Analytical Method—Ranking

The non-analytical systems of job evaluation place jobs in a grading hierarchy. The objective is to assess the importance of each job as a whole or unit in relation to all the other jobs being compared. The jobs are not broken down by factors for evaluation purposes. In small organizations, all jobs are taken and ranked as a group. In larger companies the ranking is done by department. For greater acceptance and a more accurate and unbiased evaluation, the ranking is usually done by a committee.

The ranking system has one distinct advantage over all other methods of job evaluation in that it is the simplest method of evaluation (Fig. 3.1). The raters usually work from their overall knowledge of the job and this information is backed by a written job description outlining the duties of the job. The raters simply compare each job against the other jobs, determining whether it is

more demanding
as demanding
less demanding

As a result, a grading of the jobs is obtained.

Fig. 3.1
Comparison of Ranking to Job Classification

Ranking	Job Classification
This informal method requires nothing more than a subjective judgment	Sometimes referred to as the grade description method because grade levels are defined for benchmark job. The formal systems identify and define compensable factor gradations for each applicable grade level

Characteristics	Characteristics
Ranks whole job against others	Evaluates whole job against others
The first used and the simplest	Utilizes pre-determined number of pay grades or pay grade increments
Requires extensive knowledge, by the evaluator, of all jobs in the organization	Basically an extension and improvement of ranking system
Best applications in relatively small organizations with well-established and understood jobs	Requires comprehensive knowledge of benchmarks and/or compensable factor gradations
Often is the final judgmental test before using more sophisticated systems	Best application in organizations with well-established or rather constant and understood jobs
	Evolved from Federal Classification act of 1923 and is used by most government and academic institutions

Source: American Compensation Association, *Booklet #45,* Feb. 1978. ACA, P.O. Box 1176, Scottsdale, Arizona, 85252.

RANKING

The following might be an approach to a ranking system for a small warehouse terminal.

The warehouse has the following four jobs, with 16 employees on the payroll.

Job	Number of employees on the job
janitor	1
electrician	1
fork lift operator	6
car and truck loader	8

In using the ranking approach, we probably could surmise that the lowest paying job would be the janitor and that the highest paying job would be that of the electrician. The question arises, however, whether the fork lift operator has a more important or more demanding job than does the car and truck loader. The one job entails operating equipment, while the other job is responsible for the final count and shipping of the merchandise. Let us assume that the grading is listed as follows.

Grade	Job title
1.	janitor (lowest in pay)
2.	car and truck loader
3.	fork lift operator
4.	electrician (highest in pay)

The system of ranking has established the hierarchy of the four jobs, but it is weak in several areas.

In a larger company, it would be impractical to try to rank many diverse jobs, say 35 different jobs, located in four different departments, and having totally different job contents. For example, jobs in a warehouse department would vary completely from those in the production department or in quality control. Ranking jobs in a very small company or by departments is relatively simple, but merging the department list into one listing becomes complicated and reduces the accuracy of the system.

How much pay differential should there be between grades one, two, three, etc.? In the foregoing example, should the car and truck loader be placed in pay grade two and the fork lift operator in pay grade four, since there is a great deal of difference in their jobs; or are they properly ranked as pay grades two and three? The question concerning pay is how important is the job to the company in meeting its objectives. The rate of pay should be fixed accordingly. Since the grading system is non-analytical, it is difficult to arrive at a proper pay differential.

Since jobs are studied as a whole, it is a relatively simple task to rank such familiar jobs as those of janitor and electrician, but what happens if a different type of job is added to the payroll or if a different level of skill is needed in a "trade" job such as an electrician. For example, how does one compare a quality control inspector, a bookkeeper, and a crew leader, or a top grade electrician with an apprentice electrician? These jobs or levels of skill are not as well known by the committee, and it is much more difficult to slot properly little-known or technical jobs. One of the weaknesses of the ranking system is that the person or committee doing the evaluating needs a great degree of personal knowledge concerning all of the jobs.

INSTALLING A RANKING SYSTEM

Whenever a company installs a formal job evaluation program, there are several steps it should take prior to actually doing the evaluating. The first five steps of installing a program are always the same, no matter which method of evaluation is going to be used.

1. Notify all employees of the pending program.
2. Update the organizational structure of the company.
3. Assign duties in each area or department.
4. Prepare a job questionnaire for each position.
5. Write job descriptions.

These five steps will be explained in detail in Chapters 7, 8, 9, and 10.

The ranking of jobs as a method of job evaluation does have a place in our business society. If it is properly applied, it can be a most useful tool.

Ranking of jobs may be done by one of several approaches.

Ranking by a Committee Using Average Scores   A job evaluation committee studies the descriptions of the jobs to be evaluated. Each member then ranks each job with a numerical value, (1) being the highest rated job, (2) the second highest, and so on. After all the jobs have been ranked, an average score is determined for each job. This score is the ranking of that job. As was explained earlier, the ranking method of evaluation compares the whole job, not segments or factors of the job [1]. This approach to ranking was used in the example of the small warehouse.

Ranking by Use of Index Cards   A second approach to ranking is to prepare a set of index cards with the job titles written on them. By comparing the jobs, the committee then places the cards in sequential order with

---

1. Burgess, Leonard R. *Wage and Salary Administration in a Dynamic Economy.* New York: Harcourt, Brace, 1968, p. 31.

the least demanding (important) job on the bottom and the most important one on the top. All other jobs are slotted between these two in order of importance.

Ranking by Paired Comparison Using X's   A third approach is achieved by using paired comparisons. Every job is compared to all other jobs in the grouping. The procedures for making the comparison are:

1. A listing of all jobs is placed in the same sequence, in both a vertical and a horizontal row.

2. The rater then compares the jobs in the vertical row against the same listing of jobs in the horizontal row. If the job listed in the vertical row is more important and/or difficult than the job listed in the horizontal row, an X is placed in that square. In making the comparison, the question that might be asked by the rater for each of the jobs being reviewed is "What job is more important to the functioning of this department?"

3. After all comparisons have been made, the number of X's are totaled on each horizontal level. The job that receives the most X's is the most demanding job in the group. The one that receives no X's is the least demanding. The others are ranked according to their point scores [2]. (See Fig. 3.2.)

Fig. 3.2
Paired Comparison Using X's

Job	Janitor	Electrician	Fork lift operator	Car and truck loader	Inspector	Total
Janitor	—					0
Electrician	X	—	X	X	X	4
Fork lift operator	X		—			1
Car and truck loader	X		X	—		2
Inspector	X		X	X	—	3

2. Otis, J. and R. Leukart. *Job Evaluation, A Basis for Sound Wage Administration,* 2nd ed. New York: Prentice Hall, 1959, p. 77.

The ranking for these jobs then becomes

1. janitor (least important or demanding)
2. fork lift operator
3. car and truck loader
4. inspector
5. electrician (most important or demanding)

Ranking by Paired Comparison Using Point Values   The fourth approach, actually a variation of the paired comparison, is to assign point values to the ratings. This method tends to refine paired comparison and gives a slightly more accurate review of the ranking.

A table similar to the one shown in Fig. 3.2 is prepared, but instead of placing X's in the columns, a numerical score is used.

If a job is considered to be more demanding than the one it is compared with, it scores 3 points. If both jobs have the same demand, it receives 2 points. One point is allocated to the job if it has less demand or skill requirements than the job being compared [3]. Figure 3.3 shows the results using point values.

Fig. 3.3
Paired Comparison Using Numbers

Job	Janitor	Electrician	Fork lift operator	Car and truck loader	Inspector	Total
Janitor	—	1	1	1	1	4
Electrician	3	—	3	3	3	12
Fork lift operator	3	1	—	2	1	7
Car and truck loader	3	1	2	—	2	8
Inspector	3	1	3	2	—	9

3. British Institute of Management. *Job Evaluation, A Practical Guide for Managers.* Management Publication Limited: 5 Winsley Street, London, WI, England. 1970, p. 1.

Fig. 3.4
Ranking Jobs by Department

Warehouse	Service	Office	Engineering	Production
Janitor	Custodian	Receptionist	Laborer	Laborer
Fork lift operator	Yard maintenance	Clerk–typist	Apprentice carpenter	Machine operator
Receiver	Grounds equipment operator	Mail clerk	Apprentice electrician	Inspector
Car loader		Key punch operator	Carpenter B	Cook B
Final checker	Lead custodian	Secretary	Electrician B	Cook A
	Gate guard	Administrative clerk	Carpenter A	
	Patrolman	Senior accounting clerk	Electrician A	
			Electronic technician	

Any one of the four approaches will rank the jobs in order of importance. The fourth (most refined) method makes for greater ease in slotting jobs that are very similar in importance to the company.

As stated earlier, the ranking approach to job evaluation is quite adequate in very small companies, but other methods of job evaluation give more accurate results as the number and complexity of jobs increase. If, however, management wishes to use the ranking system for a medium size company, the following approach might be used.

1. Proceed through the five steps outlined in Chapters 7 through 10.
2. Divide the company into functional departments (grouping of similar tasks into one department, such as production, engineering, warehousing, etc.).
3. Rank all the jobs department by department.
4. Prepare a listing of the ranking of the job in each department (Fig. 3.4).
5. Assign pay grades to the listing (Fig. 3.5).

Fig. 3.5
Assigning Pay Grades to the Ranking

Grade	Warehouse	Service	Office	Engineering	Production
1	Janitor	Custodian	Receptionist	Laborer	Laborer
2		Yard maintenance	Clerk–typist		
3	Fork lift operator	Grounds equipment operator	Mail clerk		Machine operator
4	Receiver	Lead custodian	Key punch operator		Inspector
5	Car loader	Gate guard	Secretary	Apprentice carpenter	Cook B
6	Final checker	Patrolman	Administrative clerk	Apprentice electrician Carpenter B	Cook A
7			Senior accounting clerk	Electrician B	
8				Carpenter A Electrician A	
9				Electronic technician	

Once the jobs have been placed into pay grades, money values may then be assigned to each pay grade. Establishing the wage structure is covered in Chapters 15 through 19 in the section on the weighted-in-points approach to job evaluation.

Review Questions

1. What are the first five steps to be taken before installing any job evaluation program?

2. Prepare a chart that compares the advantages and weaknesses of the ranking method of job evaluation.

3. What are the basic criteria for using the ranking method of job evaluation?

4. List four methods of job evaluation.

5. Explain the technique of paired comparison as used in the ranking method.

6. Are job descriptions really necessary when using the ranking method of evaluation?

7. Explain the benefits that can be obtained from a formal job evaluation program.

8. Is the paired-comparison approach to ranking superior to the index card method? Explain.

9. Explain how the ranking method can be applicable to larger organizations.

10. Should all jobs in an organization be evaluated by the same job evaluation program? Explain.

Work Exercise

1. The following are abbreviated job descriptions for a company [4]. Practice evaluating the jobs by using:
   a. the index card ranking system,
   b. the average score ranking system,
   c. the paired-comparison system using X's in the box score,
   d. the paired-comparison system using point values in the box score.

Job: *Yard Maintenance*

Function: To provide manual and some semi-skilled work in the care and culture of plants and flowers, and the maintenance of the grounds.

Tools and Equipment: Tractor, mower, lawn mower, edger trimmer, rake, hoe, shovel and other small tools used in maintenance of a yard, trees, shrubbery, etc.

Directs the Work of Others: None

Typical Duties and/or Working Procedures:
1. Maintains the lawn, shrubs, trees, and flowers as needed.
2. Mows the grass when needed.
3. Applies fertilizers and insecticides to grass, flowers, and trees as needed.
4. Periodically checks various plants against plant disease, and takes corrective action if they are diseased.
5. Sow grass, and plant new flowers, shrubs, trees as required.
6. Care for indoor plants as required.
7. At times, may work on other custodial jobs as assigned by his supervisor.

---

4. Source: Region One, Education Service Center, Edinburg, Texas, 78539. Descriptions as they appeared in Sept. 1977.

Job: *Mail Clerk*

Function: Responsibility for processing of all incoming and outgoing mail. Picks up mail from U.S. Post Office; sorts, records, and delivers mail to offices. Picks up and receives in-house mail; stamps, records, and delivers to U.S. Post Office. When not occupied in this capacity, assists in library by preparing incoming materials for shelves, van and/or mail delivery.

Tools and Equipment: Various size scales, stamp machine, adding machine, typewriter, and small office tools such as stapler and scissors.

Supervises and/or Directs the Work: None

Typical Duties and/or Working Procedures:
1. Drives to U.S. Post Office and signs for mail. Then loads letters, films, and parcels, and returns to Service Center.
2. At Service Center, unloads and immediately delivers by mail cart all films and bulk parcels to proper department obtaining signature for accountable mail.
3. Returns to mail department, sorts and bundles letter mail by department, then delivers to department, at the same time picking up outgoing mail.
4. Sorts and stamps outgoing mail, keeping record of postage charges by department, and recording all insured mail. Then loads outgoing mail for the U.S. Post Office.
5. Drives vehicle to U.S. Post Office, unloads mail, separating it for local or out-of-town delivery, and clearing accountable mail with U.S. Postal Clerk.
6. In addition, handles dissemination of the minor amount of parcels from sources such as United Parcel.
7. Monthly maintains stamp machine, posts departmental stamp charges, disseminates news record and calendars to schools, and delivers postage meter to U.S. Post Office for updating of postal account.
8. When not performing mail room duties, assists Dissemination Component by working in library putting newspapers on rack, packing and unpacking news records and calendars, shelving books, typing labels and other routine library clerical chores.

Job: *Printer A*

Function: Responsible for the scheduling, duplicating, delivery, and billing for varied material printed by the company. Most of work done on Multilith Offset printing presses. Directs the work of others in getting the total task completed.

Tools and Equipment: Multilith Offset printing presses, electrostatic copier, collators, punching and binding machines, gluing and taping machines, a duplicator, electric paper cutter, photo direct camera and processor.

Directs the Work of Others: Directs the work of Printer B

Typical Duties and/or Working Procedures:
1. Schedules all incoming work to be duplicated on the various machines to meet the required completion dates.
2. Performs the duties of operating the various duplicating and auxiliary equipment.
3. Trains new employees in how to operate the various machines and then assigns them to the various duplicating assignments to meet the proper completion date of work in progress.
4. Makes minor adjustment to machines as required. When machine is seriously malfunctioning, calls in a service man.
5. Performs daily cleaning, plus a thorough weekly "break-down" and cleaning of all presses, converter, and copier. During this process inspects machinery for wear and tear so as to avoid major breakdowns.
6. Maintains inventory of supplies and materials on hand and prepares requests for Supervisor's signature for additional supplies and materials as needed.
7. Maintains files for such items as supplies, orders, maintenance work performed, etc.
8. Prepares plates for two-tone printing jobs, and more sophisticated printing work such as photographs, one- or two-colored ink jobs, etc.
9. Counsels supervisors concerning their printing needs as it pertains to layouts, format, and printing costs.

Job: *Accounting Clerk*

Function: Responsibility for maintaining accounts receivable. Also computes in-house billing and performs other duties related to financial accounting of the company.

Tools and Equipment: Calculator, typewriter, and copier.

Directs the Work of Others: None

Typical Duties and/or Working Procedures:
1. Maintains accounts receivable. This includes:
   a) Maintains accounts receivable files, including files on invoices that are current and past due.
   b) On a weekly basis collects invoices and assigns codes (such as, customer number, revenue account number, fund code, and transaction code) and then mails out one copy to the customer, files two copies, and batches the remaining copy according to code for computerization.
   c) Sorts the customers monthly computerized statements for mailout.
   d) Processes incoming check payments by pulling the invoices, noting payment, filing paid invoices, and writing coded message for adjustment of the account on the computer.
   e) Answers inquiries related to customer invoices and statements.
   f) Sends second notices for customer accounts that are past due.

2. Computes individual departmental billing for charges on supplies (on a monthly basis), printing (weekly), telephone (monthly), and postage (monthly).

3. Maintains fixed asset inventory system.

4. On an annual basis, bills schools for special education commitment, bills departments for rent and IBM maintenance, and assists in the mailout for the purchasing coop.

5. Occasionally performs other duties of a clerical nature, such as: typing payment authorizations and purchase orders for the business office and the print shop, distributing supplies, and making change from the lunch box petty cash.

Job: *Electronic Technician A*

Function: To repair many different types and models of audiovisual equipment. To train and later direct the work of a lesser skilled technician.

Tools and Equipment: Various types service repair equipment such as Signal Generator, Oscilloscope, VTVM, small machine shop equipment as grinders, drill presses, plus the small assorted hand tools, typewriter and a calculator.

Directs the Work of Others: Yes, the work of a less skilled technician.

Typical Duties and/or Working Procedures:
1. Receives incoming equipment needing repairs, sees that it is properly identified and placed in the schedule for repairs.
2. Evaluate the extent of malfunction and determine repairs necessary to restore equipment to its original working order.
3. Trouble-shoot actual defect in equipment to determine defective components in both solid state and conventional vacuum tube circuitry. Determine necessary steps required to either prefabricate a dependable repair of the old component, or replace with a new one.
4. Employ the use of technical test equipment common to the trade of repair to audiovisual equipment such as a Signal Generator, VTVM meters, Oscilloscopes, frequency meters and various devices used to calibrate and adjust special circuits operating automatic functions for remote control modes.
5. Repair or replace defective wiring and associated cabling in the audiovisual equipment in general use.
6. Perform necessary mechanical lubrication and adjustment for smooth operation of all associated mechanical mechanisms involved in tape recorders, projectors, record players, and a variety of other audiovisual equipment.
7. Makes sure that the replacement parts necessary for repair jobs scheduled are either on hand or on order.
8. Trains lesser skilled technicians in the department and directs and coordinates their activities in getting the best efficiency in the work being performed.
9. Performs general electrical work in the building and/or equipment in the building as required.

Job: *Key Punch Operator B*

Function: To transmit information from various-type forms via a keypunch/verifier to a computer card. Performs general office clerical work when requested.

Tools and Equipment: Keypunch/verifier, computer terminal, printer, reader, decollator, burster, copier, calculator, typewriter.

Directs the Work of Others: None

Typical Duties and/or Working Procedures:
1. To process information from raw data to a finished keypunched computer card.
   This involves the following:
   a. Check the raw data for accuracy and completeness. This involves learning information concerning approximately 90 to 100 different forms used in finance, payroll, tax scheduling, grade reporting, accounts receivable, etc.
   b. Memorizing the formats of each job request and to punch and verify applicable data.
   c. Delivering the finished card to the terminal operator for further processing.
2. Reports the malfunctioning of any equipment to supervisor.
3. Relieves other personnel in the area for lunch and/or vacation time, such as employees assigned as terminal operators, secretaries, etc.
4. During peak period for work in the Terminal Room (Sept., Nov., and Dec.), does general office work of printing, trimming, decollating, bursting, packing, and shipping.

Job: *Keypunch Operator A*

Function: To coordinate the work of several keypunch operators in seeing that all incoming keypunching assignments are properly scheduled and in turn completed in an accurate and prompt manner. Also acts as the secretary for the area.

Tools and Equipment: Keypunch/verifier, typewriter, burster and decollator, calculator, and other general office-type equipment.

Supervises and/or Directs the Work: Directs the work of other keypunch operators.

Typical Duties and/or Working Procedures:
1. Receives, reviews, and assigns priorities to incoming work.
2. Assigns work to be keypunched. All payroll, finance, tax accounting, accounts receivable, student scheduling, and grade-reporting keypunch assignments are processed through this office.
3. Reviews all keypunch operators' work in regard to accuracy and volume of work. Refers serious personnel problems to the supervisor.
4. Is in charge of the filing system for the department. This includes:
    a. Maintaining daily records for annual reports.
    b. Files on schools that are participating—commitment forms, all billings, flow of material.
    c. Records of van delivery receipts and bus weigh bills on incoming and outgoing data.
    d. A calendar of keypunch workload at all times and making sure that the jobs are received according to schedule.
    e. Maintain an up-to-date inventory of supplies on hand.
    f. Daily Logs Job Control Language for media booking system for billing purposes.
5. Performs all secretarial duties for the area.
6. Relieve keypunch operators when necessary (sickness, break-time, lunch, etc.).
7. Initiates action to get mechanical repairs to the equipment that is not functioning properly.
8. Assists in training keypunch operators for the department, and occasionally assists local school districts in training personnel to keypunch.

Job: *Clerk–typist*

Function: To provide basic clerical and typing support for the performance of varied office tasks of limited complexity. May perform a variety of jobs that are each easy to learn.

Tools and Equipment: Typewriter, Xerox duplicating machine, calculator, academically related machines such as film projectors, transparency machines etc., and other standard office machines.

Supervises and/or Directs the Work: None

Typical Duties and/or Working Procedures:
1. Types routine correspondence, form letters, agendas, memos, requisitions, lists and tables.
2. Answers telephone and takes messages.
3. Opens mail, and sorts and routes correspondence or forms.
4. Does filing, Xeroxing, proofreading, collating and other related tasks.
5. Performs other duties of a support nature including: running errands, maintaining supply inventories, tabulating cumulative reports, keeping checklists, and maintaining activity calendars.

Work Table for Work Exercise 1b

	Rater A	Rater B	Rater C	Rater D	Rater E	Average for Committee
Yard maintenance						
Mail clerk						
Printer A						
Accounting clerk						
Electronic technician A						
Key punch operator B						
Key punch operator A						
Clerk–typist						

Work Table for Work Exercise 1c

	Yard maint.	Mail clk.	Printer A	Acc't clk.	Elec. tech.	Key P–B	Key P–A	Clerk–typist
Yard maintenance								
Mail clerk								
Printer A								
Accounting clerk								
Electronic technician A								
Key punch operator B								
Key punch operator A								
Clerk–typist								

Work Table for Work Exercise 1d

	Yard maint.	Mail clk.	Printer A	Acc't clk.	Elec. tech.	Key P–B	Key P–A	Clerk–typist
Yard maintenance								
Mail clerk								
Printer A								
Accounting clerk								
Electronic technician A								
Key punch operator B								
Key punch operator A								
Clerk–typist								

4

Non-Analytical Method—
Job Classification

This method of job evaluation is sometimes called a grading system or a rating system. Like the ranking method of job evaluation, it too is a non-analytical approach to evaluation. The total job is evaluated, usually by a committee, and is placed into job grades that have been predetermined and arranged in a hierarchy of importance. Each job is evaluated by the committee and placed into the grade where the grade description most closely fits the particular job being evaluated.

We might gain a clearer understanding of this by reviewing a very elementary type of job classification method: a general warehouse terminal that receives, stores, and later ships the merchandise to local retail stores in the area might use this approach for evaluation.

The jobs being reviewed might be classified into three levels, i.e., unskilled, semi-skilled, and skilled. Consequently, all jobs being evaluated would be placed into one of these three levels or grades. To aid in the slotting or placing of the jobs, a definition would be written for each of the levels. The descriptions might be as shown in Fig. 4.1.

After the jobs are properly slotted or placed into grades, a money value would be assigned to each level. The following is an example of the type of jobs assigned to each grade and the pricing for each grade.

Fig. 4.1
Job Classification Schedule — Warehouse Employees

Level or Grade	Definition
1	*Unskilled work* Performs work that is learned after brief oral instructions. Tasks may be of a repetitive and routine nature. Learning period — Less than one month Supervision — Close
2	*Semi-skilled* Work may include a variety of tasks, many of which may be elementary in nature, but must be done accurately, such as record keeping of cases shipped. Work may involve the operation of equipment in the performance of the work. Learning period — One to six months Supervision — Close
3	*Skilled* Work involves the use of independent judgment and of problem solving. The responsibility is great, in that the jobs assigned to this level involve working with the finished product just prior to its leaving the warehouse. The work must be done accurately since these employees are the last to see the product before the customer receives it. The job may include the coordinating and/or directing the work of others. Learning period — Over six months Supervision — General

The level of pay and the increment between grades are arbitrarily assigned in the example below, just to explain the system. How to determine these factors is covered in detail in Chapter 17.

    Grade one — $3.50
        janitor
        messenger
    Grade two — $4.00
        fork lift operator
        receiver
    Grade three — $4.70
        shipper
        inspector

Fig. 4.2
Job Classification Schedule — Maintenance Repair Crew

Level or Grade	Definition
4	*Technical* The work may involve extensive technical training and/or specialized schooling involving broad knowledge of a trade or training of a very specialized kind. Learning Period — Over one year Supervision — General

If the warehouse is large enough to have its own maintenance repair crew, then a fourth level might be established covering this level of skill. A definition for this group might be as shown in Fig. 4.2.

The rate of pay for this grade would be approximately $5.60 per hour based on a geometric progression approach to the pricing of the wage schedule. Geometric progression involves the assignment of money to the pay grades by an increasing amount. The progressive differential between these four pay grades is 50 cents, plus an additional 20 cents at each succeeding pay grade. Thus, the increment is 50 cents, 70 cents, and 90 cents. Consequently, grade four is set at $5.60 ($4.70 for grade three plus 90 cents). If there were to be a grade five, the rate of pay would be $6.70 ($5.60 of grade four plus $1.10 or 20 cents added to the previous increment of 90 cents).

This example of a job-classification evaluation system, of course, is very elementary, but the steps taken to install such a system are the same regardless of the complexity or the size of the work force being evaluated. These steps are:

1. Notifying all employees of the pending program
2. Updating the organizational structure of the company
3. Assigning duties in each area or department
4. Preparing a job questionnaire for each position
5. Writing job descriptions
6. Selecting the number of levels (grades) to be defined and used in the program

7. Writing grade definitions describing each level of skill required

8. Having the job evaluation committee review each job description, compare it to the various grade definitions, and place or slot the job into the grade the committee feels most closely defines it

9. Assigning a money value to each grade level

10. Notifying the payroll department, the supervisors and the employees of the outcome of the evaluation system in order to begin paying the new rates

In companies having many different work assignments and more complex jobs, there is a need for many levels in the classification schedule. Under these circumstances, a more elaborate and a more detailed definition for each grade must be given. The job evaluation committee must determine the number of levels that are definable and then write the definitions. This is the most exacting and complicated part of the program. It is extremely important that the grade definitions are properly and clearly written so that the job evaluation committee can place each job at the correct level. Figure 4.3 shows a job evaluation schedule that might be used for production employees.

An important feature of the job-classification approach to job evaluation is that different rating schedules or scales can and should be prepared for the different types of work. One system would not work well for grouping jobs in production, clerical, sales, and supervision. The same principle would also hold if one were to try to group technical and sales into one program. The reason these different types of jobs should not be mixed is that there is no sure way to write properly the grade definition to cover the diverse types of work that are offered in such broad categories.

In view of this, a separate definition schedule should be written for the various categories of work. In this way, definitions may be written for each level for the production jobs and all jobs in the production area are compared against this schedule. Another schedule would be written for the office, etc. In this way, all jobs in the company would ultimately be ranked in their group and assigned to their respective grade levels. Later, management can assign money values to each pay level in the company. The coordinating of the wage structures for several job evaluation programs within the same company is covered in detail in Chapter 17.

Fig. 4.3
Job Classification Schedule — Production Employees

Grade	Definition
1	Very simple repetitive tasks or non-repetitive tasks involving little directed thinking.
2	Tasks require only brief instructions to learn. No experience necessary, because tasks can be learned on the job. Work is performed under close supervision.*
3	Tasks may be varied or routine in nature, but the procedures are established by the company's policies and work rules. Work is performed under general supervision.† Tasks may require some decision making, but the decisions are few and limited. Occasionally may require the use of independent judgment.
4	Tasks are varied and are learned only after considerable experience on the job. May frequently demand the use of judgment and independent thinking. Work is done under general supervision.
5	Tasks may be technical or specialized in one area. Independent judgment frequently needed. Work may be done under general supervision. Work may involve directing several other employees.
6	Tasks involve a high degree of responsibility, using independent judgment and the application of highly specialized or technical training. Work is done under general supervision. May involve directing and coordinating the work of a small crew.

*Close supervision — an employee is told what to do and, in some detail, how to do it.

†General supervision — an employee is told what to do with only a brief explanation as to the specific method or, in some cases, with no explanation.

The Federal government uses the job classification method for grading its clerical, administrative, scientific, and professional employees. The program is known as the General Schedule and has 18 different job classes. The classes or grades differ in the level of difficulty, the kind of work responsibilities, qualifications, and the amount of supervision required. Figure 4.4 shows examples of the first ten grades in the schedule.

Fig. 4.4
Examples of General Schedule Descriptions for Federal
Government Job Classification System

Grade	Definition
GS-1	Includes those classes of positions the duties of which are to perform, under immediate supervision, with little or no latitude for the exercise of independent judgment — (A) the simplest routine work in office, business, or fiscal operations; or (B) elementary work of a subordinate technical character in a professional, scientific, or technical field.
GS-2	Includes those classes of positions the duties of which are — (A) to perform, under immediate supervision, with limited latitude for the exercise of independent judgment, routine work in office, business, or fiscal operations, or comparable subordinate technical work of limited scope in a professional, scientific, or technical field, requiring some training or experience; or (B) to perform other work of equal importance, difficulty, and responsibility, and requiring comparable qualifications.
GS-3	Includes those classes of positions the duties of which are — (A) to perform, under immediate or general supervision, somewhat difficult and responsible work in office, business or fiscal operations, or comparable subordinate technical work of limited scope in a professional, scientific, or technical field, requiring in either case — (i) some training or experience; (ii) working knowledge of a special subject matter; or (iii) to some extent the exercise of independent judgment in accordance with well-established policies, procedures, and techniques; or (B) to perform other work of equal importance, difficulty, and responsibility, and requiring comparable qualifications.
GS-4	Includes those classes of positions the duties of which are — (A) to perform, under immediate or general supervision, moderately difficult and responsible work in office, business, or fiscal operations, or comparable subordinate technical work in a professional, scientific, or technical field, requiring in either case — (i) a moderate amount of training and minor supervisory or other experience;

Grade	Definition
	(ii) good working knowledge of a special subject matter or a limited field of office, laboratory, engineering, scientific, or other procedure and practice; and
	(iii) the exercise of independent judgment in accordance with well-established policies, procedures, and techniques; or
	(B) to perform other work of equal importance, difficulty, and responsibility, and requiring comparable qualifications.
GS-5	Includes those classes of positions the duties of which are — (A) to perform, under general supervision, difficult and responsible work in office, business, or fiscal administration, or comparable subordinate technical work in a professional, scientific, or technical field, requiring in either case —
	(i) considerable training and supervisory or other experience;
	(ii) broad working knowledge of a special subject matter or of office, laboratory, engineering, scientific, or other procedure and practice; and
	(iii) the exercise of independent judgment in a limited field;
	(B) to perform under immediate supervision, and with little opportunity for the exercise of independent judgment, simple and elementary work requiring professional, scientific, or technical training; or
	(C) to perform other work of equal importance, difficulty, and responsibility, and requiring comparable qualifications.
GS-6	Includes those classes of positions the duties of which are — (A) to perform, under general supervision, difficult and responsible work in office, business, or fiscal administration, or comparable subordinate technical work in a professional, scientific, or technical field, requiring in either case —
	(i) considerable training and supervisory or other experience;
	(ii) broad working knowledge of a special and complex subject matter, procedure, or practice, or of the principles of the profession, art, or science involved; and
	(iii) to a considerable extent the exercise of independent judgment; or
	(B) to perform other work of equal importance, difficulty, and responsibility, and requiring comparable qualifications.

Fig. 4.4 (continued)

Grade	Definition
GS-7	Includes those classes of positions the duties of which are — (A) to perform, under general supervision, work of considerable difficulty and responsibility along special technical or supervisory lines in office, business, or fiscal administration, or comparable subordinate technical work in a professional, scientific, or technical field requiring in either case —
	(i) considerable specialized or supervisory training and experience;
	(ii) comprehensive working knowledge of a special and complex matter, procedure, or practice, or of the principles of the profession, art, or science involved; and
	(iii) to a considerable extent the exercise of independent judgment;
	(B) under immediate or general supervision, to perform somewhat difficult work requiring —
	(i) professional, scientific, or technical training; and
	(ii) to limited extent, the exercise of independent technical judgment; or
	(C) to perform other work of equal importance, difficulty, and responsibility, and requiring comparable qualifications.
GS-8	Includes those classes of positions the duties of which are — (A) to perform, under general supervision, very difficult and responsible work along special technical or supervisory lines in office, business, or fiscal administration, requiring —
	(i) considerable specialized or supervisory training and experience;
	(ii) comprehensive and thorough working knowledge of a specialized and complex subject matter, procedure, or practice, or of the principles of the profession, art, or science involved; and
	(iii) to a considerable extent the exercise of independent judgment;
	(B) to perform other work of equal importance, difficulty, and responsibility, and requiring comparable qualifications.
GS-9	Includes those classes of positions the duties of which are — (A) to perform, under general supervision, very difficult and responsible work along special technical, supervisory, or adminis-

Grade	Definition
	trative lines in office, business, or fiscal administration, requiring —
	(i) somewhat extended specialized training and considerable specialized, supervisory, or administrative experience which has demonstrated capacity for sound independent work;
	(ii) thorough and fundamental knowledge of a special and complex subject matter, or of the profession, art, or science involved; and
	(iii) considerable latitude for the exercise of independent judgment;
	(B) with considerable latitude for the exercise of independent judgment, to perform moderately difficult and responsible work requiring —
	(i) professional, scientific, or technical training equivalent to that represented by graduation from a college or university of recognized standing; and
	(ii) considerable additional professional scientific, or technical training or experience which has demonstrated capacity for sound independent work; or
	(C) to perform other work of equal importance, difficulty, and responsibility, and requiring comparable qualifications.
GS-10	Includes those classes of positions the duties of which are — (A) to perform, under general supervision, highly difficult and responsible work along special technical, supervisory, or administrative lines in office, business, or fiscal administration, requiring —
	(i) somewhat extended specialized, supervisory, or administrative training and experience which has demonstrated capacity for sound, independent work;
	(ii) thorough and fundamental knowledge of a specialized and complex subject matter, or of the profession, art, or science involved; and
	(iii) considerable latitutde for the exercise of independent judgment; or
	(B) to perform other work of equal importance, difficulty, and responsibility, and requiring comparable qualifications.

Source: U.S. Civil Service Commission, U.S. Government.

Although a class (or grade) may appear to be similar to the class above or below it, this is not the case. There are in each class definition certain phrases that differentiate it from the other classes. The different wording may be in one of several areas. Basically, the differences are in the areas of difficulty of the work, job responsibility, qualifications and training required, amount of supervision received, and the need for the use of judgment. Table 4.1 points out these differences.

Table 4.1 illustrates the technique the Federal government uses in writing grade definitions so as to be able to differentiate the level between grades. Private companies also use the same approach. The

Table 4.1
Key Wording that Differentiates One Class from Another in the Federal Government Job-Classification Program

Class	Difficulty	Responsibility	Qualifications	Supervision and judgment
1	simplest routine work		elementary work	
2	routine work		some training or experience	immediate supervision with limited latitude on use of judgment
3	somewhat difficult	somewhat difficult	some training and working knowledge	immediate or general supervision
4	moderately difficult work	moderately responsible work	moderate training and good working knowledge	general supervision, independent judgment in accordance with policies and procedures
5	difficult work	responsible work	broad working knowledge	general supervision, independent judgment in a limited field
6	difficult work	responsible work	considerable training, broad working knowledge, special and complex subject	general supervision, independent judgment

items most often used in the definitions for differentiating between levels are:

1. difficulty
2. responsibility
3. supervision
4. knowledge
    a. general
    b. special
    c. technical
5. training and/or experience
6. judgment

The key to having a successful job classification evaluation program is the writing of the definitions. If they are clear and concise, then the evaluation committee can properly slot or place all the jobs. As will be explained in Chapter 15, the committee is required to slot the jobs into the different pay grades. There is no set procedure for the slotting of jobs under this type of evaluation. However, some committees select key jobs, (benchmark jobs) and slot them first. Slotting these jobs first allows the committee the opportunity to grade any job against the grade definition as well as to compare the jobs to the key jobs.

Advantages of the Job-Classification Method

When comparing the job classification method to a weighted-in-points program, the job-classification method has the following advantages.

1. A fewer number of definitions are required. In the weighted-in-points method, the committee must define four to seven levels for each of the factors used in the program. This means that a total of 25 to 40 definitions must be written. In the job-classification method only five to ten definitions need be written.

2. The time required by the committee to review a job against six to ten factors in the weighted-in-points program is many times greater than under the job-classification system. Other services, such as typing, reproducing copies of each page used, are also greatly reduced.

3. Next to the ranking method, the job-classification program is the most economical program to install.

4. This system is a very good one to use when there are relatively few levels of skill required in the group being evaluated, such as the example of the evaluation for the warehouse employees.

5. Since the total manual for classifying a job under the job-classification system is less than two pages in length (the definitions for the various levels), most employees can understand how the system operates and tend to accept the slotting of the jobs in their respective grades.

Disadvantages of the Job-Classification Method

The following are disadvantages of the job-classification method.

1. Defining each level of grade is difficult. The wording must be exact enough to allow the committee to determine at what level the job should be placed. When there are many levels of grades desired, the defining of each level, especially the middle grades, is very difficult.

2. The whole job is evaluated at one time against each grade definition. This requires that each member of the committee have a thorough knowledge of what each job does, to be able to do a proper job of evaluating. Finding such committee members is not an easy task.

3. When jobs are evaluated in a point system, the jobs are reviewed against six to ten factors. The committee gets an opportunity to review the job six to ten times and the total score for the job is the summation of the points received on these factors. Under the grade classification system, the job is viewed only once against the grade definitions and then "slotted" accordingly. It is possible that some job might be improperly graded with only the one review of the job. The possibility of bias creeping into the evaluation is also more prevalent with only one review of the job.

4. As the job-classification method is a non-quantitative system to job evaluation, the program is more subjective in nature and when applied to more complex type work is not as exacting or as accurate as a weighted-in-points program.

5. If definitions for each level of grades are written in too-general terms, it is difficult to slot properly the jobs. On the other hand, if

the definition is too lengthy and tends to cover many aspects of the work, it becomes difficult to use.

6. Under the weighted-in-points system, a job can have a very high rating on one factor and a low rating on other factors. An example might be the rating on the factor of hazard for a painter. For this factor, the job would be rated high because the painter might have to work on scaffolds hanging on the outside of a building many feet above the ground. If the job of painter was viewed as a whole, as it is done under the job classification method, this part of the job could be watered down or perhaps overlooked entirely.

Review Questions

1. In the job-classification method, why should the committee slot the key (benchmarked) jobs first?

2. Give five examples of key (benchmarked) jobs.

3. Who should determine which jobs are key jobs? What criteria should be used for the determination?

4. If a company is operating reasonably well without a formal job evaluation system, should one be placed into effect? Explain.

5. List the steps to be taken to place into effect a job-classification evaluation program.

6. Explain the difference between close and general supervision. Why is this differential important in the job evaluation process?

7. List the advantages of the job-classification method of job evaluation over that of the ranking method. List the disadvantages.

8. The writing of the grade definition is the most difficult and also the most important part of the job-classification method of evaluating. Explain why these grade definitions are so important.

9. Write a five-level grade definition for non-exempt office-type work.

Case Problem

1. A very wealthy person has just moved to your section of the state and has decided to open ten new convenient (quick service—open 24 hours a day) grocery stores with a filling station at each store. He plans to have the following employees working at each store.

1 store manager

1 assistant store manager

2 shelf stockers and cleanup personnel

1 filling station attendant

1 mechanic

6 workers assigned to five positions.

Problem: You have been asked to recommend a suitable job evaluation method. Select either the ranking or job-classification method and give reasons for your selection. You may add any additional points or assumptions to come to a conclusion.

Follow through with the program by actually making a hierarchy of the jobs by using the method of evaluation that you choose.

If you choose the job-classification method, use the grade definitions shown in Fig. 4.3.

Work Exercise

1. Read the following ten descriptions of key production jobs. Using the definitions in Fig. 4.3 slot these jobs in their proper grades.

Warehouse Lift Truck Operator

Function

Operate various types of fork lift truck including Pul-Pac trucks to move and stack materials in storage or to load or unload carriers.

Tools and Equipment

Various types of fork lift trucks including trucks equipped to vertically lift wood pallets 210 inches or Pul-Pac unit load paper 185 inches, automatic vertical pallet lift, clip board, forms, bridge plate, trailer jacks, wheel chocks and truck or railroad boards.

Materials

Wood pallets or Pul-Pac unit load paper of materials such as finished case goods, raw materials or advertising and stationery stock.

Working Procedure

1. Obtain shipping, storing, transferring or receiving instructions from Supervisor.

2. Operate various types of fork lift trucks including trucks equipped vertically lift wood pallets up to 210 inches high or Pul-Pac slip sheets 185 inches high, requiring operation of hand controls for traveling forward and reverse, selecting a choice of up to four (4) speeds plus neutral, hoisting load up and down or sideways, tilting load backward and forward, clamping or unclamping Pul-Pac paper, pulling or pushing unit load into position and foot controls for applying power brakes to move partly filled and full loads of materials and empty wood pallets throughout warehouse; and to stack pallets of finished goods.

3. Operate automatic vertical pallet lifts by setting switch for automatic or semiautomatic operation, pushing call or send button as necessary and start and stop pallet conveyor.

4. Maintain orderly storage of stock by tearing down and rebuilding stacks of pallets and cases on full and partly filled pallets by hand.

5. Drive fork lift truck with care to prevent damage to surrounding equipment and materials and to reduce hazard.

6. Identify, count and record all necessary information concerning unloaded, stored, transferred or loaded orders including hand stacking of goods onto pallets and indicating quantity by marking case with chalk.

7. Use fork lift truck or Pul-Pac truck to move goods or materials into and out of storage, load and unload automatic elevator, automatic palletizers, railcars or trailer trucks.

8. Use lift truck to place bridge plates, dock boards and pontoons in position at truck or car or place empty pallets in pallet loaders.

9. Perform miscellaneous duties assigned by supervisor such as moving and stacking empty pallets, advertising and stationery stock, and picking up damaged pallets.

Dining Room Help "A"

Function
Serve a variety of food, perform general clean-up in dining rooms and act as Cashier when needed.

Tools and Equipment
Coffee urn, rags, cash register, dish washer, meat slicer, knife, and dollie wagon.

Materials
Prepared food, dishes and silverware.

Working Procedure

1. Clean tables and chairs throughout dining room.

2. Arrange silverware and dishes in preparation for distribution.

3. Operate meat slicer when necessary to prepare meat for sandwiches.

4. Dish out pies, puddings, fruits, bread and butter.

5. Help clean up dining room, including washing dishes and wiping tables.

6. Act as Cashier when needed.

7. Serve on service line when required.

Construction and Maintenance Electrician

Function
Install electrical equipment.

Tools and Equipment
Pipe benders, wrenches, threaders, cutters, electric hammer and drill, chain block, work trucks, drill press, ladder, hand tools such as pliers, screwdriver.

Materials
Wire, tape, motors, starters, controllers, switches, pushbutton stations, lights, conduit, fittings and similar electric equipment and parts.

Working Procedure
1. Read blueprints and sketches; make sketches for job layout.

2. Read wiring diagrams and connecting charts.

3. Select, measure, cut, thread, bend and erect conduit.

4. Cut and drill angle iron and make brackets.

5. Do installation work such as:
   a. Mount and connect controls, starters, fuses, breakers, pushbuttons, relays.
   b. Mount, align, fasten and connect motors and generators with help of Millwright or Machinist as necessary.
   c. Install substations, switchboards, P.A. systems, lights.
   d. Do construction wiring, as for elevators.
   e. Install meters and recorders.
   f. Install and know function of proximity switches, electric eyes and probe controls, electric counters.

6. Select proper size wire and conduit for various needs and proper size fuses, circuit breakers and other protective devices.

7. Check connections as job progresses and is completed; test as necessary.

8. Generally perform duties of maintenance electrician.

Multi-Die Cap Press Attendant

Function

Prepare bundles of tinplate for the Multi-Die Cap Press. Measure bundle to insure proper registration with feed system. Load bundles into feed section, operate start-stop controls and remove jams in order to maintain steady production of quality caps. Keep lined end packer properly supplied with packing containers.

Tools and Equipment

Hand lift truck, pinch bar, wire cutter, Multi-Die Cap Press and Liner, scrap truck, skids, corrugated or wood boxes, case roller conveyor, magnetic stick, crayon, pencil, production forms, paper cap sleeves, tape measure.

Materials

Electrolytic tinplate or tin free steel sheets with or without enamel coating or lithographed printing in mill bundles.

Working Procedure

1. Remove and set aside all outside wrappings from bundles of tinplate utilizing wire cutters to cut wire.

2. Place metal and cardboard wrapping in proper disposal barrel.

3. When the previous bundle is completed, lower elevator, dispose of empty pallet and load new bundle onto the sheet feeder.

4. Check double sheet detector for proper functioning at start of each bundle of plate.

5. Operate start-stop controls of the Multi-Die Press to maintain a steady production flow of caps to the two cap liners.

6. Stop the press to remove bent or damaged sheets from the feed section. Call mechanic when adjustments or repairs are required.

7. Record on stock ticket and on mill ticket, if available, the meter reading at the start of each bundle.

8. Occasionally tamp the scrap in the scrap bin and assist in changing the scrap bin when it is full.

9. Seal and load filled corrugated cases onto platform and move platform by hand lift truck to storage area when loaded.

10. Record date, time and production ticket number on production ticket when each platform load is moved to storage.

11. Keep working area clean and orderly.

Job Title	Job Number
Nurse's Helper	0400422

Function

Prepare medical materials; assist in attending minor cases; record accidents in log book then later transfer to permanent record card; sterilize instruments and dressings; perform specimen tests and eye examinations; prepare patients for doctor's examination; take charge of office procedures during relief periods as required.

Tools and Equipment

Instrument sterilizers, heat pack, muscle massage stimulator, heat lamp, eye testing machine, typewriter, file cabinets, miscellaneous laboratory equipment.

Materials

Gauze, cotton, tape, permanent history cards, loose leaf daily record book, log book, various chemical solutions, miscellaneous office materials.

Working Procedure

1. Assist with washing, dressing and removing dressings in minor cases under the direction of the nurse.

2. Record all accidents in current log book and then transfer the data to the employee's permanent history card. Code history cards for allergies, cardiac conditions, diabetes, epilepsy, etc. Submit monthly report to Factory office.

3. Assist with medical examinations by preparing patient for Doctor's examination, performing specimen analysis, operating eye testing machine and recording results.

4. Sterilize instruments and dressings by boiling or steaming.

5. Unpack and count incoming supplies, count-out or weigh medical supplies from stock into individual containers.

6. Keep hospital area and equipment clean and orderly.

7. Take charge of office procedures during relief periods or emergencies.

Packing Line Help

Function

Feed full tins or jars onto conveyors to labeling machines, inspect labeled and capped containers, form fibreboard cases and pack ready for sealing, stack or form cases for packer or feed and operate semi-automatic packing machines.

Tools and Equipment

Chutes, conveyors, sterilizing baskets on trucks, semi-automatic packing machines (side packing or drop packing), roller conveyors, and packing tables.

Materials

Labeled and capped containers of a variety of finished products and cases.

Working Procedure

1. Check codes on containers for conformance with variety being labeled and signal others when code changes.

2. Repetitively pick up and place containers in chute or on conveyor to maintain continuous flow to labeler.

3. Wipe jar tops, remove and dispose of defective or broken containers and remove minor jams before or after the labeler.

4. Inspect containers pass on conveyor, remove unacceptable containers and recondition when possible. Advise others of poor labeling.

5. Push full cases along roller conveyor or place onto conveyor.

6. Remove or replace packing case separators.

7. Operate controls on conveyors to prevent jams.

8. Pack containers on or off retort trucks and set cases aside periodically for sample collections.

9. Operate controls on can unscrambler or booster.

10. Pick up, form and place cases for semi-automatic packers, adjust flap and case separators and set damaged or imperfect cases aside.

11. Feed and operate semi-automatic case packer for tins or jars, replace jars or tins missed by packer and shove full case on conveyor to sealing operation.

12. Keep work place clean and orderly and clean conveyors and equipment.

Printer Operator

Function

To operate and load a corrugated shipping case printer, scorer and slotting machine, and make all the necessary adjustments that will assure that the printed flat shipping cases conform to specifications.

Tools and Equipment

Amatex printer, scorer and slotter, printing mats, ink viscometer and small hand tools such as wrenches and screwdrivers.

Materials

Corrugated blanks, ink, printed flat shipping cases.

Working Procedure

1. Prior to start-up of each printing order:
   a. Mount printing mat on printing cylinder.
   b. Fill ink reservoir if needed and correct the ink viscosity if out of tolerance.
   c. Make a carton test run and verify that the printed flat shipping cases conform to specifications.

2. Start printer, set counter, commence printing cases and continue to load corrugated blanks into the magazine until the production run is complete.

3. Performs periodic checks during the production run, to be sure the printed flat shipping cases conform to specifications.

4. After each printing schedule has been completed:
   a. Remove the printing mat and have it washed by the Printer Helper. Maintain inventory of printing mats.

5. When the day's printing schedule has been completed:
   a. Remove the printing mat and have it cleaned.
   b. Empty the ink reservoir.
   c. Flush out the ink delivery system.
   d. Clean up the printer.

6. Make all the necessary adjustments to convert case sizes.

7. Maintain a daily production report.

8. Notify Supervisor when: printing dies become worn, ink supply needs to be replenished, and when the printer malfunctions.

9. Direct the activities of the Printer Helper.

10. Periodically perform a detailed cleaning of the printer, including putting oil in the reservoir cups.

11. Keep work area neat and clean.

Case Palletizer Operator

Function

Operate more than one automatic case palletizer and related conveyors to provide a continuous flow of correctly stacked full pallets.

Tools and Equipment

Automatic case palletizers such as Von Gal, pallet dispensers, pencil and paper.

Materials

Cases of finished goods and wood pallets.

Working Procedure

1. Start the automatic case palletizers, pallet dispensers and related conveyors at the beginning of each shift, after each label change, and after removing jammed cases.

2. At the completion of each variety and account production run:
   a. Stop the automatic palletizing cycle.
   b. Record number of cases palletized.
   c. Manually operate start/stop controls to: clear the remaining cases from conveyors, palletize last layer, move partial pallet onto the pallet conveyor, and cycle in an empty pallet.
   d. Reset pallet pattern.

3. In the event a case becomes jammed in the palletizer:
   a. Stop the automatic palletizing cycle.
   b. Open the air pressure control valve to relieve the air pressure build-up.
   c. Remove the jammed case.
   d. Close the air pressure control valve.
   e. Manually operate start/stop controls to: complete stacking the partial layer, move the partial pallet onto the pallet conveyor, and cycle in an empty pallet.
   f. Record number of cases removed because of jam-up.
   g. Reset pallet pattern.

4. Remove any open, torn or turned case before it enters the palletizer.

5. Periodically check the pallet dispenser to assure pallet uniformity in the magazine. Remove any damaged pallet.

6. Keep work area clean and orderly.

7. When required, place a Pul-Pac slip sheet on empty pallet.

Cook's Helper

Function

Measure or weigh out batches of a variety of prepared ingredients into drums and buckets. Deliver batch containers to cooking kettles and mix ingredients for cooking. Assist Cook with a number of duties such as mixing and dumping ingredients.

Tools and Equipment

Platform scales, table scales, drums, buckets, scoops, electric hoists, drum dollies, electric mixers and tanks, kettles, four-wheeled trucks, can openers, knives, hatchets, spice wagons and containers, tables, gauge rods, stirring paddles, grinders, dicers, pumps, pulpers, scrapers, strainers, casks and electric or hand transporters.

Materials

All ingredients used in cooking such as meat, chicken, flour, cereals, dairy products, spices, vegetables, tomato pulp or paste, chocolate, and sauces.

Working Procedure

1. Push truck or move platform or pallet loads of ingredient materials to weighing and mixing area on hand or electric transporters.
2. Open bags, cans, drums, barrels or crates of materials. Place stock tags on file hook or box.
3. Measure or weigh out ingredients according to recipe card or oral instructions.
4. Strain and dump specified quantity of ingredients into Day Mixers, tanks or kettles and mix according to directions. Discharge and weigh out into batch lots and place on trucks. Open and fill casks with sauce mixtures.
5. Move filled batch containers to cooking kettles on trucks, dollies or in retorts.
6. Help Cook dump containers into kettle by hand or with aid of electric hoists. Place containers on platform for Cooks.
7. Operate controls on mixers and stirrers, operate pumps to transfer liquid mixtures and pulps from tanks to kettles or from mix kettles to cooking kettles or pulpers. Check quantity of ingredients in tank and kettles.
8. Dice, grind or cut up meats, vegetables, cheese, etc., and distribute in batch lots.
9. Works under close direction of Cook or Supervisor.
10. Move retorts to filler chute and dump or shovel mixture into chute.
11. Flush and scour out kettles and know operation of kettle controls.
12. Fold ingredient containers, stack on trucks, and deliver waste and containers to elevator. Keep working area clean and in an orderly condition.
13. Inspect and remove any foreign materials as batch lots are prepared.
14. Keep records of materials used or batches prepared.
15. Open, dump, and rinse out cans of pulp or juice into drums or tanks.
16. Help Cooks where necessary and have supplies on hand ahead of each kettle batch.

Research Analyst "A"

Function

Set up and calibrate laboratory apparatus to conduct experiments in laboratory or pilot shop. Follow, record and report results of experiments.

Tools and Equipment

A wide variety of laboratory apparatus necessary in food technology research such as a pH Meter, Amylograph, distillation equipment, Colorimeter and vacuum equipment, pilot shop research equipment, etc.

Materials

All types of raw ingredients through to finished goods in tins, jars, or other containers.

Working Procedure

1. Set up, calibrate and operate a wide variety of laboratory apparatus to evaluate raw materials and finished goods for quality factors.

2. Operate specialized equipment such as distillation equipment for fractionation and concentration of flavors.

3. Assist in conducting preliminary laboratory tests prior to institution of larger scale pilot plant tests. Cook small laboratory batches, assist in developing recipes.

4. Conduct experimental tests in pilot plant to determine practicability of using new products, raw materials; processes.

5. Assist in transferring pilot plant operation to production operation. Instruct Factory Personnel in proper operating techniques as required.

6. Supervise storing of samples, laboratory equipment and supplies in laboratory storeroom.

7. Maintain written records of all experimental work in addition to making out routine data sheets.

Part II

Quantitative Systems of Evaluation

5

Quantitative Systems— Factor Comparison

It is generally accepted that the non-quantitative job systems (ranking and job classification) are subjective in nature and leave a lot to be desired when applied to a large number of diversified jobs. In companies with a small number of jobs or positions on the payroll, or in one that has a limited amount of resources, these approaches, especially ranking system using the paired comparison with point values, can be adequate.

All evaluation systems have both strong and weak points, and the selection of the system depends on the following factors, to name just a few.

number and complexity of the jobs

availability of funds

level of the jobs to be evaluated

availability of knowledgable persons to be in charge of the program

acceptance of job evaluation by the employees

(To overcome some of the weak points in the non-quantitative programs, two main techniques, factor comparison and weighted in points, were developed for evaluating jobs in a quantitative manner.)

Fig. 5.1 Comparison of the Weighted-in-Points Method
to the Factor-Comparison Method

Factor-Comparison Method	Weighted-in-Points Method
A quantitative method of evaluating jobs against others without a pre-determined scale. Jobs are related by factorial comparison.	Measures a job factor by factor against a pre-determined scale of relative value and provides a quantitative job-to-scale measurement. Jobs are related by factorial analysis.

Source: American Compensation Association, *Books 46 and 47*. ACA, P.O. Box 1176, Scottsdale, Arizona, 85252.

The two approaches are in reality merely variations of the same system, in that they both break down the jobs into factors or job characteristics (Fig. 5.1). The only difference between the two is that the factor-comparison method compares job against job and the weighted-in-points evaluation compares the job against a point scale.

WEIGHTED-IN-POINTS METHOD

A point rating system compares each job against a pre-determined job factor (characteristic) and assigns a point value for that characteristic.

Fig. 5.2 Characteristics of the Weighted-in-Points Method

> Most popular of the formal plans
>
> Provides a scale or yardstick
>
> Utilizes compensable factors common to the group
>
> Utilizes differentiating degrees or graduations for each factor
>
> Defines and weights factors and degrees
>
> Measures jobs in component parts
>
> Adapts to large organizations
>
> Adapts to diverse job groups

Source: American Compensation Association, *Books 46 and 47*. ACA, P.O. Box 1176, Scottsdale, Arizona, 85252.

Generally speaking, as few as five and as many as 20 factors may be chosen, and each job is compared against these factors and points assigned accordingly. The job that receives the most points is considered the most demanding and/or important and receives the most wages. The other jobs are ranked according to their point value and assigned to a computed wage schedule. This method will be explained in greater detail starting in Chapter 6. Statistics show that over two-thirds of all evaluation systems are prepared in the point rating manner (Fig. 5.2).

FACTOR-COMPARISON METHOD

This quantitative approach is different from the point system in that a group or set of factors is chosen and is given a pre-determined weight (ranking of importance in relation to 100 percent). The factors most generally chosen are:

skill
responsibility
mental requirements
physical requirements
working conditions

All jobs are ranked in importance in each of these factors and receive a money value for their position in rank. The total money value for the five rankings for each job is the wage rate to be paid for that job. This approach to job evaluation has several advantages over the point rating system as well as some disadvantages (Fig. 5.3).

The remainder of this chapter will be devoted to explaining the advantages and disadvantages of the factor-comparison system and how this system is developed and functions within a company. Chapter 6 will do the same for the weighted-in-points evaluation system.

Proponents of the factor-comparison system of job evaluation feel that the proper way of paying for services received is to compare one job against the other jobs in the program. They feel that this is the best way of obtaining the true worth of the various jobs.

Advantages and Disadvantages of the Factor-Comparison System

Usually only five basic factors are used: skill, responsibility, mental requirements, physical requirements, and working conditions. As you

Fig. 5.3 Characteristics of the Factor-Comparison Method

Utilizes significant compensable factors usually 3 to 5

Utilizes key jobs selected to represent each major level of duties, responsibilities, and skills encompassed within range of jobs to be evaluated

Compares jobs factor by factor and ranks from low to high

Proportions total current pay to each in correlation to ranking

Establishes factor money scale

Evaluates other jobs to key benchmark values

Adds factor values to determine total job value

Source: American Compensation Association, *Books 46 and 47*. ACA, P.O. Box 1176, Scottsdale, Arizona, 85252.

can see by the titles, there is very little overlap between the factors. This is not always the case under the point rating system. For example: is there a clear-cut division between judging on the factors of experience and training and judging on the factor of job knowledge?

There is no writing of definitions under the factor-comparison method. Each job is ranked in importance on the factors being used and a money value set to their ranking. Under the point method, if seven factors were used and each were divided into four to seven levels, then approximately 35 to 40 different definitions would have to be written. This is time consuming and is difficult to do correctly.

Managers who favor the factor-comparison method feel that the biggest recommendation for this method is that it is custom-made for the company. It is the ranking of jobs compared to each other, and not to a factor description. They feel that this is the crux of job evaluation, that the program should decide which jobs in your company are more important and thus should receive more pay. The author can agree to this premise, but is the factor-comparison method defensible in the following areas?

1. In handling a grievance concerning the status of a particular job, can the company management really explain why one job was ranked higher or lower than another job? Under the point rating method, this is easier and more systematically handled.

2. In ranking of jobs, two jobs may be ranked eighth and ninth, but in reality there is a smaller difference between seven and eight than between eight and nine. However, the jobs are merely ranked 7, 8, and 9. Under the point rating method for this factor, job seven may receive 30 points, job eight 50 points, and job nine 60 points. The ranking system implies only that one job is higher than another on a certain factor, but not to what degree it is higher. Under the point rating system, the difference is taken into consideration by placing the job in the correct degree level.

In most factor-comparison systems the money values are allotted to the ranking the jobs receive. On the one hand, this is very good because the employee understands money allocation much better than when the computation is done in points and/or percentages and then converted to a money value. On the other hand, direct allocating of money has one major drawback in that employees might try to manipulate or negotiate as much as possible the rankings that they realize affect the money values. The assigning of money to each job on each factor under the factor-comparison method is an extremely difficult task.

Since the factor-comparison method compares one job against the other jobs rather than a part of the job compared to a paragraph definition, the discussion becomes very general and not specific in nature. Consequently, there may be confusion and frustration on the part of the employee if he does not realize why his job was ranked above or below other jobs he has in mind.

The factor-comparison system is tied somewhat to the existing pay schedule and thus it is more easily understood and accepted, being similar to something the employee has previously had. Under the point rating method, similarly rated jobs are grouped into grades and then the grade is assigned a money value. Some personnel managers feel that sometimes there is too much of a tendency to fit the new system to the present pay scale rather than determining what is the proper pay scale—the very thing a job evaluation program is supposed to do.

INSTALLING A FACTOR-COMPARISON JOB EVALUATION PROGRAM

The first five steps in this method are identical with those of the ranking and job-classification methods.

1. Notify all employees of the pending program.
2. Update the organizational structure of the company.
3. Assign duties in each area or department.
4. Prepare a job questionnaire for each position.
5. Write the job descriptions.

They are explained in Chapters 7, 8, 9, and 10.

Step 6—Prepare Job Specifications

There should be a job specification to accompany each job description. This writeup explains the minimum requirements for each job in terms of the factors being used. A form such as the one shown in Fig. 14.4 is prepared for each job description. This job specification, together with the accompanying job description, permits the rater to systematically and logically compare one job with all the others in the group. A review on the preparation and use of job specifications can be found in Chapter 14.

Step 7—Select the Factors

Under the weighted-in-points method of job evaluation any number from five to 20 might be used in making the job evaluation program. This is also true in the factor-comparison approach, but usually only five factors are used:

mental requirement
skill
physical requirements
responsibility
working conditions [1]

These factors, originally selected by Benge, have basically been used in most factor-comparison programs for the past 40 years. Additional factors can be added, but then there can be overlapping. These

1. Benge, Eugene J., Samuel H. Burk, and Edward N. Hay. *Manual of Job Evaluation.* New York: Harper and Brothers, 1941.

same basic factors are also used in the weighted-in-points plan, but are generally broken down into sub-factors, with each sub-factor being assigned a certain percentage of weight in the overall plan. Adopting more than five factors for the factor-comparison method would make it extremely difficult to work with, as money values must be assigned to each of the jobs in accordance with their rank in each factor. With many factors this would be quite difficult and very time consuming.

Step 8—Define the Factors

Definitions must be prepared for describing each factor. In other words what do we really mean when we are ranking jobs on the factor of working conditions? Does the factor only mean whether the job is clean, dirty, hot, cold, damp, noisy; or does it also include such items as hazardous work, mental stress, or some other disagreeable element? A definition must be written to define what the factor actually is measuring. These definitions should be custom made for each company although a general definition might be adapted from another company.

Following are the five major factors and examples of their definitions.

Mental Requirements   The knowledge to do the job may be inherent or acquired. It is the part of the job that requires the person to use intellect. On some jobs it may be in the form of specialized or technical training such as industrial engineering, food chemistry, accounting, or statistical quality control.

Examples are:

1. The knowledge needed by a skilled craftsman to diagnose a problem with a piece of equipment and then have the knowledge to repair it.
2. The knowledge and judgment needed by a crew leader to solve a current production problem and the ability to get the members of the crew to perform a fair day's work.

Skill   This factor is not to be confused with mental requirements. Mental requirement means having the mental ability to do the job; skill refers to the manual skill needed to perform the work. This includes the manual dexterity/coordination, the experience, and/or the practice time to do the work quickly and accurately. This factor also includes the sensory skills that may be required to do the job satisfactorily. Examples are:

1. A fork lift operator must have the skill to operate swiftly and accurately a fork lift truck. In addition, he or she must also have good depth perception so as not to damage the case goods.
2. A secretary must have the manual dexterity to type accurately 50 words per minute.

Physical Requirement   This factor refers to the physical demand placed on the employee. It takes into account the degree of physical effort and whether the demand is continuous or intermittent. Such conditions as lifting, standing, climbing, walking, etc. are evaluated.

Responsibility   This factor appraises what the holder of the job is held accountable for such as records, equipment, materials, safety of others, training, or supervision.

Work Conditions   This factor appraises both the working conditions and the hazards of the job. Those conditions that tend to make the work pleasant or disagreeable such as heat, cold, dampness, noise, odor, ventilation, illumination, dirt, fumes, and unsanitary conditions are taken into consideration. Those conditions that tend to make the work unsafe, such as working with high voltage, working at excessive heights, or doing heavy physical work are also considered [2].

Step 9—Select the Key Jobs

When first establishing the comparison scale table the new jobs being ranked are compared to certain key jobs in the company and ranked either above or below them. Key jobs are significant in establishing the program because *all jobs are evaluated and rated against them.* To qualify as a key job, sometimes called a benchmark job, a position should meet the following requirements:

1. It should be well known throughout the organization. Titles such as janitor, fork lift operator, and electrician meet this requirement,

2. *Ibid.*

as most employees have a basic idea of what duties these jobs require.

2. There should not be any dispute as to the proper level of pay for this job. This is an *absolute must*, for if there are questions or grievances being filed over its level of pay, it is not a proper job to be used as a key example for the program.

3. There should be more than one employee assigned to the job. This is not absolutely necessary, but is desirable, since a job with only one employee assigned to it is not generally very well known by other employees in the plant.

The number of key jobs to be chosen depends on the total number of jobs to be evaluated. If possible, 10 to 15 jobs should be selected. Once other jobs have been ranked against the selected key jobs, they, too, become part of the system. Jobs still to be ranked must also be ranked against all of the jobs in the system at the time of their ranking. Example: If there were 15 key jobs, then the first job to be ranked would be compared to the 15. The second job, however, now would be compared to the 16 total jobs, then to 17, etc. If there were 53 total jobs, then the 53rd to be ranked would be compared to the 52 jobs already ranked into the system, not just to the original 15 benchmarked jobs.

All of the committee members should be in agreement on the terminology used in the job descriptions, the definitions of the factors, and the compensation rates for these key (benchmarked) jobs.

At this stage of implementing a factor-comparison system, the following items should have been completed:

1. a written job description for all the jobs to be in the program
2. job specifications for all of the jobs
3. a definition of each factor being used in the evaluation
4. ten to fifteen key (benchmark) jobs selected and agreed upon by the evaluation committee

Step 10—Review Job Descriptions and Factor Definitions

A review should be made by the evaluation committee of the job descriptions for the key jobs. It is important that each job description is clear and understood by each of the committee members. The committee then critically studies the definitions of the factors being used.

There should be complete agreement among the committee members as to job requirements for each job, and each person on the committee should have a good understanding of what the factor definitions really mean. These two steps are extremely important before any ranking of jobs can be started.

Step 11—Rank by Factor

Using the job descriptions and the job specifications for each job, the committee ranks the key jobs in the order of their importance on each of the five factors. To be sure all raters are comparing to the same

Fig. 5.4
Average Rank of Benchmark Jobs

| Job title | Average Rank as Determined by the Committee | | | | |
	Skill	Mental requirements	Physical requirements	Responsibility	Working conditions
Yard maintenance	1	1	8	1.1†	8
Key punch operator B*	4	3	4	2.4	5
Mail clerk	2	4	7	5.3	4
Printer A	7	7	6	6.7	7
Clerk-typist	3	2	2	3.8	1
Key punch operator A*	6	5	3	4.1	6
Electronic technician A	8	8	5	7.9	2
Accounting clerk	5	6	1	7.1	3

*It is not good practice to have two levels of abilities of the same job as benchmark jobs, but these examples were used to show how to handle the problem when all of the jobs are being ranked. Since the key punch operators work in the same general location, the working conditions are practically the same, but Operator A was ranked higher on this factor because of the stress of the job.

†In the column for responsibility, the ranking is shown as it would be if the committee averaged its score to obtain the ranking.

measuring stick, an understanding should be reached by the committee as to what they feel the definitions actually mean. Any one of the ranking approaches as discussed in Chapter 3 may be used, but the comparison system using numbers seems to produce the most accurate results. As a last resort, averaging may be used by the committee to reach an agreement on the ranking. If a particular job appears to be completely out of line in the ranking, it probably is a sign of misunderstanding or intentional bias, and a detailed review should be made of the job.

Figure 5.4 shows a ranking of the key jobs in a company. The ranking for these jobs was facilitated by reviewing the job descriptions in the Chapter 3 Work Exercise.

Note from Fig. 5.4 that in the factor column mental requirement, the highest rank (8) is given to the job of Electronic technician A while the lowest rank (1) is assigned to the job of Yard maintenance. On the other hand, in the factor column physical requirement, the highest rank (8) was assigned to the job of Yard maintenance and the lowest rank (1) is assigned to the job of Accounting clerk.

Step 12—Assign Money Values to Factors for Each Key Job

The committee now establishes the base wage rate for all the ranked key jobs (to be shown in Fig. 5.6). The money value for each of the jobs is divided among the five factors in accordance with how the committee believes each factor relates to the total job.

This step is probably the most important one of the system and it is also the most difficult one to carry out in any of the different job evaluation methods. Money values must be assigned to each factor for each job.

Assuming that the Electronic technician A receives $5.83 an hour, the Accounting clerk $4.23 an hour, and the Yard maintenance $3.35 an hour, the money values might be distributed for each factor of these three jobs as shown in Fig. 5.5.

To aid in the allocation of money to each of the five factors, the committee may prepare a job comparison scale (see step 13). This scale reveals how much money is assigned to each factor for each job. For example the ranking and money value for the lowest four jobs on the factor responsibility could be as shown in Table 5.1.

The assigning of 45 cents for this factor for Clerk–typist was not an absolute must, but the money value had to be somewhere between the number 2 ranked job, Key punch operator B at 38 cents, and the

Fig. 5.5
Money Values Apportioned to Five Factors for Three Key Jobs

Factor	Three Key Jobs and Assigned Money Rates		
	Electronic technician A	Accounting clerk	Yard maintenance
Skill	1.45	1.10	.40
Mental requirements	2.81	2.15	1.20
Physical requirements	.50	.10	1.00
Responsibility	.95	.75	.20
Working conditions	.12	.13	.55
Total base rate	5.83	4.23	3.35

Table 5.1
Responsibility Factor

	Rank	Rate
Yard maintenance	1	$.20
Key punch operator B	2	.38
Clerk–typist	3	.45
Key punch operator A	4	.50

Table 5.2
Physical Requirement Factor

	Rank	Money value
Accounting clerk	1	$.10
Clerk–typist	2	.28
Key punch operator A	3	.30
Key punch operator B	4	.43

number 4 ranked job of Key punch operator A at 50 cents. The ranking
of the jobs determines the wage range within which an individual job
rate may be placed.

Another example of how to assign money values might be made by reviewing the ranking and money assignments for the jobs in Table 5.2 on the factor of physical requirement.

As stated in Table 5.2, it is not absolutely necessary to assign 28 and 30 cents to the jobs of Clerk–typist and Key punch operator A, but the amount must be located somewhere between the number 1 rank job of Accounting clerk, at 10 cents, and the number 4 rank job of Key punch operator B, at 43 cents. The exact location on the money scale for this factor may be shifted a few cents either way to slot the job in its proper ranking and money value as shown in column two in Fig. 5.6.

By ranking all of the key jobs and assigning a money value to each factor for each job, a table (Fig. 5.6) can be prepared. The table is established in the following manner.

1. All key jobs are listed in the left column, starting with the highest paid job and ending with the lowest.
2. The hourly wage base rate determined by the committee is placed in column 2.
3. The ranking for each factor for each job and the distributed money values are placed in columns 3 through 12.
4. The total distributed money values for each factor, added horizontally, must equal the established base rate.

The distribution of money is first made for the benchmarked jobs. This table is then used as a guide for all the remaining jobs to be evaluated. This part of the evaluation appears to the author to be a weakness in this approach to job evaluation. It tends to tie the money value to the present rate system—the very factor that the evaluation program is attempting to judge for fairness and equity. Invariably, after years under the personal rate approach, some jobs in a company will be either too low or too high. The factor-comparison system because of sticking close to the rates of the key jobs does not correct this inequity as well as the other three approaches to job evaluation.

Once all the benchmarked jobs have had money values assigned to them, the table should be checked to see if the dollar values are in synchronization with their vertical ranking. If these values are correct, then the values for each job on each factor should be checked horizontally to ascertain if they also add up to the present wage rate of the job.

Fig. 5.6
Ranking and Money Values

1	2	3	4	5	6	7	8	9	10	11	12
	Hourly Base Rate	Skill		Mental requirements		Physical requirements		Responsi- bility		Working conditions	
Job title	Rate	Rank	Rate	Rank	Rate	Rank	Rate	Rank	Rate	Rank	Rate
Electronic technician A	$5.83	(8)	(1) 1.45	8	1 2.81	5	4 .50	8	1 .95	2	7 .12
Printer A	5.07	(7)	2 1.25	7	2 2.31	6	3 .56	6	3 .65	7	2 .30
Accounting clerk	4.23	(5)	4 1.10	6	3 2.15	1	8 .10	7	2 .75	3	6 .13
Key punch operator A	4.06	(6)	3 1.20	5	4 1.85	3	6 .30	4	5 .50	6	3 .21
Mail clerk	3.75	(2)	7 .76	4	5 1.60	7	2 .67	5	4 .55	4	5 .17
Key punch operator B	3.60	(4)	1.06	3	6 1.55	4	5 .43	2	7 .38	5	4 .18
Clerk-typist	3.41	(3)	6 1.05	2	7 1.53	2	7 .28	3	6 .45	1	8 .10
Yard maintenance	3.35	(1)	8 .40	1	8 1.20	8	1 1.00	1	8 .20	8	1 .55

Factor Ranking and Money Values

Step 13—Evaluate All Other Jobs

The assigning of rates and the ranking for each factor for each key job has now established a measuring stick (Fig. 5.6) for ranking jobs and evaluating factors in money values. The committee is now ready to complete the evaluation of all jobs by comparing them with the key jobs. This process is aided by constructing a job comparison scale (Fig. 5.7). On this chart, the title of each job is placed opposite the money level to which the job was assigned for that factor. Each job title appears on the chart five different times and at five different locations on the money scale. There has to be a money rating for each factor. The five money ratings add up to the total value for the job.

All remaining jobs to be evaluated are ranked or compared against the job comparison scale. Usually the committee considers one job at a time in its relative position to the key jobs and their evaluated ranking and money values. The evaluation continues in the following manner.

The committee reads the job description for the job being evaluated and compares it with the job descriptions in the general area where the committee believes the job will rank. For example, if the committee feels that the job being evaluated compares very favorably with the job of Printer A on the factor of responsibility, the committee will review the job descriptions of three jobs—Accounting clerk; Printer A; and Mail clerk (the key jobs ranked above and below the job of Printer A as shown on the job comparison scale). By reviewing these three jobs, the committee can determine if the new job does rank in this general area, and then can set a money value for the job being evaluated. Each time a job is evaluated and the money values assigned, the job is listed in its respective position on each of the factors on the job comparison scale. Other jobs to be evaluated are then compared to the key jobs as well as to all the other jobs on the job comparison scale. As soon as all jobs in the group have been slotted in each factor and money values are assigned, the evaluated program is completed.

Step 14—Assign Jobs to Pay Grades

Since the wage rate for each job is set by adding the money values for the five factors, there is no real need to group jobs into pay grades. If a company feels, however, that it has too many individual pay levels, it may group jobs with similar pay levels into a pay grade and assign one level of pay for these jobs. The grouping would be done as when working with points as will be shown in the weighted-in-points method.

Fig. 5.7
Job Comparison Scale

Money value	Mental requirements	Skill	Physical requirements	Responsibility	Working conditions
$2.81	Electronic technician A				
2.50					
2.47					
2.44					
2.41					
2.38					
2.35					
2.32	Printer A				
2.29					
2.26					
2.23					
2.20					
2.17					
2.14	Accounting clerk				
2.11					
2.08					
2.05					
2.02					
1.99					
1.96					
1.93					
1.90					
1.87					
1.85	Key punch A				
1.82					
1.79					
1.76					
1.73					
1.70					
1.67					
1.64					

Value				
1.61	Mail clerk			
1.58	Key punch B			
1.55	Clerk-typist			
1.52				
1.49				
1.46				
1.43		Electronic technician	Electronic technician	
1.40				
1.37				
1.34				
1.31				
1.29				
1.26		Printer A		
1.23				
1.20	Clerk-typist	Key punch A		
1.17				
1.14				
1.11		Accounting clerk		
1.08		Key punch B		
1.05		Clerk-typist		
1.02				
.99			Yard maintenance	
.96				
.93				
.90				
.87				
.84				
.81				
.78				
.75		Mail clerk		
.72			Mail clerk	
.69				Accounting clerk
.66				Printer A
.63				
.60				

Fig. 5.7
Job Comparison Scale (continued)

Money value	Mental requirements	Skill	Physical requirements	Responsibility	Working conditions
.57			Printer A		
.54				Mail clerk	Yard maintenance
.51					
.48			Electronic technician	Key punch A	
.45				Clerk-typist	
.42					
.39		Yard maintenance	Key punch B	Key punch B	
.36					
.33					
.30			Key punch A		Printer A
.27			Clerk-typist		
.24					Key punch A
.21				Yard maintenance	Key punch B
.18					Mail clerk
.15			Accounting clerk		Accounting clerk
.12					Electronic technician
.09					Clerk-typist
.06					

Summary

As stated earlier, the factor-comparison job evaluation program does have some distinct advantages:

1. It is custom made for each particular company.
2. Once the evaluation scales are established, it is relatively easy to evaluate other jobs and to slot them into the program.
3. Jobs are compared to other jobs within the company and a relationship is established between them.

On the other hand, the system has some serious disadvantages:

1. It is imperative that proper key jobs are selected and that these jobs do not change in job content. If they do, the rating scale becomes obsolete.
2. It is difficult to establish the money values for the five factors for each job. Each money value must be within the price range for that particular job's position in the ranking for that factor.
3. Installing the system does take a considerable amount of time.
4. If a union is involved, there may be much disagreement and argument over the assignment of money values for each factor on each job.

Review Questions

1. List the five factors generally used when evaluating by the factor-comparison method.

2. What is the difference between a quantitative and a non-quantitative job evaluation program?

3. What general advantages do the quantitative methods of job evaluation have over the non-quantitative methods?

4. Why is it unrealistic to use ten to fifteen factors when using the factor comparison method of evaluating?

5. Explain the difference between the factors of mental requirements and skill.

6. List the criteria that you think should be met in selecting a job evaluation method.

Case Problem

1. From the job descriptions in the Chapter 3 Work Exercise, proceed through the necessary steps under the factor-comparison system to have a finished job comparison scale similar to Fig. 5.7.

Quantitative Systems—
Weighted in Points

The weighted-in-points method is the most popular approach to job evaluation. Two out of three programs, particularly for employees on the hourly payroll, are evaluated in this way. Since it is the leader of the four approaches to job evaluation, it will be discussed in much greater detail. In fact the rest of the book, excluding wage and salary administration and employee performance appraisal, is devoted to the weighted-in-points job evaluation program.

As stated earlier, this method compares each job against a predetermined job factor (characteristic) and assigns point values for that characteristic. The job that receives the most points is considered the most demanding and/or important and receives the most wages.

In establishing the factors against which the jobs are compared, a great deal of study is made as to what factors can best be used in comparing the jobs. Once the factors have been chosen, it is then possible to refine the process further by "weighting" the factors. This procedure allows the assigning of the proper value that each factor contributes to the overall value of the job. It is thought that by comparing a job to a factor definition nearly all bias is removed from the evaluation because the individual employee's approach to the work is not part of the evaluation process.

ADVANTAGES OF THE WEIGHTED-IN-POINTS METHOD

There are many advantages to the weighted-in-points method. They will be discussed first followed by a list of the disadvantages.

The committee doing the rating of the jobs can do so very satisfactorily without knowing all of the jobs in the company. The rater studies the job description and then evaluates one job against the definitions defining each factor. A point value for a job on a factor is then determined. Compare this with the factor-comparison approach where the raters must compare each job against all the other jobs in the program and thus must be knowledgable about all of the jobs. Such a committee is hard to find, especially in a large company that perhaps may have 200 or more different jobs.

Once the definitions for the factors have been established, they are usable for a long time. It is true that it is time consuming to first write these definitions, but it is a one-time task and the definition manual lasts for many years.

Using point values and evaluating all jobs against the same factors is a very systematic approach. It simplifies slotting new jobs into the program as well as reevaluating existing jobs. For example, if working conditions were a factor and the working conditions of a particular job changed, the job evaluation committee would need only to reevaluate this job on the one factor "working conditions." If the point rating were changed, then the total points would be changed. If the point change was sufficient to place the job into a higher or lower pay grade, such a change would be made. Under the factor-comparison system, the "changed" job would be compared on a total basis with all the other jobs in the work group to see if this change in work conditions would warrant a change in its position of rank on this factor.

The weighted-in-points system is more free of bias because the committee is comparing a job against 5 to 20 different factors; therefore, if a judgment were swayed either up or down, the effect would not be carried over into other factors. On the other hand, when comparing one total job with other jobs, there is more chance for bias. In addition, the raters may not be too familiar with all of the jobs and tend to rate the jobs they know higher than the ones about which they know very little.

With the point system, the total point score is obtained for each factor and each job; therefore, a comparison system can also be used when all of the jobs have been evaluated. At that time, a box score, explained in detail in Chapter 14, can be established. By comparing point scores for such jobs as secretary, typist, file clerk, and receptionist on each of the factors, the committee can immediately determine if an error was made when each job was individually evaluated. If all the workers on these four jobs worked in the same room but one of the group got a higher rating on work conditions, then this rating should be restudied just to be sure an error had not been made when the job was originally evaluated. This comparison of points on each factor, in regard to jobs of similar skills and importance, provides a double check to be sure an error was not made.

With each job being evaluated against each of the factors, the rater must review each job in exactly the same way. This gives consistency of evaluation. This consistency is not present in the factor-comparison system, in which the total job is viewed against the other jobs in the system.

In the factor-comparison system, one or two jobs may be ranked ahead of a particular job, but this ranking does not necessarily determine the degree of difference between the two jobs. Under the point system, each job ultimately receives a total point score. The differences between the two scores show a more exacting position. A point spread of seven is quite different than one of 33. Of course the pay increment should also reflect this exacting difference.

The handling of grievances concerning the evaluation of a job is simpler under the point system. If an employee wishes to compare his job evaluation against another job in the work force, he needs only to review the point values for each factor. If, for example, there were seven factors used and the two jobs were rated equal on five of the factors, then the discussion could be centered on the two factors that tended to favor the other job, placing it in a higher pay grade. This narrows the area of discussion to only those two factors. Under the factor-comparison system, the rater again views the total job against the other jobs on each of the factors. The decision is more subjective and less defensible under this approach.

In the weighted-in-points evaluation program, after the evaluation has been completed and the point scores established for each job, it is a relatively easy assignment to group similarly rated jobs into pay grades and assign money values. For instance, all jobs under 150 points would be assigned to grade one, 151 to 170 points to grade two, 171 to 190 points to grade three, etc. Each grade level would be assigned a money value. This is not a difficult task under the factor-comparison system, since the results are in terms of money, but many feel that there is a tendency to "fit" the program to the present rate structure rather than to create a totally new one.

Over a period of time, jobs do change in content. Is the change sufficient to warrant a change in grade? This, of course, is the big question. Under a point rating system it is possible to study a portion of the job that affects only one or two of the factors. The same is not true in the factor-comparison system where one must compare the *total* job against the other jobs. This approach prevents studying only the part of the job that has changed. One disadvantage of the point rating system that Benge did not mention is the difficulty in defining the various levels of each factor. It is important to have a clear-cut definition for each level within a factor. If there are to be six levels or degrees within a factor, then each must be carefully defined so that all raters may consistently judge that the same job definitely belongs on the same level. In the point method, there is no way of evaluating a job at 2 1/2 or 2 1/3. The rating must be either at level two or at level three. There is no interpolation between levels.

In reviewing the four approaches to job evaluation—ranking, job classification, factor comparison, and weighted in points—we find that each has some very strong points as well as some that may be termed a disadvantage. As stated earlier, the *selection of a system to be used at any one company depends on many factors.*

DISADVANTAGES OF THE WEIGHTED-IN-POINTS SYSTEM

Eugene J. Benge, considered by many to be the first to sponsor the factor-comparison system, discusses in his book, [1], reasons why he feels that the factor-comparison system is superior to the weighted in points system. The weaknesses of the point system as seen by Benge are:

1. A fixed number of factors, for which points will be assigned, must be established. Hence, the point system assumes that all jobs are composed of those factors and only those factors.

1. Benge, Eugene J. *Job Evaluation and Merit Rating.* New York: National Foremen's Institute, 1943, pp. 18–21. Quoted in Otis, J. and R. Leukart. *Job Evaluation, A Basis for Sound Wage Administration,* 2nd ed. Englewood Cliffs, N.J.: Prentice Hall, 1959.

2. The assignment of point values for varying degrees of each factor is arbitrarily done.

3. Upper limits of the points to be assigned to the several factors must be arbitrarily established.

4. The point system sets up seeming refinements that are not inherent in the judgments made by use of them.

5. A unit is created that is undefined. This unit is a point.

6. Factors are frequently undefined. [This may have been true at one time, but does not seem to be true today.]

7. Under the point system the job analysis itself tends to set the value of the job rather than the job comparison.

It is true that selecting and weighting the factors to be used in the point system is the critical part of the system, but it also has good advantages over other approaches to job evaluation. In selecting the factors against which jobs are compared, there is not a set number that is required. If a certain factor (job characteristic) is shown as being present in most of the jobs in the company, then that factor should be chosen to be used. Some systems have as many as 20 factors being used. The weighting of the factors is done in the same manner if you have 7 or 17 factors. The total percentage used for all the factors must add up to 100 percent. The author feels that the advantages and value of the weighted-in-points system far exceed those of any other methods, especially for hourly paid and non-exempt office jobs. The weaknesses as listed by Benge can be minimized by carefully studying the job descriptions and selecting the necessary factors that will evaluate the jobs. The factors used for office employees would be different than those used for jobs in production, professional, management, etc. *Unusual jobs are difficult to slot properly, regardless of the system that is being used.*

A summary of the steps followed when establishing a weighted-in-points system is shown in Fig. 6.1.

Fig. 6.1 Steps in Establishing a Weighted-in-Points Job Evaluation Program

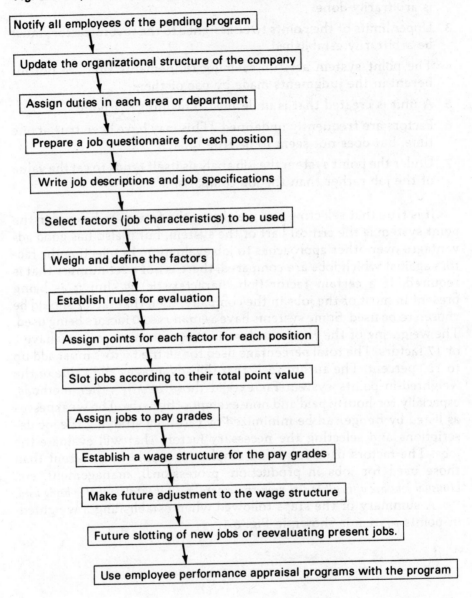

Notify all employees of the pending program

Update the organizational structure of the company

Assign duties in each area or department

Prepare a job questionnaire for each position

Write job descriptions and job specifications

Select factors (job characteristics) to be used

Weigh and define the factors

Establish rules for evaluation

Assign points for each factor for each position

Slot jobs according to their total point value

Assign jobs to pay grades

Establish a wage structure for the pay grades

Make future adjustment to the wage structure

Future slotting of new jobs or reevaluating present jobs.

Use employee performance appraisal programs with the program

Review Questions

1. When comparing the factor-comparison method to the weighted-in-points method, do the disadvantages outweigh the advantages? Explain.

2. Explain briefly the four basic methods of job evaluation. Under what conditions would you recommend ranking, job classification, factor comparison, or point rating?

3. List in chronological order the steps necessary to complete a weighted-in-points job evaluation system.

4. Speculate on the reasons why the weighted-in-points job evaluation program is used in over two-thirds of all evaluation systems.

5. Prepare a chart that shows the advantages and disadvantages of the four job evaluation methods described in this text.

6. Why is "weighting" of the factors important in the weighted-in-points method of job evaluation?

7. Why would it be unrealistic to change the "weight" of the factors after the program was in existence?

8. Defend the position that the weighted-in-points method of job evaluation is more free of bias than any of the other programs.

Case Problem

1. You are the Personnel Manager of a company that has 81 different production jobs with 419 employees assigned to the jobs. Your company president has asked that you recommend a formal job evaluation program. You presently have an informal program that closely resembles a personal rate structure. Which of the following methods would you choose, ranking, job classification, factor comparison, or weighted in points? Defend your selection.

Notifying All Employees of the Pending Program

Except where an entirely new company is concerned, most formal job evaluation programs replace an existing informal structure where the wage was paid on a personal basis. In a small company, the entire task of actually preparing the job evaluation program usually will be assigned to one individual. It will be his or her responsibility to see that the program is understood and accepted both by management and by the employees. This can be accomplished only by explaining to them what the program is supposed to accomplish, how it will be used, and what it is not supposed to do. Certain principles and procedures concerning the evaluation should be explained.

The new program should be thoroughly explained to all supervisors, and their cooperation with getting it installed should be solicited. Supervisors who have employees working on jobs to be reviewed may become involved in getting the job questionnaire completed; they can then review each questionnaire for accuracy before forwarding it to the person in charge of the evaluation program.

In small companies (20 to 100 employees), other than getting the job questionnaire completed and reviewed, one person will do all the work concerning a job evaluation program. In installing a program in larger companies (100 or more employees), a committee approach should be used. One person is assigned the responsibility, but he recruits members from management and from hourly rated jobs to serve on the committee. A member from each segment of the business is assigned, and they are in a position to exercise great influence on the remainder of the work force when the program is actually put into effect. They are in a position to answer questions from their constituency on how the program will function and to represent their department's point of view concerning the evaluation of jobs from their respective areas. Any committee size above seven begins to become unwieldy, but it is important to have representation from the major departments of the plant if full employee acceptance is to be obtained.

Prior to the selection of the committees, certain communication steps should be taken.

Announcement of the Plan

The way the announcement is made will depend on the size of the unit. A good approach is to have the supervisors, who previously have had the plan explained to them, explain it to each of their employees. This might be done on an individual basis or, if the number of employees to be covered is rather large, on a departmental basis. The meetings, whether on an individual basis or in groups, should be started at the same time throughout the company. Many companies prepare a pamphlet that gives a detailed explanation of the program, and then either give it to the employees after the departmental meetings or else mail it to their homes. The written material is issued so that the employee will have something to review and later ask questions about. It also establishes the company's position on all points. Everyone is aware that information may be presented incorrectly or misunderstood when presented in departmental meetings.

Contents of the Letter

The pamphlet or letter should include the following points in explaining the new program.

1. Explain the need for the change from the present system to the pending system.

2. Indicate the person who is in charge of the program and tell where to go to get more information about the program.

3. Make it clear that the job evaluation program is being prepared to establish a proper wage structure and has nothing whatsoever to do with the number working at the location.

4. Stress the fact that no employee will be laid off as a result of the job evaluation program.

5. Explain that the new pay scale will go into effect on a certain date and that all employees will be paid according to the new rate from that time on. Any employee whose job is upgraded will be promoted immediately. It is possible that some jobs will be placed at a lower grade than they currently are receiving. The employees in these jobs will not be cut in pay, but will be placed on "red circle" rates in the pay scale. Every attempt will be made to get these employees transferred to a job having a rate level comparable to their former rate. More on red circle rates will be covered in Chapter 19.

6. The letter should emphasize *what the program is.*
   a. It evaluates the *job,* not the employee.
   b. It *compares* one job to the other in the unit.
   c. It establishes a *ranking of jobs* that may be set into *pay grades,* and then money values are assigned to the pay grades.
   d. It eliminates personal wage rates by establishing rates for a job.

7. The letter should also emphasize *what the program is not.*
   a. It *does not set* the number to be working at the company.
   b. It *does not measure* the *ability* or effectiveness of an employee.
   c. It *does not cut* the *pay* of any employee.

8. The letter should also mention that the job questionnaire must be completed. Employees should be encouraged to complete the questionnaire and to return it to their supervisor by a cutoff date. They should be urged to answer the questions as completely as possible, since it is to their advantage to explain thoroughly the tasks and conditions of their job.

The following letter is an example that might be used to be sent to the homes of employees after the proposal had been announced at the work place.

**NORMAN BARTLEY
MANUFACTURING COMPANY**

Jan. 10, 19 ____

Dear Fellow Employee:

For the past several years, our organization has grown so much in size that it has become difficult and impractical to continue with our present way of assigning wages. For this reason, we have decided to install a job-ranking job evaluation program. This type of evaluation compares or ranks one job with the other jobs in the company.

The new program will establish a fair and equitable way of comparing the requirements for one job to another. It is an evaluation of the job, not of the individual worker. It does not determine the size of the work force, and it does not attempt to evaluate any employee's job performance. No employee will lose his job because of the evaluation. The evaluation program does not set wage rates; it is a way of comparing the value of your job to the other jobs in the company. As soon as all the jobs have been evaluated, they will be slotted into a pay schedule, and at that time money values will be set to the pay grades. No employee will receive a cut in pay, but it is possible that certain jobs may receive an increase in pay and that the employees assigned to these jobs will get the increase.

In order to evaluate the jobs, we will prepare a job questionnaire to gather information about the work you do and the conditions under which you work. It is to your benefit that you complete the questionnaire to the best of your ability. Please answer each question in detail, because it could make a difference if something of importance were omitted. Do not be concerned with grammar or punctuation.

Mr. D. Pietrini has been assigned the responsibility of the job evaluation program, and you will be receiving information from him in the near future. If you have any questions concerning the program, see your supervisor or Mr. Pietrini.

Because of the amount of work to be done, the new wage schedule will probably be placed into effect about July 1st. A general announcement will be made at a later date announcing the exact time.

Sincerely Yours,

Review Questions

1. Should all the facts about job evaluation be explained to the employees? If not, which facts should be omitted?

2. If management were to prepare a list of guidelines that should be followed in announcing a new job evaluation system, what should they include?

3. What is so important about communicating the pending job evaluation program to the employees?

4. What is necessary to make a job evaluation program more likely to be accepted by employees?

5. How many members should there be on a job evaluation committee? If a union is involved, should it have representation? If so, to what extent?

6. Is a job evaluation program more important to the employee or to management? Defend your position.

7. In what way should a job evaluation program be announced to the employees of a company of 50 employees, 300 employees, 1000 employees?

8. When is a "one man's program" of job evaluation undesirable?

9. In what way can a job evaluation program make the supervisor's point of view more objective?

10. What is the difference between job evaluation and employee appraisal?

11. The supervisors or foremen can be very important to the success of the program. How might they be motivated to do a good job?

12. Prepare a list of reasons why it is important to keep employees informed about installing or altering a job evaluation program.

Work Exercise

1. You are the Personnel Manager of a company that has 430 production employees, all working at one location. The company president has just announced to you that he wishes to install a weighted-in-points job evaluation program and would like for you to create a plan to best explain the program to the employees.
   a. Outline step by step procedures for announcing the new program.
   b. If the procedures include a letter to the employee's home, prepare the letter.
   c. What possible negative reaction might you receive from certain employees? How would you deal with it? Be specific.

2. Your job is that of Office Manager for a small plant of 90 employees. Part of your work is taking care of the personnel work for the company. The owner of the company has just informed you that he has hired a consultant to install a "ranking" job evaluation system. The president would like for you to prepare a letter to be sent to all hourly paid employees, advising them that a job analyst has been hired by the company and that he will be visiting them in the near future concerning the evaluation of their jobs. Prepare such a letter for his signature.

8

Updating the Organization's Structure and Assigning Duties to Employees

UPDATING THE ORGANIZATION'S STRUCTURE

Too often a company is structured in a certain manner and continues to operate in this way whether it is proper for the business at the present time or not. To avoid complacency, at the outset of establishing a job evaluation program, top management should review the organization's structure to ascertain if it is correct for managing the business. The company objectives should be established for the business for the next several years and, following this, the organizational structure should be reviewed to see if it will meet these objectives. It would be of very little value to install a job evaluation program and then eight months later to reorganize the company completely, reassigning duties to other departments and different jobs. This organization review may mean establishing new departments or abolishing departments or sections of departments. Once the proper structure and job alignment are established, employee placement should be reviewed.

ASSIGNING DUTIES IN EACH DEPARTMENT—
PLACING EMPLOYEES

There are differing opinions as to whether a company should establish the tasks for a job and then assign the person to fill the job or if the company should write the tasks around the incumbent on the job. One of the basic principles of organization is that the work fits the job, the job does not fit the worker. Generally the approach used for writing tasks for hourly paid jobs is to establish the tasks and then to assign and to train employees for these tasks. For management positions, particularly in small firms, often because of the special skills and talents of a particular salaried employee, the job description is written around what the person does. If this employee leaves that post, then the work assignments are re-assigned to the new management group and new job descriptions are written, and the job re-evaluated. One thing is certain—every major task to be performed must be assigned to one of the jobs within the company.

By reviewing the job questionnaire and, later, the job description, one can ascertain what duties each employee is performing. The supervisor then can reassign duties to best fit the needs of the department. The diagram on page 6 helps to explain how the job questionnaire might point out tasks that should be excluded or included into duties for a particular job. The job questionnaire and job descriptions are two instruments that will help to improve the communication process between the employee and management.

An attempt has been made to get the support of both top management and supervisors, to put into effect the organizational structure that is needed to meet the company's objectives, and to assign the various tasks to all of the employees in the company. It is now time to start evaluating the jobs.

Review Questions

1. Why is the task of updating the organization's structure important prior to starting a job evaluation program?

2. When shifting from personal rates to a formal job evaluation program, why is it important to get top management behind the project?

3. Why should the company's objectives be kept in mind when establishing the company's organization structure?

Work Exercises

1. List the advantages and disadvantages of assigning duties that are similar in nature as well as degree of complication to one job.

2. Write the pros and cons for
   a. assigning duties to a job and then assigning and training an employee, compared to
   b. writing the job description and describing the tasks the employee is actually performing

   Would the size of the organization affect your answer in regard to your method of assigning tasks? Explain.

9

Preparing Job Questionnaires and Job Analysis

To evaluate a job under this weighted-in-points method, it is necessary to compare every job against the same job characteristics or factors. For simplification, the term factor will be used throughout the remainder of the manual. Examples of factors are job knowledge, working conditions, hazard, complexity, responsibility for equipment, responsibility for materials, etc. Selecting the proper factors for use in evaluating the various types of work forces will be discussed later. In comparing jobs, certain information is needed for the job descriptions and, to obtain this information, specific information must be asked of the employees performing the work. For this purpose it is necessary to prepare a job questionnaire.

WHAT IS JOB ANALYSIS? WHAT IS ITS PURPOSE?

Job analysis is the systematic process of collecting and making certain judgments about all of the pertinent information relating to a specific job. The purpose of job analysis is to provide a job-related basis for management decisions that involve recruiting, selecting, placement, training, advancement, *compensation*, and other personnel functions [1]. An analysis is made through a job questionnaire.

1. *Job Analysis, Key to Better Management.* U.S. Civil Service Commission, BIPP-32, Sept. 1973.

Each question in the questionnaire should be worded in such a way that the person preparing the evaluation will fully understand how each job might be rated on each factor. Generally speaking, the person in charge of the project should have a good idea of what factors are to be used so that questions seeking information about these factors can be included. However, the final selection of the factors should be made after all the questionnaires are in and the job descriptions have been written.

The questionnaire should be designed to allow each employee's tasks to be graded against the various factors that are being considered for use. The questionnaire should be long enough to obtain the necessary information but should be kept as short as possible, particularly for employees assigned to hourly paid positions. Most of these employees do not like to be bothered with paper work. All questions used should be relative to the evaluation. If most of the jobs involve to some degree a particular factor, then that factor is acceptable. If only one or two jobs out of the total number of jobs relate to this factor, then the factor is not valid and should not be used. An example would be decision making. If 22 out of 25 jobs being evaluated were in the bottom level of this factor and the other three jobs in the top level, the characteristic would fail on the basis that it was not representative of most of the jobs being reviewed. It might be valid if managerial-type positions were being evaluated, but it would not generally be valid for evaluating hourly paid positions. This is discussed in Chapter 11, but it is relevant here because the questionnaire *must include questions that will give information on the factors being considered.*

PREPARING QUESTIONNAIRES FOR HOURLY PAID EMPLOYEES

A questionnaire should be completed for each job in the work area being reviewed. If more than one employee is assigned to a particular job, it is not necessary to get a questionnaire from every employee, but at least three employees should complete questionnaires in order to get different approaches to what the employees feel the job requirements are. Sometimes the same job might be slightly different if it is performed on the second or third shifts. Consequently, when more than one shift is operating, a questionnaire should be completed by at least one employee from each shift. In other words, if five or ten employees are assigned to a particular position, it is not necessary to get all employees to complete a questionnaire, but a representative sample should be obtained to see what the employees think the job requirements are. After a questionnaire is completed by an employee, it is submitted to the supervisor for review. Figures 9.1, 9.2, and 9.3 are examples of job questionnaires that might be used for hourly paid or non-exempt salaried jobs. In addition to these questions, the following questions and/or methods of asking questions might also be considered when preparing a questionnaire.

1. If your job is part-time, seasonal, or for a limited duration, please explain _____ .

2. Describe the kind and amount of training and experience you believe is necessary to learn and perform your job duties. If specific training, skill, or experience is required (e.g., welding, operator's license, etc.) record it below _____ .

3. Education required (place an X in the appropriate space).

YEARS OF EDUCATION

None	8	12	12 Tech.	13	14	16	Masters	Doctorate

4. Experience (how much work experience does a person need to fill a position like yours? Place an X in the appropriate space.)

None	Less than 3 months	3 months to 1 year	1–2 years	Over 2 years

5. Job Summary—What is the overall purpose of your job?

6. How is it done and why?

7. Mental and/or visual demand. Describe any degree of mental or visual concentration or attention that is required as part of your job (minimum, close work, constant attention, etc.).

8. Responsibility for equipment or tools. What is your responsibility, in dollars, to protect or to prevent loss of or damage to equipment, tools, etc?

9. Responsibility for materials or products. What is your responsibility, in dollars, to protect or to prevent spoilage of material or waste of products in handling, storage, producing, inspection, selling, etc?

10. Responsibility for safety of others. What is the nature and extent of your responsibility to maintain safe conditions for others?

(Continued on page 103)

Fig. 9.1

NORMAN BARTLEY MANUFACTURING COMPANY
Job Questionnaire   Date _____

NAME _____   JOB TITLE _____

DEPARTMENT _____   SUPERVISOR _____

GENERAL DUTIES
  Describe clearly the work you perform. Divide the regular or main duties from those duties
  that you occasionally are required to do. Estimate the percentage of time during the week
  that is required for each task.

1. REGULAR OR MAIN DUTIES REQUIRED WEEKLY (attach additional sheets if necessary)	% of Time
1.	
2.	
3.	
4.	
5.	
6.	
7.	
8.	
9.	
10.	

2. OCCASIONAL DUTY—Performed at infrequent intervals. Explain duty and how much time
  it takes to do the job and how frequent during a year is the job required, such as to check
  equipment, prepare tax statements, minutes, reports, etc.
  1.
  2.
  3.
  4.

Fig. 9.1 (continued)

3. Which of the tasks requires the greatest skill? Explain _____
_____
_____

4. What machines-equipment or tools do you operate _____
_____
_____

5. Hours worked per day _____ per week _____ Shift starts at what time of day
_____

6. Describe the kind and amount of training you believe is necessary to learn and perform your
   job duties. If specific training is required, such as welding, record it.
   Amount of training   Less than a week _____
                                               1 to 4 weeks _____
                                               3 months _____
                                               4 to 12 months _____
                                               over a year _____
   Kind of training—explain _____
   _____

7. In doing your work, state the general surroundings. (This would include exposure to different weather conditions, temperature, odor, noise, etc.) Example—working outdoors
   _____
   _____

8. In doing your work state any hazard that you might be exposed to. (This would include working around machinery, at heights, around chemicals, steam, fire, etc.) _____
   _____

9. What physical activity is required in doing your job? (This would include stooping, bending,
   kneeling, lifting, etc.) List if you do the activity frequently, less than six times an hour or just
   occasionally as once or twice a day. _____
   _____

10. How often or frequently do you receive instruction in your work? Explain _____
    _____
    _____

11. Give the number and job titles of employees you supervise.
    I do not supervise anyone _____
    I supervise _____ employees, the job titles for these employees are _____
    _____

    Signature of Employee _____

Fig. 9.2

JOB QUESTIONNAIRE   Date _____
Wade Manufacturing Company

NAME: _____   JOB TITLE _____

DEPARTMENT: _____   SUPERVISOR _____

GENERAL DUTIES

   Describe clearly the work you perform. Estimate the percentage of time during a week that is required for each task.

   1. Rank the jobs in the area below with the job taking the most time listed as number 1, the task taking the second amount of time as number 2, etc.

   2. In Column 2 rank the tasks according to the priority of attention each should receive.

   3. In Column 3 rank the tasks according to what you consider to be their importance or value to your department.

DUTIES REQUIRED WEEKLY	1 Percentage of time	2 Priority of attention	3 Value of department
			NOTE: *Numbers as shown below only given as an example of completing this form after the tasks have been written by the employee.*
1.	25	3	2
2.	15	8	6
3.	12	1	3
4.	12	6	1
5.	10	2	4
6.	8	9	9
7.	8	10	5
8.	5	4	8
9.	3	5	7
10.	2	7	10

Fig. 9.3

JOB QUESTIONNAIRE
KANE MANUFACTURING COMPANY

NAME _____   JOB TITLE _____

DEPARTMENT _____   JOB NUMBER _____

SUPERVISOR'S NAME _____   SUPERVISOR'S TITLE _____

1. *SUMMARY OF DUTIES:* State in your own words briefly your main duties. If you are responsible for filling out reports/records, also complete Section 8.

   _____

   _____

2. *SPECIAL QUALIFICATIONS:* List any licenses, permits, certifications, etc. required to perform duties assigned to your position.

   _____

   _____

3. *EQUIPMENT:* List any equipment, machines, or tools (e.g., typewriter, calculator, motor vehicles, lathes, fork lifts, drill presses, etc.) you normally operate as a part of your position's duties.

   MACHINE   *AVERAGE NO. HOURS PER WEEK*

   _____

   _____

   _____

4. *REGULAR DUTIES:* In general terms, describe duties you regularly perform. Please list these duties in descending order of importance and percent of time spent on them per month. List as many duties as possible and attach additional sheets, if necessary.

   _____

   _____

   _____

5. *CONTACTS:* Does your job require any contacts with other department personnel, other departments, outside companies or agencies. If yes, please define the duties requiring contacts and *how often.*

   _____

   _____

Fig. 9.3 (continued)

6. *SUPERVISION:* Does your position have supervisory responsibilities? (   ) Yes (   ) No. If yes, please fill out a *Supplemental Position Description Questionnaire for Supervisors* and attach it to this form. If you have responsibility for the work of others but do not directly supervise them, please explain.

_____

_____

7. *DECISION MAKING:* Please explain the decisions you make while performing the regular duties of your job.

_____

_____

_____

(a) What would be the probable result of your making (a) poor judgment(s) or decision(s), or (b) improper actions?

_____

_____

8. *RESPONSIBILITY FOR RECORDS:* List the reports and files you are required to prepare or maintain. State, in general, for whom each report is intended.

(a)   *REPORT*   *INTENDED FOR*

_____

_____

_____

(b)   *FILES MAINTAINED*

_____

_____

9. *FREQUENCY OF SUPERVISION:* How frequently must you confer with your supervisor or other personnel in making decisions or in determining the proper course of action to be taken?

(   ) Frequently   (   ) Occasionally   (   ) Seldom   (   ) Never

10. *WORKING CONDITIONS:* Please describe the conditions under which you work—inside, outside, air conditioned area, etc. Be sure to list any disagreeable or unusual working conditions.

_____

_____

11. *JOB REQUIREMENTS:* Please indicate the minimum requirements you believe are necessary to perform satisfactorily in your position.

(a) Education:
    Minimum schooling _____

Number of years _____

Specialization or major _____

(b) Experience:

    Type _____

    Number of years _____

(c) Special training:

TYPE	NUMBER OF YEARS

(d) Special Skills:

    Typing: _____w.p.m.   Shorthand_____w.p.m.

    Other: _____

12. *ADDITIONAL INFORMATION:* Please provide additional information, not included in any of the previous items, which you feel would be important in a description of your position.

_____

_____

_____

EMPLOYEE'S SIGNATURE _____ DATE: _____

(Continued from p. 97)

11. Work Conditions

Percent of your time spent standing _____ walking _____ sitting _____ lifting _____ climbing _____ bending _____ kneeling _____ other _____ .

12. Days of traveling out of town _____ per week _____ per month _____ per year.

The questionnaire on the Wade Manufacturing Company, Fig. 9.2, shows a somewhat different approach to writing the job questionnaire in stressing the importance of a particular task. The incumbent, in addition to stating percentage of time, also shows priority of attention and value to the department. This approach may give additional information that might be helpful in writing the job description.

Additional questions concerning working conditions, hazards, physical effort, etc. would be on the back of the questionnaire. Questions similar to those in Fig. 9.1 would be used.

PREPARING QUESTIONNAIRES FOR
MANAGERIAL POSITIONS

In general, the kind of questions used for managerial positions are different from those used for hourly paid or clerical jobs. This is necessary because the factors to be used will be different also. Figures 9.4 and 9.5 are examples of this type of questionnaire (compare them with Figs. 9.1 through 9.3).

Other questions not used in these two questionnaires but meaningful for evaluating managerial type jobs are:

1. To what extent do you make decisions in your job? (Place an X on proper line.)
   _____ little or no decision making is required
   _____ some decision making
   _____ perform several duties that require initiative in making decisions
   _____ standard methods and procedures are not always available and it is sometimes necessary to work toward desired results
   _____ the work situations or conditions are frequently changing and the duties are complicated and technical and not covered by standard procedures

2. Contacts—What people do you have to deal with in your daily work?
   _____ employees in your department
   _____ employees in other departments
   _____ with all departments
   _____ with department heads
   _____ general public
   _____ other professional people
   _____ other—explain _____

3. What qualifications should one possess to fill this position when future vacancy arises?
   1. Education _____
   2. Experience _____
   3. Personal _____

4. Indicate the physical and/or mental-emotional demands or pressures of this position. _____
   _____

5. Is the work confidential in nature? If so to what degree? _____

_____

6. Are there special communication skills involved? If so explain.

_____

7. Special qualifications—list any licenses, permits, certificates, etc. required to perform duties assigned to your position.

8. Decision making—explain the decisions you make while performing the regular duties of your job as it pertains to the following:
   a. extent that decisions are controlled by company policy or by law

_____

_____

   b. the consequence of error in judgment _____

_____

   c. the level of review of your decisions _____

_____

9. What are the most important duties of this position? _____

_____

_____

10. How many positions and levels of supervision do you supervise?

_____

_____

11. Are your supervisory responsibilities varied and/or complex or are they more routine in nature? Explain. _____

_____

_____

12. Performance guides—describe the representative and extreme to which the work is governed by standard policy, methods, procedures, and practice or precedent. Indicate the type and availability of assistance and the type of degree of original or creative thinking required based on general principles and techniques.

13. Judgment—describe the representative and extreme job requirements for judgment and indicate the purpose, basis or criteria and information evaluated, the variety of judgment, the effect and significance, and the ratio or percent required for the total job.

14. Decisions—describe the representative and extreme types of decisions, reasoning, determinations, and conclusions required to accomplish the objectives of the job, and indicate their significance or effect.

15. Complications and difficulties—describe the type and significance of complications and difficulties related to the typical duties and responsibilities of the job. Indicate the frequency with which they might occur.

16. Accuracy and consequence of error—is the job requirement for accuracy and use of proper techniques to achieve assigned job objectives within acceptable standards and precautionary measures; are there precautions to prevent error, and is there representative continuity required for the total job?

17. Accuracy—describe the most representative and extreme job requirements for accuracy and/or use of proper techniques. Indicate the type of accuracy and technique, the degree required, typical problems, normal precautions to prevent error, and the representative continuity required for the total job.

18. Consequence of error—describe the most representative and extreme level of job assigned responsibility for error. Indicate the type of error, the likelihood of detention, and prevention, the reasonable probability the error may occur, the magnitude or effect and the cost or problems of correction if undetected.

19. Working relationships outside—is the requirement of the job to contact and deal effectively with the general public, suppliers, regulatory agencies, and others outside the organization? Describe representative and significant types of contacts and indicate
    a. whom you contact
    b. the nature and purpose of the contact
    c. the frequency of the contact
    d. how the contact is made such as personally, through correspondence, or by telephone
    e. the requirement, if any, for tact and skill to influence others, and
    f. the overall ratio of time required by such contacts to the total job

20. Working relationships internal—is the requirement of the job to contact and deal effectively with employees of the organization who work in other departments and outside of the immediate work group? Answer same questions as outlined in the previous factor [2].

2. Source: Items 12 through 20 are used courtesy of American Compensation Association, P.O. Box 1176, Scottsdale, Arizona, 85252.

Fig. 9.4

D. Pietrini Company
Administrative or Managerial Position Questionnaire

NAME _____   TITLE OF POSITION _____

DEPARTMENT _____   IMMEDIATE
                                  SUPERVISOR _____

1. General statement concerning the work you perform. _____
   _____
   _____
   _____

2. Regular significant duties consist of. _____
   _____
   _____
   _____

3. Special or occasional duties (state only the important ones and list the frequency with which they occur).
   _____
   _____
   _____
   _____

4. Supervisory responsibilities (include level of employees supervised and number of employees at each level, close or general supervision, complexity of work).
   _____
   _____
   _____
   _____
   _____
   _____

5. Responsibilities for relations within the company. (What impact does your decision or action have within the company?)
   _____
   _____
   _____
   _____

Fig. 9.4 (continued)

6. Responsibilities for relations with other companies and general public. (What impact does your decision or action have outside the company?)

_____
_____
_____
_____

7. Confidentiality of duties. _____
_____

8. Level of decision making (are decisions mostly covered by company policy).

_____
_____

9. Safety and working conditions (to include both physical and mental demand plus emotional stress).

_____
_____
_____

10. General points of interest about your work not covered in the above items.

_____
_____
_____
_____

Fig. 9.5

ADMINISTRATIVE POSITION QUESTIONNAIRE

_____   _____   _____
Title of position   Name of incumbent   Telephone

_____   _____   _____
Department   Supervisor's name   Telephone

_____   _____
Division   Number of months on job

1. General statement of position.

2. Regular—most significant duties—please list in order of magnitude and indicate which percentage of the total job each duty comprises.

3. Occasional duties—duties that occur infrequently such as end-of-year reports, special projects, committees, etc.

4. Supervisory responsibility—please comment on the level and difficulty, how varied and complex the functions are, and how many subordinates are supervised directly or indirectly.

Fig. 9.5 (continued)

5. Responsibility for relations
   a. Please explain your position's responsibility for internal relations with students, faculty, staff, and employees outside your department, and

   b. for external relations with the general public, state agencies, federal agencies, etc.

6. Confidentiality of duties and safe keeping of records.

7. General
   a. What level of education is required for a person starting in this position?
   _____ high school _____ college _____ other, Explain _____

   b. Does experience play a vital role in the performance of your duties? Explain _____

   c. Is specialized training required for your position? Explain _____

   d. Indicate the order of importance of the communication skills.
   _____ Verbal _____ Written. What percent of time is spent in communicating on a one to one basis? _____ %.
   e. How many employees do you supervise? Directly _____ Indirectly _____
   How many levels _____ ?

8. Decision making
   a. To what extent are your decisions controlled by law, University policies, and procedures?

   b. If an incorrect decision is made—What is the consequence of the error?

c. Is innovativeness helpful in making decisions for your position? Explain _____

_____

d. What is the level of the review of your decisions?

9. Work conditions—please describe
   a. The physical demands for your job.

   b. The environment in which the majority of your duties are carried out.

   c. The mental or emotional pressures from your job.

10. If additional space is needed, please use extra pages.

REVIEW OF QUESTIONNAIRES BY SUPERVISORS

After a job questionnaire has been completed by an employee, it should be reviewed by the employee's supervisor. This review gives the supervisor the opportunity to:

1. Review what the employee has said and to see that an accurate picture of the job content has been presented.
2. Evaluate whether the worker is doing all the tasks that the supervisor thinks the job should include; also, to decide if the employee is doing some tasks that the supervisor feels should not be performed or that should be transferred to another employee and/or department.

The supervisors' questionnaires (Figs. 9.6 and 9.7) reveal the type of questions that might be asked of them. When completed, the questionnaire should be attached to the employee's questionnaire being evaluated and forwarded to the person in charge of the job evaluation program who, in turn, will write a job description for the job.

Fig. 9.6

NORMAN BARTLEY MANUFACTURING COMPANY

To be completed by immediate supervisor

1. To the best of my knowledge, all preceding entries are true and complete and I have no corrections or comments, except as follows: _____
   _____
   _____

2. What are the most important duties of this position? _____
   _____
   _____
   _____

3. What are the nature and extent of instructions given? _____
   _____
   _____

4. If the position were vacant, what qualifications would you consider most necessary for the person hired as a replacement?

   Minimum requirements

Education	
Experience, kind and length, in months	
Special knowledge, abilities or skills	
Special requirements	

5. Indicate the physical demands of the position. _____
   _____

6. Indicate unusual environmental or working conditions on the job. _____
   _____

7. Signature of Immediate Supervisor   Title of Immediate Supervisor
   _____   _____

Fig. 9.7

KANE MANUFACTURING COMPANY

Supervisor Questionnaire

   To be completed by the supervisor for each position in the department. If more than one employee is assigned to the same position, then no more than three job questionnaires should be reviewed by the supervisor for each position.

1. Are all parts accurate or complete? Please comment. _____
_____
_____
_____

2. Please indicate the amount of independent action and decision making ability that is associated with this position. _____
_____
_____
_____

3. What degree of supervision is required by you for the employee on this job? _____
_____
_____
_____
_____

_____
Supervisor's Signature

_____
Date

Review Questions

1. What are the major elements in a job questionnaire?

2. Why is each of the elements important?

3. What is the significance of the job questionnaire to the job description? To the job specifications?

4. In what way can a company make sure that the job information obtained in the job questionnaire is accurate? Complete?

5. Explain why the job questionnaire for hourly paid employees must be different from the questionnaires for managers.

6. If a company were working three shifts and they had 12 employees on each shift performing the same job, how many job questionnaires should be completed for this one position? Explain.

7. For hourly paid employees, is it better to have "check the right answer type of question" or essay. Defend your answer.

Work Exercise

1. You are the Personnel Manager of a small company manufacturing plastic bags. Your company has 500 hourly paid production, maintenance, and service employees working on 51 different jobs. At the present time the company is manufacturing on two shifts. The necessary preliminary steps (1 through 3) have been taken to install a job evaluation program and it now is time to prepare the job questionnaire form for the program.

   Design and prepare the form for these hourly paid jobs.

   How would these forms differ from the forms you would prepare if you were also going to evaluate the 18 different positions of management at the company? Explain the reason why the two sets of forms are different.

10
Job Descriptions

Once each job questionnaire is completed, it is reviewed by the employee's supervisor. He or she verifies the accuracy of the responses, altering or amending as necessary, and then submits both the questionnaire and review to the person in charge of the evaluation program who, in turn, prepares a job description for each job covered in the program.

Job descriptions should include information on the following items.

1. The overall objective of the job. (The functions of the job and why it exists.)

2. The tasks, duties, or accountabilities for the job.

3. The nature of supervision received and/or given.

4. The conditions under which the job is performed.

5. Special features of the job such as special skills required to operate certain types of equipment, or certain experience or educational requirements necessary for the employee to be successful on the job.

One style of description is used for all the jobs. Figures 10.1 through 10.4 are examples of descriptions for hourly paid employees and Figs. 10.5 and 10.6 are for salaried employees (Figs. 10.1 through 10.6 are at the end of this chapter).

The style used is not a critical part of the program, but the information in the description must reflect exactly what the employee does and must contain information that the committee can compare against the factors selected. It is better to include questions in the questionnaire (and, later, statements in the tentative job descriptions) that may not be used than to leave out some questions that would necessitate going back to all employees with a second questionnaire just to get more information.

Certain basic information is needed in each description in order that relevant facts may be found, read, and interpreted quickly. The following chart (a detailed explanation of it follows) shows how the information may be catalogued (see Fig. 10.1 for a completed example).

Name of Company	Effective Date (1)	Revised (2)	Department Approved (3)	Written by (4)
Position Title (5)		Department or Division (6)	EEOC Occupation Classification (7)	Job Number (8)

1. The date the job description became effective.
2. If this square has a date, it shows when the description was last revised.
3. The name of the supervisor approving the latest description.
4. The name of the person on the job evaluation committee who prepared the latest job description.
5. The name or title given to the position.
6. The name of the department or division to which the job is assigned.

7. Equal Employment Opportunity Commission (EEOC) Occupation Classification—when a company is operating under an Affirmative Action Program, it must file certain reports with the federal government. The report requires the company to itemize the number of employees in certain occupational categories. This block on the job description form indicates to which classification the job is assigned. The categories and descriptions of the categories are:

Management: Includes all persons whose assignments require primary (and major) responsibility for management of the company, or a customarily recognized department or subdivision thereof. Assignments require the performance of work directly related to management policies or general business operations of the company. It is assumed that assignments in this category customarily and regularly require the incumbent to exercise discretion and independent judgment, and to direct the work of others. Includes the Executive and Administrative classification under the Fair Labor Standards Act.

Professional: Occupations requiring either college graduation or experience of such kind and amount as to provide a comparable background including: accountants and auditors, architects, librarians, mathematicians, natural scientists, registered professional nurses, personnel and labor relations workers, physical scientists, physicians, social scientists, and teachers. Correlates to the Professional status under the Fair Labor Standards Act.

Technician: Includes all persons whose assignments require specialized knowledge or skills that may be acquired through experience or academic work such as is offered in many two-year technical institutes, junior colleges, or through equivalent on-the-job training. Includes computer programmers and operators, drafters, engineering aides, junior engineers, mathematical aides, licensed, practical, or vocational nurses, dietitians, photographers, radio operators, scientific assistants, technical illustrators, technicians (medical, dental, electronic, physical sciences), and similar occupations that are not properly classifiable in other occupational activity categories, but are institutionally defined as technical assignments.

Sales: Occupations engaging wholly or primarily in direct selling. Includes advertising agents and salesmen, and sales clerks.

Office–Clerical: Includes all persons whose assignments typically are associated with clerical activities or are specifically of office-type work. Includes personnel who are responsible for internal and external communications, recording and retrieval of data (other than computer programmers) and/or information and other paper work required in an office such as bookkeepers, stenographers, clerk–typists, office-machine operators, statistical clerks, payroll clerks, etc.

Craftsmen (Skilled): Manual workers of relatively high skill level having a thorough comprehensive knowledge of the processes involved in their work. Exercise considerable independent judgment and usually receive an extensive period of training. Includes the building trades, hourly paid foremen and leadmen who are not members of management, mechanics and repairmen, skilled machining occupations, electricians, motion picture projectionists, pattern and model makers, and stationary engineers.

Operative (Semi-skilled): Workers who operate machine or processing equipment or perform other factory type duties of intermediate skill level that can be mastered in a few weeks and require only limited training. Includes apprentices (auto mechanics, carpenters, electricians, machinists, mechanics, plumbers, building trades, metalworking trades, printing trades, etc.), photographic process workers, stationary firemen, truck and tractor drivers, and welders.

Laborers (Unskilled): Workers in manual occupations that generally require no special training, perform elementary duties that may be learned in a few days and require the application of little or no independent judgment. Includes gardeners (except farm), and grounds-keepers, and laborers performing lifting, digging, mixing, loading, and pulling operations.

Service Workers: Workers in both protective and nonprotective service occupations including attendants (hospital and other institution, professional and personal service, including nurses aides, and orderlies), charwomen and cleaners, cooks (except household), counter and fountain workers, guards, watchmen, and door-keepers, stewards, janitors, policemen and detectives, porters, and waiters and waitresses.

8. The number of this particular job. Usually this is a four digit number, the first two digits reflecting the pay grade and the last two a particular job in that pay grade. For example Job 1101 would be pay grade eleven, and the first job written at that level. The other jobs in pay grade eleven would be 1102, 1103, 1104, etc. Usually all jobs are filed in the job evaluation manual in sequence, from job number 0101 through the highest number used. An index sheet is made listing all jobs by grade; consequently, one may refer to this list to obtain the job number. Since all jobs are placed in numerical order in the job evaluation manual, each description can easily be found. (See Fig. 15.3 for an index of jobs.)

In writing descriptions for hourly paid jobs, it is good to place the following sentence on the bottom of page one of each description: The above duties describe the chief functions of the job and are not to be considered a detailed description of every duty of the job.

No description is written to include all the duties of the job; just the major functions are recorded. This is all that is needed to arrive at the proper evaluation. Incidental duties are seldom written into the description. The above statement prevents the employee from refusing to perform a certain task just because it was not recorded as part of the duties. The job description, however, should be rewritten if major changes were made in the types of tasks assigned. Rewriting of existing jobs that have been changed in job content is covered in Chapter 19.

Job descriptions are essential for establishing a rational basis for preparing a wage structure; however, they may benefit an organization in many other ways. Table 10.1 shows some of these additional uses.

The purpose for which job descriptions will be used help to determine how they should be written. If they are to be used only as a means for a better understanding of the employee's present job, then they would be written in greater detail than if they were to be used for some other purpose such as the basis for comparison between jobs for a job evaluation program. The main use for job descriptions is the systematic recording of information to facilitate the comparison of jobs. The job questionnaire is designed to obtain all the information concerning a particular job, but when it comes time to write the description a personal observation of the job is desirable. This allows the person writing the description to verify the facts on the questionnaire and be in a better position to describe the job.

Table 10.1
Uses of Job Descriptions

To clarify relationships between jobs, thus avoiding overlaps and gaps in responsibility

To help all employees on all levels acquire greater understanding of their present jobs by analyzing their duties.

To help revise the organization's structure on any level

To re-assign and fix functions and responsibilities in the entire organization

To evaluate job performance by comparison between what the employee does and what the job description says should be done

To introduce new employees to their jobs

To assist in hiring and placing employees in the jobs for which they are best suited

To set forth lines of promotion within all departments and at all levels

To forecast the training needs for a particular function

To maintain continuity of all operations in a changing work environment

To provide data as to proper channels of communication

To help in the development of job specifications

To serve as a basis for human resource planning

To improve the work flow

To review critically the existing practices in the organization*

To act as the basis for job evaluation

To assist in the cataloging of jobs for compiling of data for the EEOC report to the government

*Berenson, C. and R. D. Ruhnke. *Job Descriptions, How to Write and Use Them.* Reprinted with permission from *Personnel Journal* © 1976, p. 14.

JOB DESCRIPTIONS FOR HOURLY PAID JOBS

When comparing jobs for hourly paid employees, there are two cardinal principles to adhere to:

1. The statements should be brief and concise
2. Only the major or main elements of the job should be described.

In general, all descriptions should have the following items:

1. A chart or table at the very top of the description showing the title of the job and other pertinent information about the job. (See Fig. 10.1 for an example.)

2. A brief statement about the purpose of the job. Usually this is in very general terms and may include the scope of the job. (See Fig. 10.4 for an example.)

3. A section indicating to whom the holder of this particular job reports and if this job has any other job reporting to it. (See Figs. 10.4 and 10.5 for examples.)

4. A listing of duties broken down into two types:
   a. Typical duties and/or working procedures—the main duties performed each week, and
   b. Periodic or seasonal duties—these are important aspects of the job but they may be required only on a monthly, seasonal, or yearly basis. These infrequent duties must be recorded, however, since some may be quite important and can favorably affect the point score of a job.

5. A listing of the tools and equipment used on the job. For certain jobs (such as tradesmen) filled by hourly paid employees, this general heading may be quite important. In jobs where tools and equipment are not involved, the absence of such skills becomes immediately apparent. Generally speaking, this heading is not used when describing management positions.

6. Separate headings should be used for all other specific factors such as experience, responsibility for materials, physical demand, or working conditions.

In writing the description of an hourly paid job certain terms are often used. The list on the following pages shows some of the more frequently used terms. Examples of how they are used are found in Figs. 10.1 through 10.4.

Most job descriptions for hourly paid personnel are one to two pages in length. Descriptions for some salaried positions may reach three pages in length. The intent of descriptions is to record the major and important elements of the work, not all of the tasks assigned.

Arrange	Load	Replace
Assemble	Lubricate	Replenish
Assist	Maintain	Report
Check	Make out	Represent
Clean	Mark	Reset
Compile	Measure	Sample
Complete	Move	Seal
Conduct	Monitor	See that
Determine	Negotiate	Select
Direct	Obtain	Separate
Dismantle	Open	Service
Distribute	Operate	Set up
Drive	Perform	Sort
Dump	Pick up	Stack
Enter	Place	Start
Exercise	Position	Store
Fabricate	Posts	Study
Fill out	Prepare	Supply
Identify	Process	Take
Inspect	Push	Take necessary action
Install	Receive	Train
Insure	Recommend	Unfasten
Keep records	Record	Use
Lift	Regulate	Weigh
	Remove	

Writing Job Descriptions for Differences of Skill on One Job

Whenever there is only one level of work for a particular task, that particular job can be written accurately and evaluated very carefully and systematically. A special problem exists, however, in evaluating several levels of expertise for the same trade or skill. These types of jobs are found in the mechanical areas and in the offices of a company. To illustrate: Plumber C is the entry level for plumbing work, Plumber B is a higher level of skill, and Plumber A is the top level of skill required.

The same system also serves for evaluating Accounting clerk C, B, and A, or any other type of work that involves several levels of skill. The basic skills are required for the lowest level, job C, and the B and A levels of the job require more expertise and skill than the beginning job. The basic knowledge and skill required is written into the C description. The B and A job descriptions show a higher rating for these jobs on several of the factors used. The higher ratings contribute to a higher number of total points and, consequently, to a higher pay grade.

Usually the A description is properly evaluated and the other two levels are worded so as to place them in reasonable relationship to other jobs in the program and in relationship to the A classification. This procedure will be covered in more detail in Chapter 15.

The following paragraphs are excerpts from job descriptions covering different levels of skill for the same general type of work. They present one approach to establishing a differential in the total points for each job. The part underlined in the description of the function and scope of Plumbers B and A should place each of these jobs in a higher rating on the factors used, thus giving them higher ratings and qualifying them for additional compensation. These changes will be reflected in writing the duties required in the three levels of work. (Before reading the illustration please review the job description for Plumber A in Fig. 10.1.)

0405 Plumber C
Function: To *provide physical assistance and some skill* in maintenance, installation, and repair of plumbing facilities.

Scope: Does the *manual labor* necessary for operation and maintenance of plumbing facilities and systems and installation in minor construction projects, *while learning the skills* of the plumbing trade.

0605 Plumber B
Function: To *assist plumber* in maintenance, installation and repair of plumbing facilities.

Scope: Responsible for *operation* of plumbing facilities and systems.

0806 Plumber A
Function: To provide *journeyman-level skills* in maintenance, installation, and repair of plumbing facilities.

Scope: Is *responsible for operations* of plumbing facilities and systems, and for *design and construction in minor construction projects.*

Basically, the three levels of expertise shown are a journeyman plumber, an apprentice plumber learning the trade and performing routine operational functions, and a beginner whose responsibility is to do the heavy manual work required and to assist in any way he can the more highly skilled workers. Writing the description allows each level of expertise to be evaluated and to be assigned a certain number of points.

Another example of writing descriptions for the same basic skill but for various levels of the skill is illustrated by these accounting jobs.

0202 Accounting clerk C
General statement of duties: Performs *routine clerical* accounting duties; does related work as required.

Distinguishing feature of the class: An Accounting clerk C engages in *repetitive* clerical–accounting work. *Detailed instructions* are given for new or difficult assignments and work is reviewed in process or upon completion, for accuracy. Since this is the *beginning class in the account–clerk series,* alertness and a willingness to learn and to prepare for assignments of progressively increasing difficulty are essential. An Accounting clerk C *may check* the work of other clerks for accuracy but does not exercise direct supervision except on occasion.

0502 Accounting clerk B
General statement of duties: Performs *difficult clerical tasks* in keeping financial accounts and records; does related work as required.

Distinguishing features of the class: The work involves *performance of account-keeping, auditing, or related tasks within clearly defined limits.* Similar problems are constantly recurring and their solutions are routine, having been previously determined. *Unusual cases are checked by supervisors.* Supervisors are available for consultation and give detailed instructions on all new assignments. Positions in this class require familiarity with the office to which assigned or a background in bookkeeping and related clerical–accounting tasks. *Immediate supervision may be exercised* over the work of the Accounting clerks or Clerk–typists.

0806 Accounting clerk A
General statement of duties: Performs highly responsible clerical account-keeping and subprofessional accounting tasks; does related work as required.

Distinguishing features of the class: An Accounting clerk A is required to *perform subprofessional accounting and supervisory tasks* in maintaining major revenue and expenditure accounts of the City. This position is of such a nature that routine problems are handled without referral to a supervisor. *Supervision is exercised* over subordinate Accounting clerks C and B. Assignments are received and work is reviewed by the Manager.

By referring to the points underlined above in the three different job descriptions, one can see that there are three levels of skills being applied on the three jobs described. Because of this, the three accounting jobs will receive different levels of pay, and are placed in pay grades 2, 5, and 8. This is reflected in their job numbers 0202, 0502, and 0806.

Although most small companies would not have need for three levels of skill for secretaries, this next example is included to show a third way of writing a job description when several levels of skill are involved. Since everyone has a general idea of what the duties of a secretary are, this job is used only as an example to show how the job descriptions can be changed. The same approach may be used on any type of production, service, office jobs, or mechanical jobs where several levels of the same type of skill are required (e.g., operating equipment: fork lift, pick up truck, small delivery trucks used in the local vicinity, and over-the-road long-distance hauling semi-trailers).

Secretary C
Function: To provide basic secretarial and clerical skills as required in various departments. This is a repetitive, *clerical-type* work performed in accordance with prescribed routine. Work is performed under *close* supervision.

Secretary B
Function: To provide basic secretarial and clerical skills as required in the various departments. *Occasionally assignments require the use of some independent judgment.*

Secretary A
Function: To provide basic secretarial and clerical skills as required for the job. *Frequently* must use *independent judgment and planning* to relieve the administrator of many routine administrative matters.

Several points listed will make a change in the total point score of the three jobs. Secretary C does very basic *repetitive* and routine office work, requiring close supervision. For Secretary B the job assignments increase in complexity, since the work no longer is routine or repetitive, but *occasionally* requires the use of independent judgment. In Secretary A the job requires *frequent* use of independent judgment as well as the use of planning.

By showing that the higher level jobs are no longer routine and that they require additional talent and skill to satisfactorily fulfill the tasks, the B and A positions will receive a higher evaluation score, i.e., a greater total number of points.

In addition to stating changes to the general duties in the functions of the job, additional changes would be listed in the section of the description outlining the typical duties of the job. An example would be as shown in writing part of the section for the duties and/or working procedure for Secretary C, B, or A.

0305 Secretary C
Typical duties: In this section the general duties for a secretary would be listed.

0607 Secretary B
Typical duties: In addition to the duties described for Secretary C, assumes duties of somewhat more demanding nature. Takes and transcribes dictation of letters, memorandums, reports, and other materials.

0807 Secretary A
Typical duties: In addition to the duties described for Secretary C, assumes duties of a more demanding nature. Job entails reading and routing incoming mail and the assembling of information to facilitate reply by the manager. Work involves information of very confidential nature.

Determining on what level a particular employee is capable of working is another problem and is not part of the job evaluation. The following, however, is one company's approach to assigning a maintenance employee to a certain level.

1. An employee was assigned as a journeyman plumber (0805) if he could perform most of the job assignments that he was requested to do.
2. He would be on Job #0605–Plumber B if he could perform all of the minor tasks or jobs assigned and most of the major tasks. Even if he had the talents to be a journeyman, he would not be given the rate unless he was given the major jobs or tasks that accounted for 51% of his work time.
3. He would be placed on the Plumber C Job #0405 when he started on the job and would be given the learner rate. As he personally grew

in skill, his job assignments would change, and once he performed regular plumbing tasks on his own and was performing such jobs for at least 51% of his work time, he would be considered for promotion to Plumber B.

JOB DESCRIPTIONS FOR ADMINISTRATIVE OR MANAGERIAL JOBS

Job descriptions covering salary-exempt personnel are written in different ways, depending on the type of evaluation system being used. For salaried positions evaluated under weighted-in-points system the style and type of descriptions would be similar to the descriptions written for hourly personnel. The questionnaires must ask the type of questions that will allow evaluating the job against the factors to be used. As stated earlier, the factors for this type of work will be very different from those used for hourly paid and clerical work. Generally speaking, management jobs should never be a part of the job evaluation program used for hourly paid jobs. Figures 10.5 and 10.6 show examples of job descriptions for management jobs.

Some terms often used when describing salaried positions are listed here.

Act as	Establish	Plan and develop
Administer	Examine	Prepare
Advise	Exercise	Prescribe
Analyze	Formulate	Provide
Approve	Guide	Recommend
Assist	Identify	Represent
Assure	In charge of	Research
Attend	Initiate	Review
Audit	Insure	Schedule
Authorize	Investigate	Search for
Calculate	Is available for	Select
Conduct	Is responsible for	Serves as
Confer	Keep abreast of	Study
Coordinate	Keep staff informed on	Supervise operations
Counsel with	Maintain	Train
Delegate	Monitor	To collaborate
Design	Negotiate	To develop
Develop	Obtain	To safeguard
Direct	Oversee	Use
Encourage	Participate	Visit
	Place into	

The following is an outline of the basic features of a job description used by a large corporation for the job of Area sales manager.

1. Function
2. Responsibilities and Authorities
    a. Management responsibility
    b. Control and financial responsibility
    c. Organizational responsibility
    d. Marketing responsibility
    e. Personnel responsibility
3. Relationship to
    a. Collaborates with
        1. Product manager
        2. Market research manager
        3. Distributor relations manager
        4. Advertising manager
    b. Cooperates with other regional sales managers
    c. Reports to Regional Manager—Marketing Division [1].

As explained earlier, when preparing job descriptions for management jobs, the method used is important in only two respects:

1. The same style or format should be used for all jobs in the program.
2. Complete information should be listed in the description so that the evaluating committee can compare each job against the factor definitions; it is essential that after reading a job description the evaluator has an idea where this job rates on each of the factors used in the program.

Review Questions

1. How does the job description differ between one written for hourly paid jobs and one written for management jobs?

2. Why are job descriptions so important to the success of a weighted-in-points job evaluation plan? Explain.

1. Sperling, JoAnn. *Job Descriptions in Marketing Management.* New York: American Management Association, Inc., 1969, pp. 157–161.

3. Are job descriptions as important for a ranking job evaluation program as they are for a weighted-in-points program?

4. What can be done to avoid the difficulty of an employee's refusing to perform a task assigned by management that is not written into the job description?

5. When you are preparing a job description if you find that the job is not being performed in the correct manner, should you write the job as it is being performed or as it should be performed? Why?

6. What are some uses other than job evaluation that the job descriptions may be used for?

7. Why are accuracy and completeness essential in writing job descriptions?

8. As part of the job description, of what importance is the title? Explain.

9. In preparing job descriptions for management jobs, there are some examples of glamorizing a particular job. Is this good practice? Why or why not?

10. Job descriptions can be written in very specific or general terms. What are the problems encountered under each approach?

11. Explain the difference between the terms *tasks* and *job EEOC classifications*, and *semi-skilled* and *skilled*.

12. Why are A, B, and C job classifications difficult to evaluate? How can each level be properly written?

13. What are the dangers of an incomplete job description in regard to the evaluation, to relationships between employees working in the same area, and to future changes in job content and possible re-evaluation?

14. If a company is unionized, a correct job description is extremely important. Explain.

15. If the job questionnaire does not give the committee enough information on how to write the job description, how else can the committee obtain this information?

16. What is the advantage of writing a "tentative" job description (i.e., one that is prepared and then checked by both the employee on the job and the supervisor for the job. This checking is done before the description is finalized)?

Work Exercises

1. Prepare a job description for a Fork lift operator handling case goods in a warehouse.

2. Prepare a job description for a Manager of personnel of a factory of 600 hourly and 75 salaried employees. This is a one-plant corporation. There is no "home office" guidance or assistance for the Manager of personnel.

3. Prepare a job description for the position of President of a large university having 15,000 students and 600 faculty members.

4. Prepare a list showing the major differences in preparing the three job descriptions asked for in Work Exercises 1, 2, and 3.

5. List seven purposes for writing job descriptions for a company.

Fig. 10.1

JOB DESCRIPTION				
Petrini Manufacturing Company	Effective 9-1-74	Revised 10-1-78	Approval D. Levis	Described DB
Position Title Plumber A		Department Maintenance	EEOC Occupation Classification Craftsman	Job Number 0805

SUMMARY

Function
— To provide journeyman level skills in maintenance, installation and repair of plumbing facilities.

Scope
— Responsible for operation of plumbing facilities and systems and design and construction in minor construction projects.

DUTIES

Typical
— Installs, repairs, and maintains water, air, gas and sewer lines, pipes, traps, washbowls, fittings, drains, sinks, valves, faucets, hot water units, gas heaters, vents, toilet fixtures, fountains, and water treatment systems. Checks for preventive maintenance, assures supply of plumbing materials, and estimates plumbing jobs when needed.

Periodic
— Flushes water heaters and checks steam system and sump holes. Occasionally assigned to special events and/or emergencies.

SUPERVISION

Received
— Work coordinated by Lead Plumber and/or Supervisor of Utilities.

Given
— Coordinate the work of assistants.

EDUCATION

Required
— High school degree with Journeyman's license in plumbing.

Preferred
— High School degree with Master's license in plumbing.

EXPERIENCE

Required
— Two years plumbing work as a journeyman plumber and an operator's license.

Preferred
— More than two years as a journeyman plumber.

EQUIPMENT
— Use of sewer snakes, power pipe threader, manual pipe threader, electric drills, acetylene torch, propane torch, pipe wrenches, copper tubing flare kit, pipe cutter and pipe joiner kit.

WORKING CONDITIONS

Usual
— Dampness, dirt, close quarters requiring body discomfort, exposed to heat, cold, disagreeable odors and mud.

The above duties describe the chief functions of the job and are not to be considered a detailed description of every duty of the job.

Fig. 10.2

JOB DESCRIPTION				
Norman Bartley Manufacturing Company	Effective 7-1-74	Revised 6-1-78	Approval DLB	Described W. Smith
Position Title Stockroom Attendant		Department Maintenance	EEOC Occupation Classification Office-Clerk	Job Number 1018

FUNCTION

Maintain inventory of stock and inventory files. Perform miscellaneous stockroom duties.

TOOLS AND EQUIPMENT

Hammer, nail puller, pinch bar, wire cutters, hand trucks, hoist, hand saw, step ladder, forms, parts books, pencils.

MATERIALS

M.R.O. Stockroom supplies such as unions, couplings, collars, nipples, bearings, drive chains, gears, pulleys, sprockets, bushings, nuts, bolts, washers, valves, gaskets, etc.

WORKING PROCEDURE

1. Unload and open boxes of incoming materials and dispose of waste.

2. Check all incoming materials against order, notify Head Stockroom Keeper or Supervisor if incorrect.

3. Put materials in proper stock location.

4. Keep records as to stock location and inventory. Notify Head Stockroom Keeper or Supervisor when items are to be reordered.

5. Maintain file of completed forms such as 2-B (Purchase Requisition) and 485 (Stores Requisition).

6. Issue materials from stockroom and execute proper forms.

7. When necessary, receive and check returned materials and execute proper forms.

8. Take periodic inventory.

9. Assist other stockroom personnel with miscellaneous stockroom work.

10. Use power tools to cut stock when necessary.

11. Keep stockroom neat and orderly.

The above working procedure describes the chief functions of the job and is not to be considered a detailed description of every duty of the job.

Fig. 10.3

<table>
<tr><td colspan="5" align="center">JOB DESCRIPTION</td></tr>
<tr>
<td>Kane Manufacturing Company</td>
<td>Effective
6-1-75</td>
<td>Revised
8-1-78</td>
<td>Approval
N. Wade</td>
<td>Described
R. Douglas</td>
</tr>
<tr>
<td>Position Title
Automobile Mechanic</td>
<td colspan="2">Department
Maintenance</td>
<td>EEOC Occupation
Classification
Craftsman</td>
<td>Job Number
1203</td>
</tr>
</table>

GENERAL STATEMENT OF DUTIES: Repairs and maintains a variety of makes and models of passenger automobiles, trucks and street maintenance equipment; does related work as required.

DISTINGUISHING FEATURES OF THE CLASS: Employees in this class perform difficult and skilled mechanical work to automotive equipment. Employees are expected to plan their work and make decisions within established policies and procedures. Although an employee in this class must exercise independent judgment, general supervision is received from the Street Superintendent.

EXAMPLES OF WORK: (Illustrative only)
Diagnoses defects of automobiles, trucks and general or specialized automotive equipment;
Repairs or overhauls chassis units including brake systems, transmissions, differentials and front and rear axles;
Repairs and maintains various types of mowers, tractors, trucks and road graders;
Inspects, adjusts, and replaces necessary units and related parts;
Times camshaft and ignition;
Adjusts connecting rods and main bearings;
Removes and installs engines, transmissions, differentials, clutches and steering assemblies;
Paints vehicles;
Performs body work on vehicle;
Repairs street signs and barricades;
Prepares and files maintenance records.

REQUIRED KNOWLEDGE, SKILLS AND ABILITIES: Thorough knowledge of standard practices and equipment of the automotive mechanic trade; good knowledge of the principles of operation of gasoline engines and of mechanical repair on heavy trucks and construction equipment; good knowledge of the occupational hazards and safety precautions of the trade; ability to understand and carry out complex oral and written instructions; ability to adapt available tools and repair parts to specific repair problems; skill in the use and care of hand and machine tools employed in motor repair and adjustment work; skill in locating and correcting defects in automotive equipment; good physical condition.

ACCEPTABLE EXPERIENCE AND TRAINING: Considerable experience as a journeyman automotive mechanic or heavy equipment mechanic and preferably completion of a recognized apprenticeship program leading toward the rank of automotive mechanic, and completion of a standard high school or vocational school course, or any equivalent combination of experience and training which provides the required knowledges, skills and abilities.

The above duties or working procedures describe the chief function of the job and are not to be considered a detailed description of every duty of the job.

Fig. 10.4

JOB DESCRIPTION				
Wade Manufacturing Company	Effective 9-1-77	Revised	Approval B. Nelson	Described DB
Position Title Key Punch Operator B		Department Data Processing	EEOC Occupation Classification Technical	Job Number 0304

FUNCTION

To transmit information from various-type forms via a keypunch/verifier to a computer card. Performs general office clerical work when requested.

TOOLS AND EQUIPMENT

Keypunch/verifier, computer terminal, printer, reader, decollator, burster, copier, calculator, typewriter.

REPORTS TO

Program Director-Data Processing

SUPERVISES AND/OR DIRECTS THE WORK OF

None

TYPICAL DUTIES AND/OR WORKING PROCEDURES

1. To process information from raw data to a finished keypunched computer card. This involves the following:
   a. Check the raw data for accuracy and completeness. This involves learning information concerning approximately 90 to 100 different forms used in finance, payroll, tax, scheduling, grade reporting, accounts receivable, etc.
   b. Memorizing the formats of each job request and to punch and verify applicable data.
   c. Delivering the finished card to the terminal operator for further processing.

2. Reports the malfunctioning of any equipment to the supervisor.

3. Relieves other personnel in the area for lunch and/or vacation time, such as employees assigned as terminal operators, secretaries, etc.

4. During peak period for work in the Terminal Room (Sept., Nov., and Dec.), does general office work of printing, trimming, decollating, bursting, packing, and shipping.

The above duties or working procedures describe the chief function of the job and are not to be considered a detailed description of every duty of the job.

Fig. 10.5

SALARIED JOB DESCRIPTION				
Norman Bartley Manufacturing Company	Effective 5-11-75	Revised 11-1-78	Approval B. Smith	Described R. Douglas
Position Title Factory Manager		Department Manufac- turing	EEOC Occupation Classification Management	Job Number 2501

GENERAL RESPONSIBILITIES:

　　Under the general direction of the Regional Manufacturing Manager produces consistent with scheduled requirements, cost standards and quality specifications. Responsible for formulating, developing and administering management activities in accordance with established policies and procedures.

REPORTING RELATIONSHIP:

　　Reports to:　Midwest Regional Manufacturing Manager
　　Supervises:　Factory Controller
　　　　　　　　Manager-Engineering
　　　　　　　　Manager-Personnel
　　　　　　　　Manager-Production
　　　　　　　　Manager-Quality Control
　　　　　　　　Manager-Transportation and Warehousing

TYPICAL DUTIES:

A. Responsible for developing and maintaining a staff and indirectly operating personnel whose qualifications and performance meet the requirements of each assignment to a degree necessary to assure continued satisfactory operations.

B. Directs and coordinates staff functions through regular meetings to outline objectives, organize activities, clarify and assign responsibilities, interpret established policies and procedures, coordinate the thinking, adjust differences and promote improvements in operations and administration.

C. Maintains constant follow up to assure that assignments are completed, cost standards and production and quality levels are maintained, and that service divisions are adequately fulfilling their responsibilities.

D. Cooperates with and promotes the utilization by the staff of Home Office functional specialized services in studying and resolving problems, in developing new or improved methods, services, facilities and equipment to effect reductions in cost and improvements in quality of products and in the fulfillment of administrative detail.

E. Coordinates the operations of the factory with the planned program of the Operations Division in accordance with established policies and procedures; keeps the Regional Manager informed on manufacturing accomplishments and difficulties, significant cost information,

Fig. 10.5 (continued)

important personnel matters and other facts of consequence concerning the operations of the factory.

1. Directs special studies of specific phases of operations from a cost standpoint.
2. Investigates, directs development, and makes recommendation on new or modified equipment, facilities, methods or operating procedures to reduce costs or improve quality.
3. Works closely with all concerned in resolving manufacturing problems on new or changed products.

F. Gives careful attention to the factory organization, analyzing the performance and results attained, and where necessary makes recommendations for changes in the basic structure and complement of the organization.

G. Follows operations closely so as to effect reductions in costs and improvements in quality standards in products. Makes or promotes the development of technical and economic studies to substantiate recommendations to Regional Manager on equipment, facilities, methods or general operations.

H. Directs the preparation of standards for factory activities and is responsible for seeing that actual performance conforms with standards, and for taking necessary action to hold over-all expenditures within limits of standards.

I. Responsible for maintaining all buildings, equipment, and facilities in accordance with company standards and sees all necessary steps are taken to safeguard Company's properties through established security precautions.

J. Responsible for the administration of all policies and procedures concerning employee relations, including the negotiation of a proper administration of labor contracts.

K. Is familiar with and cooperates with Home Office personnel in the development of local community relations; attends civic functions as representative of the factory, and participates or promotes participation of subordinates in community affairs.

L. Responsible for factory conforming with local, state and federal laws such as labor, sanitation, zoning, etc.

M. Approves or recommends approval of expenditures within provisions of existing procedure.

N. Personnel Duties

Is responsible for the direct or indirect administration of all personnel policies and procedures concerning all employees at the factory, including their safety, health, training, benefits, compensation, promotion, employment status and general behavior.

Fig. 10.6

SALARIED JOB DESCRIPTION				
Norman Bartley Manufacturing Company	Effective 1-1-77	Revised	Approval S. McDermott	Described D. Pietrini
Position Title Senior Manager, Computer Information Processing	Department Administration		EEOC Occupation Classification Management	Job Number 2304

GENERAL RESPONSIBILITIES:

Responsible for the overall supervision, administration and coordination of the Computer Operations & Software Department and the Input Preparation & Data Communication Department. Coordinates the activities of these centralized operations with Division Headquarters, user departments, and field locations.

REPORTING RELATIONSHIP:

Reports to: General Manager — Administrative Systems
Supervises: Manager — Computer Operations and Software
Manager — Input Preparation & Data Communications
Special Assignment
Steno-Clerk

TYPICAL DUTIES:

A. Responsible for the coordination of Computer Operations & Software Department activities to insure that schedules for the running of computer applications are continuously followed to satisfy user department requirements.

B. Responsible for the coordination of input preparation functions so that input data is available for computer processing on scheduled basis while maintaining overall input equipment utilization.

C. Responsible for the coordination of data and message communication activities to insure that required data and messages are transmitted to various points in network and data is available for computer processing on scheduled basis.

D. Communicates continuously and works with user departments and field locations, i.e., factories, district offices, and distribution centers, on all problems relating data accuracy and/or systems schedules.

E. Responsible for reviewing equipment operations to insure the efficient utilization of computer hardware, input preparation equipment and data communications equipment. Participates in studies to upgrade or modify equipment under his control.

F. Responsible for reviewing systems applications to insure that computer programs are operating efficiently to achieve maximum computer thruput.

G. Directs activities performed with departments relating to manual audits and processing of documents to insure that computerized files, data bases and systems are accurately operated and maintained.

H. Reviews all new systems applications or revisions to existing computerized programs and recommends required changes to improve input and computer operating efficiencies.

I. Responsible for controlling operations within approved administrative budget, with particular emphasis on computer and data communication expenses.

11

Selecting Factors

Selecting the job characteristics or factors against which the various jobs will be compared or evaluated is a very important part of the program. The final selection of the factors is done after the job questionnaires and the job descriptions have been completed. By studying these two forms, the person in charge of the program can make the final decision as to which factors will best evaluate the jobs in question.

Since we are trying to show the differences between job requirements, it is important that all jobs be measured against the proper factors. If a factor is chosen and it is later realized that most employees rate at the same level or degree on this factor, then it is not a good factor for that group of jobs and should be discarded.

Robert Sibson in his book *Compensation* states that there are a number of requirements to be fulfilled before a factor is considered acceptable. These are:

1. Each factor must have some relationship to job difficulty or job value.
2. In combination, the factors should correlate reasonably well with job difficulty.

3. The factors selected must be both observable and measurable.

4. Important elements of every job must be measured by one or more factors.

5. Every factor should serve to help distinguish between jobs.

6. Two factors should not measure essentially the same characteristic [1].

To be acceptable for a program, a factor should have various degrees or levels.

Job knowledge is a good factor to use for most hourly paid job evaluation programs. Every job on the payroll varies in this requirement, from those jobs requiring very little job knowledge (a job that may be learned in an hour, such as common laborer) to a job requiring great expertise in job knowledge (one that takes several years of training and experience to learn, such as journey electrician). Obviously each job would rate differently on the degree scale for job knowledge.

The general factors used for evaluating hourly production work are:

1. skill

2. effort

3. responsibility

4. job conditions

These can further be broken down into sub-factors such as:

SKILL	RESPONSIBILITY
job knowledge	general
education [2]	equipment
experience	processes
initiative	material
training time	products
practice time	safety of others
manual dexterity	work of others

1. Sibson, Robert. *Compensation*. New York: AMACOM, 1974.

2. In recent years, because of some legal involvement, this factor has fallen in disfavor and consequently is being used less and less as a factor in job evaluation programs.

EFFORT
physical
mental
visual

JOB CONDITIONS
unusual working conditions
safety hazards
health hazards
pressure of the work

It is not necessary to use all of the sub-factors in the evaluation. For example, in considering the factor of skill, perhaps only job knowledge, experience, and training time might be appropriate for one particular evaluation program. In another program, with different types of work being compared, perhaps manual dexterity and practice time might be added, or one might replace one of the other sub-factors that did not fit or properly evaluate the new group of jobs.

As stated before, selecting the proper factors is a vital part of the evaluation program. Each company would want to select factors that best fit the type of work being done. The above factors (sub-factors) would fit most evaluation plans for hourly production work. They would not, however, be appropriate for someone wanting to establish a program for a retail store. For a retail store the same general factors might be established, but the sub-factors would be different as shown below.

RESPONSIBILITY
money
property
equipment
materials
service
goodwill
safety of others
direction of others

Other sub-factors that might be considered for a retail store are:

SKILL
training
technical training
experience
dexterity
precision
initiative

JOB CONDITIONS
discomfort
accident hazard
health hazard
clothing spoilage

EFFORT
perseverance
concentration
judgment
acuteness of sense
endurance

Selecting the proper factors for administrators or managers is perhaps the most difficult of all the evaluation plans. Generally speaking, a separate system should be used for the exempt positions on the payroll. Mixing production workers and supervisors on the same evaluation system usually will not be very satisfactory. The same set of factors used for hourly workers will not apply for supervisors, and vice versa.

A review of factors and sub-factors that might be considered for management work might be:

KNOWLEDGE SKILLS REQUIRED
experience
specialized training
communication skills
planning
for finance and property

IMPACT OF DUTIES
on community
on state and federal government
on employees

LEVELS OF DECISION MAKING
consequence of error
extent to which decisions are controlled by law or internal procedures
ingenuity and innovativeness required
level of review of decision

SUPERVISORY RESPONSIBILITIES OF POSITION
level of difficulty
number of direct and indirect employees supervised
variety and complexity of the department supervised
level and number supervised

WORKING CONDITIONS
physical demands
environment in which majority of duties are carried out
mental and emotional pressure
confidentiality of work

The sub-factors listed under skill, responsibility, effort, and job conditions for hourly production-type work, retail establishment, or management are suggested factors. Not all of the sub-factors would apply to a particular company; others might also be inserted. The important thing is that the factors finally chosen should apply to nearly all of the jobs in the section or area of the company being evaluated. A sub-factor listed under any of the production, retail, or management factors might be used in any of the other plans, provided all jobs in the company could be checked against it.

Review Questions

1. What are the four primary factors used in a weighted-in-points job evaluation program?

2. Why is "overlapping" of factors a serious problem in job evaluation?

3. What are two main disadvantages of having 20 sub-factors in a job evaluation program?

4. How many factors should be used for an evaluation plan for hourly paid employes? Explain.

5. If you were the Personnel Manager of a highly automated plant, what factors would you choose for your evaluation of the production and service employees?

6. Explain how the sub-factors for the primary factor of skill vary between a program for hourly paid employees and one for management.

7. What are the advantages and disadvantages of having an employee opinion poll in selecting the factors to be used in a job evaluation program?

Work Exercise

1. Prepare a table having three columns. At the top of the columns place the following headings—Production department, Bank, and Large Company that does plumbing and air conditioning work. Place in each column the factor you would choose to evaluate the type of jobs that would be necessary.

12

Weighting of Factors

Once the factors have been selected, it is necessary to "weight" (rate) each factor as to its importance compared to the other factors being used. For example: in evaluating production-type work, if job knowledge, complexity, responsibility for equipment, hazard, physical effort, and work conditions were chosen as the factors to be used in the program, what percentage of the total would each factor receive? In other words, are they all of equal importance or are some factors more important in determining what type of work is more important to the company and should thus receive more point value than the other factors. In every case each of the factors chosen may have a different total value. It is the responsibility of the person in charge of the program to either set the "weighting percentage" alone or to select a committee and solicit their input on the problem. The important thing to remember is that the factors chosen must be correct for the type of work being compared and that the relative importance of each of the factors will affect the total point score of each job.

Some years ago, under the working conditions that existed at the time, the National Electrical Manufacturing Association established the following weight for production-type work [1].

1. Source: National Electrical Manufacturers Association, Job Rating Plan—Definition of the Factors Used in Evaluating Hourly Rated Jobs. 2101 L Street, N.W., Washington, D.C. 20037.

Primary factor	Sub-factors	Percent of total	Weight
Skill	Experience	22	
	Education	14	
	Initiative and ingenuity	14	
			50%
Effort	Physical demand	10	
	Mental–visual	5	
			15%
Responsibility	Equipment process	5	
	Material or product	5	
	Safety of others	5	
	Work of others	5	
			20%
Job conditions	Working conditions	10	
	Hazards	5	
			15%
	Total	100%	100%

For production work, most companies today have reasonable working conditions. They have purchased machinery to do most jobs that require heavy physical effort. The safety hazards also have been greatly reduced. Consequently, although the factors of work conditions, safety, and physical effort are usually included in the total factor list for evaluating production-type work, they do not however receive a high percentage of the total points when the factors are weighted. The factors that usually receive the heavier weight are job knowledge, complexity, experience, etc., and the sub-factors listed under skill.

One company, for the production jobs they were reviewing, established the following weights:

job knowledge	35%
complexity	20
physical effort	12
hazard	12
responsibility for equipment	12
work conditions	9
total	100%

If, during the establishment of the job evaluation plan, one or two other factors were later considered appropriate, they could easily be added to the list. To make room for them, however, some percentage points would have to be obtained from the existing factors, as the total percentage for all of the factors cannot exceed 100.

Example: If the factor responsibility for materials was considered valid and should be added, then a new weighting must be made. Percentage points from the existing factors must be reduced to make available points for the new factor.

The new weighting would be established and points allotted accordingly. The following is an example of what might be the final allocation of percentage points when "weighting" the new list of factors.

Old weight		New weight	A reduction of
35%	Job knowledge	33%	2%
20	Complexity	20	0
12	Physical effort	10	2
12	Hazard	10	2
9	Work conditions	9	0
12	Responsibility for equipment	10	2
0	Responsibility for materials	8	0
100%		100%	8%

For the next step in developing an evaluation plan, it is necessary to sub-divide each factor into various levels. For example, job knowledge may be divided into five or six steps (levels), while work conditions might only be divided into two or three levels. In establishing points for each level of a factor, it is easier to distribute points using large numbers such as 20, 40, 60, rather than small ones such as 2, 4, and 6. One or two factors' total worth may be only six percent of the total value in the program; thus the highest point value to be received would be six if some adjustment were not made.

To overcome working with the small numbers, the actual percentages usually are multiplied by a number ranging from three to ten. It does not matter which multiplier is chosen as long as each factor is multiplied by this same number. For example, to get the factors for the production jobs previously mentioned into a more workable order, each factor's percentage point was multiplied by eight. The new point weight of each factor is now:

Factor	%	New total point value
Job knowledge	35 × 8	280
Complexity	20 × 8	160
Physical effort	12 × 8	96
Hazard	12 × 8	96
Responsibility for equipment	12 × 8	96
Work conditions	9 × 8	72
	100 × 8	800

In our sample evaluation of hourly production-type work, we have selected six factors and have assigned the total point values. If a certain job received the maximum number of points for job knowledge, that job would receive 280 points (35% of 800 points in the system). How many points should a job receive if it were not very difficult to learn? How many levels of job knowledge are there between a job that can be done after 20 minutes of instruction and a job (such as an electrician) that requires five or more years to learn?

In deciding the number of levels in any one factor, one must review the jobs being evaluated and try to determine how many levels can be identified and *adequately defined.* It is not enough just to say there are five levels in a certain factor. Each level must be clearly defined so that anyone evaluating a job and comparing it to a certain factor would be able to determine which level accurately reflects the requirements of that particular job. The factor work conditions best exemplifies this point. On most production-type work, one probably could identify three or four levels such as excellent work conditions, good work conditions, fair work conditions, and poor work conditions. On the other hand, it probably would be very difficult to identify seven different levels and write an *adequate* definition that would allow one to place that job at the right level. It would be too difficult to define the levels of the factor that would allow the evaluator to differentiate to such a fine degree.

Words like excellent, good, fair, poor, are suitable to use as a general classification, but they must always be supported by a sentence or two describing what the evaluator had in mind. Figure 12.1 is an example of a written definition for four levels of the factor work conditions.

Fig. 12.1 Definition of Work Conditions

This factor appraises the nature of the conditions under which the employee must work, i.e., the physical conditions and surroundings in which the work must be performed. These conditions may affect the mental or physical well-being of the employee and include such items as climate, ventilation, heat or cold, dirty working conditions, and noise level.

Degrees	*Points*
A *Excellent Working Conditions*—rare exposure to disagreeable elements.	18
B *Good Working Conditions*—exposure to slightly disagreeable elements or occasional exposure to a combination of disagreeable elements.	36
C *Fair Working Conditions*—frequent exposure to a disagreeable element or occasional exposure to a combination of disagreeable elements.	54
D *Poor Working Conditions*—continuous exposure to an extremely disagreeable element or frequent exposure to a combination of disagreeable elements.	72

On this particular factor, it would be quite difficult to define several additional levels of work conditions. If it was felt that certain jobs really deserved additional consideration for adverse working conditions, an adjustment could be made by installing a second chart for this factor. If this were done, the total points for both charts would also be adjusted so that the total for both charts on work conditions would be within the total for the factor. (See Figs. 12.3 and 12.4 for a complete factor description on work conditions.)

Basically, those factors that carry a high percentage of the total point value can usually be divided into six or seven levels. This is desirable, whenever possible, since it helps to differentiate the point value of the jobs being evaluated. By having more levels in the factors that carry the most points, it allows the evaluator to allocate points to the jobs more fairly.

On the other hand, if a factor only rates six percent of the total points in the program, or 48 points out of a total of 800, it would not be practical to have more than three or four levels.

Assigning point values to each level within a factor is easy once the total points for the factor have been established. The formula is merely dividing the total points for the factor by the number of levels desired.

For example, suppose there are 100 points for the factor. If you desired five levels, then the point scores would be 20 points for each level. The first level would rate 20 points, the second level 40 points, the third, fourth and fifth levels 60, 80, and 100 points respectively. If you desired six levels, then 100 divided by 6 equals 16.6 points. The respective values for the six levels would then be 16, 33, 50, 66, 83, and 100. The numbers are rounded as shown to eliminate working with decimals. *The evaluation does not have to be so accurate as to require the use of decimals in the point table.*

To complete the work on assigning points to each level of each factor, it must be decided how many levels can be defined adequately for each factor. For example, suppose that for the factors used for illustrative purpose in this manual we could adequately define the following levels:

job knowledge	5 levels
complexity	5 levels
physical effort	5 levels
hazard	5 levels
responsibility for equipment	4 levels
work conditions	4 levels

If this is the case, then a table (Fig. 12.2) would be constructed so as to allocate points to each of the levels of each factor.

Fig. 12.2
Allocation of Points to the Levels of the Factors

Factor	Weighted percentage	Total number of points allotted	Number of levels desired	Point allocation for different levels				
				1	2	3	4	5
Job knowledge	35%	280	5	56	112	168	224	280
Complexity	20	160	5	32	64	96	128	160
Physical effort	12	96	5	19	38	57	76	96
Hazard	12	96	4	24	48	72	96	
Responsibility for equipment	12	96	4	24	48	72	96	
Work conditions	9	72	4	18	36	54	72	

Once the number of levels per factor is decided and the points allocated, then it is necessary to define each level so that jobs can be compared against it. Figures 12.3 through 12.37 are examples of how a completed factor description would look. Some factors, such as job knowledge and complexity, can best be defined in essay form. Others, such as hazard and work conditions, are best understood when presented in a chart or table. Either approach is satisfactory as long as the evaluator can determine which level best describes the job being evaluated.

FACTORS OF PRODUCTION JOBS

Work Conditions

This factor appraises the nature of the conditions under which the employee must work, i.e., the physical conditions and surroundings in which the work must be performed. These conditions may affect the mental or physical well being of the employee and include such items as climate, ventilation, heat or cold, dirty working conditions, and noise level.

All jobs are evaluated in two steps.

1. A review of the job as a whole and points assigned accordingly (See Chart A) (Fig. 12.3).

Fig. 12.3 Chart A

Degrees	Points
A. *Excellent Working Conditions*—Rare exposure to disagreeable elements.	4
B. *Good Working Conditions*—Exposure to slightly disagreeable element or occasional exposure to a combination of disable elements.	8
C. *Fair Working Conditions*—Frequent exposure to a disagreeable element or occasional exposure to a combination of disagreeable elements.	12
D. *Poor Working Conditions*—Continuous exposure to an extremely disagreeable element or frequent exposure to a combination of disagreeable elements.	16

Fig. 12.4 Chart B

On each of the following items select the point value most closely corresponding to the percentage of the year for which the conditions cause discomfort. Job conditions that occur less than 10% of the time are not to be counted.

Conditions	Percent of time				
	1 None	2 25%	3 50%	4 75%	5 100%
Weather					
E. Light weather conditions characterize jobs performed indoors but without air conditioning.	0	1	2	3	4
F. Moderate weather conditions characterize jobs that are performed out of doors but not ordinarily when it is raining.	0	3	4	5	6
G. Severe weather conditions are those exposing the employee to rain or cold weather.	0	7	8	9	10
Fumes, Dust and Odors					
H. Moderate odors, dust or fumes are those that are repellent, cause considerable discomfort, or irritate eyes or respiratory passages. Moderate credit is allowed for wearing a mask or respiratory.	0	2	4	6	8
I. Strong odors or fumes are those that are so obnoxious as to create a feeling of nausea when first exposed.	0	4	8	12	16
J. *Dirt and Grease*—Credit for dirt and grease if difficult to wash off; paint, machine, grease, oil, etc.	0	3	6	9	12
Dampness					
K. Light dampness occurs on jobs requiring hands to be wet, or when employee works on damp floor or when boots are worn.	0	2	4	6	8
L. Moderate dampness occurs when the workman works in an area having puddles of water.	0	6	8	10	12
M. Extreme dampness occurs when the workman's clothes are frequently wet; this does not include dampness due to weather.	0	10	12	14	16
Noise					
N. Where the decibel readings are high enough that ear plugs are recommended.	0	10	12	14	16

2. In addition to the points earned in #1, each job may earn additional points because of specific work conditions (See Chart B) (Fig. 12.4).

Job Knowledge

This factor appraises the amount of things the employee must know in order to perform the job. As a rule, the jobs that can be learned most quickly are those that will evaluate low on this factor. Both education and experience contribute to job knowledge.

Fig. 12.5 Job Knowledge

Degree	Points
A. *Little or None.* Perform a job that is learned after brief oral instructions and observation. May be performed by a new employee or someone temporarily transferred to the job for a short period of time as a replacement for an employee off because of sickness, vacation, etc. Work may be highly routine, simple, and performed under close direction. Example: Laborer, Custodian	56
B. *Limited.* Light mental application required for performing work where the assigned tasks consist of routine or standard practices; the actions to be taken and the decisions to be made are limited to a few possibilities. May be able to perform infrequent reoccurring tasks with general direction. May do general office work with close direction. Have sufficient knowledge of a trade or skill to perform simple, familiar, or routine jobs, and/or operation of small equipment. Example: Auto mechanic C, General maintenance C.	112
C. *Moderate.* Assignments include a variety of tasks within a set procedure which require some decision making. The decisions are few and limited. Have knowledge of how to repair machines or equipment of a single type or in a single area or department. Have sufficient knowledge of the total operation of the department to work on assignments, with general direction. May prepare records or reports where some judgment is required. Example: Clerk B, Auto mechanic B.	168

(Continued)

Fig. 12.5 (continued)

D. *Advanced.* Has sufficient knowledge of a trade or skill to work under general direction in the department. Assembles, repairs, or inspects complicated machinery and equipment using a variety of gages and instruments. Judgment and initiative are required within established standards. Frequent decisions are required, but scope is limited to immediate activity. May direct the work of other craftsmen or a small crew.	224
Example: Clerk A, Auto mechanic A.	
E. *Skilled.* Has sufficient knowledge of a trade or skill to work on assignments without instructions as to a specific method. Knowledge and ability to make major decisions and/or major repairs in all phases of the work without instructions as to a specific method. Work requires considerable problem-solving ability. Duties are diversified and require the employee to meet changing conditions and problems.	280
Example: Electrician	
GUIDE RULES	
Close Direction—An employee works under close direction when told what to do and in some detail how to do it.	
General Direction—An employee works under general direction when told what to do with only a brief explanation as to the specific method.	

Physical Effort

This factor appraises the degree of physical exertion required for a full day's work. Exertions that are infrequent or that are not typical of the performance of the job should not be considered. Definitions used are:

light weight — 0 to 12 lbs

average weight — 12 to 50 lbs

heavy weight — over 50 lbs

repetitive — performing the same operation over and over without appreciable pause between cycles

frequently — more than 6 times an hour

several — from 4 to 6 times an hour

occasional — up to and including 3 times an hour

Fig. 12.6 Physical Effort

Degree	A	B	C	D	E
Light objects	Lift light weight objects, with no repetitive bending or stooping	Repetitively lift light weight objects where frequent bending or stooping alternates with lighter activities	Repetitive lifting of light weight objects with repetitive bending and stooping		
Average objects	Occasionally lift average weight objects	Frequently lift average weight objects with no repetitive bending or stooping	Repetitively lift average weight objects where frequent bending or stooping alternates with lighter activities	Repetitively lift average weight objects, with repetitive bending and stooping	
Heavy objects			Lift heavy objects several times each shift.	Frequently lift heavy objects but alternating with lighter activities	Major portion of day requires heavy lifting
Points	24	38	57	76	96

Complexity

This factor appraises the variety and complexity of this job in proportion to the requirements on this job. Consider the exercise of judgment and planning that the job requires together with the length of training time required to perform the job satisfactorily. Tasks may range from one involving a simple repetitive job to one involving independent judgment and planning.

Fig. 12.7 Complexity

Degrees	Points
A. *Minimum Complexity*—Simple re;etitive task or non-repetitive task involving little directed thinking. Exercise minimum care to prevent injuries to others.	32
B. *Moderate Complexity*—Perform a variety of tasks that require only brief instructions to learn. Not involved in planning or using independent judgment. Exercise habitual alertness to prevent injury to others.	64
C. *Average Complexity*—Perform a variety of tasks, some of which require special training, but most of job assignments are in one type of worker skill. Occasionally involved in planning or using independent judgment. Exercise a high degree of attention and care to prevent injury to others.	96
D. *Above Average Complexity*—Tasks involving work assignments in several areas or skills and tasks frequently involving independent judgment and planning. Work requires considerable problem solving ability.	128
E. *High Degree of Complexity*—Task involving heavy concentration, planning, independent judgment, and a high degree of initiative in one or a variety of areas. Duties are diversified enough to require the employee to meet changing conditions and problems.	160

Dexterity

To what degree does the job require ability to move body members rapidly, accurately, and with precision? Are these movements complex or simple, performed frequently or intermittently, repetitive or varied?

Fig. 12.8 Dexterity

Degree	Points
A. The type of tasks performed requires little or no motor ability.	
B. The job requires some motor ability, such as the occasional operation of a typewriter, adding machine, or small telephone switchboard, or occasional handling of small instruments and equipment; such operations are not a primary component of the job, nor is speed a basic requirement.	
C. The job requires repetitive or frequent exercise of moderate motor ability, such as operating an adding machine, comptometer, typewriter, or calculator; or repetitive or frequent operation of instruments and equipment—such operations being primary components of the job; speed and accuracy are desired.	
D. The job requires a high degree of motor control and coordination in order to move body members rapidly, accurately, and with precision, such as operating a large telephone switchboard or an IBM proof machine.	

Source: Courtesy of American Compensation Association, P.O. Box 1176, Scottsdale, Arizona, 85252.

Interaction with Others

On this factor, one must consider interaction of employees with members of their own department, other departments in the company, and outside companies or agencies. Contacts may be divided into two groups.

1. Contacts that have only the exchange of information, and contacts where the influencing of others is involved, with the latter having more responsibility attached to it.

2. Contacts within the department, contacts between departments in the Service Center, and contacts outside the Service Center. The weighting of these places contacts with the department as having the least importance and contacts outside the Center as having the most.

Fig. 12.9 Interaction with Others

Degree	Points
A. Performs repetitive, highly standardized office or skill functions that involve very little interchange with other employees excluding the Supervisor.	
B. Makes contacts of an information–exchange nature within the department, or has *occasional* contacts with personnel of other departments.	
C. Has on-the-job contacts requiring *frequent* exchanges of information with employees of other departments or *occasional* contacts with outside companies or agencies.	
D. Has *frequent* contacts of a minor influencing nature with other departments, or *occasional* interaction with outside companies or agencies.	
E. Frequently has contacts that require interaction with outside companies or agencies. Many of the contacts require stating the company's policy on the inquiry involved.	

Training Time

This factor evaluates the time taken by the average person to learn the job sufficiently well to be left under normal supervision. It is the time the employee needs to learn how to do the job in an acceptable manner and in sufficient quantity to be retained on the job. The total time should be based on the employee's working continuously on the job.

Fig. 12.10 Training Time

Time	Example	Degree	Points
Up to and including two weeks		A	
2 to 4 weeks inclusively	Shipping clerk	B	
1 to 3 months inclusively	Key punch operator A	C	
3 to 6 months inclusively	Quality control technician	D	
Over 6 months	Plumber	E	

Practice Time

This factor measures the additional time needed to practice any special skills until normal level of performance is reached.

Fig. 12.11 Practice Time

Time	Example	Degree	Points
Up to 1 week	Custodian	A	
1 week to 1 month	Yard maintenance	B	
1 month to 3 months	Terminal operator B	C	
3 months to 6 months	Fork lift operator	D	

Responsibility for Directing and/or Coordinating Work of Others

This factor appraises the responsibility of the worker on the job for assisting, instructing, directing, and/or coordinating the work of other employees in the department.

Fig. 12.12 Responsibility for Directing Work of Others

Degree	Points
A. Performs work with no direction and/or coordination given to other employees in the department.	
B. Performs work with *occasional* direction and/or coordination given to other employees in the department.	
C. Performs work with daily direction and/or coordination to one other employee in the department.	
D. Performs work with daily guidance, direction and/or coordination given to two, but not more than five, employees in the department.	
E. Performs work with daily guidance, direction and/or coordination given to six or more employees in the department.	

Hazard

This factor appraises the likelihood and degree of injury to the employee who uses due care and observes safety rules. Consider the past history of the job in selecting the proper level. Full consideration is to be given to all safety rules, and the evaluation is not to be based solely on a violation of the rules; however, the evaluation is to consider the degree of attention required in observing these rules. Likelihood refers to the chance of sustaining an injury of the degree specified.

Fig. 12.13 Hazard

Degrees

A. Minor cuts, burns, bruises, etc. Injury causes slight discomfort for short period of time, little inconvenience to work, and requires only simple protective dressing.

Slight skin cuts (such as result from handling metal or from broken glass), simple contact burns.

B. Severe cuts, burns, bruises, etc. Injury causes discomfort extending beyond day of occurrence, necessitates change in work pattern of job, and requires re-dressing for medical purposes.

Moderately deep flesh lacerations, small second degree burns, sore and extensive bruises, smashed fingernails, etc.

Injuries in degrees A and B are customarily handled by the First Aid Department. Those in degrees C and D customarily require outside treatment.

C. Major accidents with possible lost time. Injury may require the employee to work temporarily on another job.

Extensive second-degree burns. Severe crush wounds of toes or fingers with or without fracture.

D. Extended lost time, possible severe disability or fatality. Injury may consist of serious fractures, dismemberment, or permanent disability.

Definitions

First degree burns cause inflammation of the skin.

Second degree burns cause inflammation of the skin and formation of blisters.

Third degree burns cause destruction of skin and underlying tissue.

Fig. 12.14 Hazard (Points Allocated)

Ease of avoidance	Minor cuts, burns, bruises, etc.	Severe cuts, burns, bruises, etc.	Major accidents with possible lost time	Extended lost time Possibly severe disability
A. Little or no likelihood of injury	7	15	22	30
B. Possibility of injury exists but occurrence is easy to avoid by habitual care	15	22	30	48
C. Occasional accidents may occur but possible to avoid by conscious alertness	22	30	48	72
D. Injury is extremely difficult to avoid unless employee exercises judgment or concentrates on method of avoiding injury	30	48	72	96

Fig. 12.15 Hazard (Alternative Definition)

Degree	Points
A. Work having almost no accident or health hazards.	
B. Work having minor health hazards, accidents out-side of minor injuries such as abrasions, cuts and burns are impossible. Can be considered the same as "household" hazards.	
C. Exposure to ost time accidents, involving more serious cuts, bruises, muscle strain, allergies or some exposure to disease or contamination which would not be permanently incapacitating in nature. Rare exposure to more serious hazards.	
D. Frequent exposure to accident or health hazards that might cause incapacitation. Possibility of eye injuries, loss of fingers or serious burns. Frequent minor injuries are likely but more serious accidents are very rare.	
E. Considerable or continual exposure to disease or accidents that might result in serious permanent disability. Accidents happen frequently in spite of precautions.	

Source: Courtesy of American Compensation Association, P.O. Box 1176, Scottsdale, Arizona, 85252.

Hazards, both disease and accident, may be connected with or surround the job, even though all usual safety measures have been taken. Figure 12.15 shows an alternative way of writing a definition for hazard.

Responsibility for Processing Materials

This is the responsibility for preventing waste or loss of materials and supplies through carelessness or poor workmanship. Consider the quantity of items that may be spoiled or damaged before detection and correction, the value of the material and labor, and the possibility of salvage.

Fig. 12.16 Responsibility for Processing Materials

Degree	Points
A. Nominal. Little or no possibility of poor work or waste of materials due to poor workmanship, carelessness, or mistakes.	
B. Small losses might occur. Poor workmanship or mistakes might cause occasional losses in damaged materials, supplies, or rework up to $25.00 in a week. Poor work usually caught quickly by inspectors or other before damage is great.	
C. Substantial loss from poor workmanship or poor machine adjusting or operating could occur occasionally before ordinary checks would detect the poor work; or repeated small losses could occur. Worker must exercise care to avoid losses. Large losses possible, but losses per week should rarely go over $75.00.	
D. Considerable care on part of worker necessary to avoid damage or loss of materials. Material that could be lost represents substantial investment. Process requires careful adjustments or high degree of attention from workers. Loss or rework might occasionally run up to $300.00 in one mishap.	
E. Exacting work on expensive materials. May use machines that require exact setting and adjustments that are all made by the operator and not built into the machine. Possible losses could run over $600.00 in one mishap.	

Source: Courtesy of American Compensation Association, P.O. Box 1176, Scottsdale, Arizona, 85252.

Responsibility for Equipment

This factor appraises the employee's responsibility for preventing damage to tools and equipment. It is recognized that properly skilled employees should never permit damage to occur. However, carelessness on some jobs can result in little damage, whereas on others it can cause a greater loss. On these latter jobs, therefore, the employee's care and foresight are of greater value. In evaluating, consider the likelihood and amount of damage on any one occurrence. Consider the past history of the job.

Fig. 12.17 Responsibility for Equipment

DEFINITIONS
The material for maintenance employees is what they work on and the equipment is what they work with.
The value of purchased parts in terms of manhours is found by dividing the price of the part by the rate of the top grade mechanic.

GUIDE RULES

The size of responsibility can be measured by considering the ease or difficulty of avoiding mistakes, and the consequences of mistakes which can, and do, occur. The emphasis is on typical or usual mistakes rather than hypothetical or exceptional errors.

Degrees	Points
A. Low—Damage that can be repaired with less than two manhours of work.	
B. Medium—Damage that can be repaired in more than two and not more than 16 manhours of work.	
C. High—Damage that can be repaired in more than 16 manhours and not more than 32 manhours of work.	
D. Very High—Damage that requires more than 32 manhours to repair.	

Fig. 12.18 Responsibility for Equipment

	Degrees			
Ease of avoidance	Low	Moderate	High	Very high
A. No equipment used or Practically impossible for operator to prevent loss or to damage equipment	7	15	22	30
B. Easy to prevent loss by using habitual care and attention to job or Possible causes of loss are easily recognized	15	22	30	48
C. Alertness or close attention necessary to prevent loss or Possible causes of loss can be recognized only if employee takes specific action for this purpose	22	30	48	72
D. Employee must exercise judgment in selecting methods to avoid loss	30	48	72	96

Pressure of Work

What degree of concentration either to minute job details or to many tasks of the job is required? At what pace must the employee work? Must a large volume of work be processed within a specified limited time? Must attention be shifted frequently from one to another job detail? Are there interruptions, distractions or confusing influences? (Energy output is not necessarily involved in these considerations, but simply the required rate of performance.)

Unusual Working Conditions

What is the character of the physical conditions under which the job must be performed and to what extent do these conditions make the job disagreeable? Consider such elements as ventilation, dirt, noise, odors, unpleasant sights, etc. (Do not consider rotating shift work, for which a premium is paid.)

Fig. 12.19 Pressure of Work

Level	Points
A. Flow of work or character of duties is intermittent and requires close attention only at intervals. Tension or pressure not a part of the job.	
B. Flow of work and character of duties involves uniform mental attention. Increase in rate of performance is not usually necessary in order to reach quotas, meet deadlines, or handle emergencies, although an occasional high-speed period may occur.	
C. Requires close concentration with occasional periods during which tension caused by necessity to maintain quotas, meet deadlines, or handle emergencies is reduced.	
D. Requires constant concentration to a very large volume of work that must be completed within a limited period of time because certain deadlines must be met, emergencies must be handled effectively, or because job paces worker.	

Source: Courtesy of American Compensation Association, P.O. Box 1176, Scottsdale, Arizona, 85252.

Fig. 12.20 Unusual Working Conditions

Level	Points
A. Works regularly under desirable conditions with little or no disagreeable features. Illumination and ventilation are good and distractions are at a minimum considering the type of work performed.	
B. Works regularly under poorer-than-average conditions. Illumination, ventilation, space in which to work, or some other environmental feature is considered unpleasant or uncomfortable.	
C. Works under unusual conditions, perhaps at the sacrifice of personal health, comfort, or convenience such as excessive heat, noise, or other distractions and discomforts.	

Source: Courtesy of American Compensation Association, P.O. Box 1176, Scottsdale, Arizona, 85252.

FACTORS AND DEFINITIONS FOR MANAGEMENT POSITIONS

The factors just presented are commonly used for production work. The same general approach would be used in writing factor descriptions for exempt jobs, (supervisory positions). The following factor descriptions demonstrate additional examples of defining factors for management positions. The points are omitted, since the factors would have to be integrated into the total point structure of any program.

Experience

This factor refers to the minimum amount of work experience an average person may need to acquire the particular skills necessary to perform the job at an acceptable level. In considering this factor, it should be kept in mind that experience is of two kinds.

1. Previous experience on related work or lesser positions in or outside the company, and

2. The breaking-in time or training period on the job itself.

Fig. 12.21 Experience

Degree	Points
A. Practically no prior experience required. Can rely on education and knowledge required for the basic requirements for employment. Up to one year breaking-in time.	
B. Requires one to two years experience on this job or similar jobs. Time required to pick up the knowledge, related skills that could include management skills for leading small section or group of employees.	
C. Requires two to four years experience on this and other jobs in the field. Experience with broad management skills is required.	
D. Requires over four years experience on this job and jobs leading up to it. Progression through several job levels is usually necessary so incumbent can have intimate knowledge of the jobs below.	

Education

This factor refers to the scholastic training, either formal or informal (courses, seminars, and research) necessary to perform a job at a satisfactory level. The factor not only appraises the basic academic training, but also the necessity of remaining up to date in a field such as taxes, employment laws, labor law, environmental control, handling of student and public information, etc.

Fig. 12.22 Education

Degree	Points
A. Requires a high school education or its equivalent, with general knowledge of high school subject matter including such courses as mathematics, accounting, mechanical shop work, agriculture, etc.	
B. Requires one to two years of college or the equivalent in post high school training in a specialized area such as accounting, counseling, etc.	
C. Requires basic knowledge in a professional field in which extensive specialized training is required in order to be able to correlate information, prepare and write reports, set up detailed procedures from general requirements and make explanation of a complex nature employing technical or written expression. Work involved in the area of accounting, finance, personnel, counseling, or business administration. Examples of Degrees: B.A., B.S., B.B.A.	
D. Requires knowledge of a specialized field in order to be able to interpret and explain highly specialized business methods and techniques, or to organize, develop and coordinate activities of a complicated, diversified or highly technical nature. Information usually obtainable through post graduate study. Example: M.B.A., C.P.A., Professional Engineers License, etc.	
E. Requires extensive thorough working knowledge in a specialized field usually through extensive postgraduate work to solve highly complex problems. Example: Ph.D., M.D., L.L.D.	

Note: The factor education has come under criticism lately as to whether it is defensible under certain interpretations of the law. These definitions were written for consideration by a university where certain jobs by their very position in the organization require certain advanced degrees.

Specialized Training

This factor recognizes the degree of required training of a special skill and a comprehensive understanding of the work elements involved. It assigns a value to the training derived from training gained from actual contact and portrays the necessary accumulation of knowledge of the methods and "tricks of the trade," which can be applied in an intelligent manner.

Fig. 12.23 Specialized Training

Degree	Points
A. Elementary Where little technical knowledge is required to conduct operations and where mental application is ordinary routine in nature.	
B. Intermediate Special knowledge of operations, technical and mental skills, processes, and their effect on each other. This knowledge gained through both experience and education.	
C. Advanced Special technical knowledge beyond the routine stage which has the equivalent of a college or technical course of study in the subject. Original thought is frequently required.	
D. Skilled Extremely advanced technical or business knowledge of the subject matter; because of practice or further study, good development of technical information for intellectual application. The job requires much creativity and originality of thought.	

Responsibility for Funds and Property

This factor covers those responsibilities concerned with the conservation, protection, and economical use of the institution's assets in the form of equipment, material, and monetary resources. This includes those expenses concerned with personnel and the operating budget. This factor covers the total value of the assets and the degree of responsibility for their care and use. (Note: include payroll dollars for employees under your supervision as well as responsibility for assets.)

Fig. 12.24 Responsibility for Funds

Value of assets, payroll, and operating budget	Degree of Responsibility		
	Responsible, but has supervisory guidance	Shared	Full
Little responsibility for organization's assets	6		
Up to $100 thousand	6	18	27
Up to 1 million	12	22	32
Up to 5 million	15	26	37
Up to 20 million	18	30	42
Up to 50 million	22	35	48
Up to 100 million	26	40	54
Over 100 million	30	45	60

Source: Courtesy of American Compensation Association, P.O. Box 1176, Scottsdale, Arizona, 85252.

Consequence of Error

This factor appraises the consequence of error in proportion to the requirements of this job. How serious is a mistake or an error in judgment on the job? Would it affect the work of the individual making the error and how long will it take to correct? Might the department suffer embarrassment, financial loss, or injury to good will.

Fig. 12.25 Consequence of Error

Degrees	Points
A. Little, if any responsibility for accuracy, either because errors can be quickly and easily detected and corrected or because errors would result only in minor confusion or clerical expense for correction.	
B. Responsibility for accuracy in the performance of routine work. Errors that can be proofread and corrected. Possibility of loss through errors is low. Mistakes are detected upon the completion of the work. Probable errors usually confined to a single department.	
C. Probable errors difficult to detect and may adversely affect student, faculty, or business relationships; substantial money loss, etc. Work is usually not subject to check or detailed audit and involves considerable accuracy and responsibility. This would also involve supervisory or auditing jobs where responsibility for the accuracy of work of others is a job requirement.	
D. Responsibility for high degree of accuracy and control of details. More skill and knowledge is required to solve these types of errors. Errors may cause considerable confusion, although they may be normally detected and corrected before serious consequences result. Probable errors may involve major expenditures for equipment, materials, or major decisions involving several departments. Duties may involve the preparation of data on which top management bases important decisions.	
E. Responsibility for high factual accuracy, or the exercise of sound judgment. Thoroughness and reliability are essential because of the detailed nature of the work. Mistakes may cause considerable financial loss and loss in prestige by the company in its dealings with others. Probable errors may involve the approval, on a department or divisional basis, of data previously prepared by others, or the final development and/or administration of company policy.	

Physical Demand

This factor measures the amount and continuity of physical effort required under normal working conditions and at a normal pace. It is limited by the frequency of occurrence.

Fig. 12.26 Physical Demand

Degrees	Points
A. Light work required, very light physical effort.	
B. Light physical effort required with some of the work performed in a standing position; the job may require some walking. Occasionally lift and carry light-weight materials or packages (1 to 20 pounds).	
C. Moderate physical effort required. Job may require being out of doors and demands walking for prolonged periods.	

Confidentiality of Work

Consideration is to be given to the amount of confidential data and restricted information that the job holder controls. Confidentiality is reflected through the affect that the disclosure of this information could have upon the internal or external relations of the organization.

Fig. 12.27 Confidentiality of Work

Degree	Points
A. The data or information being held is relatively unimportant in respect to any potential harm to the internal or external relations of the organization.	
B. Disclosure of any of these data would result in only a minor effect upon the internal or external relationships since it would cause only a small amount of friction. Discretion and integrity are recognized requirements for the job.	
C. Data handled are very confidential, in that their disclosure could result in serious damage to the internal or external relations within the different departments of the university and/or with the students and faculty.	
D. Data are of an extremely confidential nature. Any disclosure of this information could have a serious affect upon the internal or external relationships of the organization in relation to students, the community or the state, and could possibly effect the department, the school or the university's future.	

Initiative and Innovation

This factor requires determining and formulating the degree of inventiveness, originality, and self-reliance needed to perform work. Also considered are the amount of decision-making, the ability to develop new methods of procedure, and the points needed for meeting situations not usually covered by usual standards or precedents.

Fig. 12.28 Initiative and Innovation

Degree	Points
A. Little resourcefulness required. Procedures simple and repetitive. Ample assistance or supervision on any variations from standard.	
B. Some originating and planning of work called for. Tasks are generally of a standard procedure. General supervision available if needed, but worker is expected to work out problems without much direction.	
C. Requires the exercise of some ingenuity to do unusual and complex duties. Standard procedure is usually inadequate in many of the situations. General supervision is available at most times, but worker is expected to work out his own problems as a rule.	
D. Requires outstanding ability to work independently toward general results. Often no standard procedure available and little help is available for carrying out assigned work. Must originate, plan, adapt, invent, and continue to accomplish tasks. Supervisor may work with rather than direct worker in completing work problems.	

Variety and Complexity of Functions

This factor appraises the variety and complexiy of functions and responsibilities involved in the job. The factor analyzes the separate duties that must be coordinated systematically in order to insure that the total work proceeds in an efficient manner. The factor also describes the level of independent thinking, planning, and judgment required relative to the degree of complexity involved in coordinating the work.

Fig. 12.29 Variety and Complexity of Functions

Degree	Points
A. Limited variety and complexity Involves directing a minimal set of routine duties that require minor supervision of employees and that do not require much coordination by the person in charge. Little planning or judgment is required in heading this work, because as a whole the tasks are repetitive or not very complex. The duties may be routine, limited, and clearly established.	
B. Moderate variety and complexity Involves directing a moderate set of duties that differ in nature and with instructing subordinates on how to carry out the assigned tasks. This requires spending time in thinking and planning the assignments of employees in order to communicate effectively what the requirements are. Some judgment in assigning and directing of tasks is involved. In sum, the tasks of employees are complex enough to require moderate supervision by the person in charge. Job duties are routine but, to some degree varied. Duties are normally within a single department.	
C. Advanced variety and complexity Involves overseeing a considerable amount of similar and different job tasks. Requires some knowledge of subordinate's tasks in order to do the instructing or correcting that is needed. Considerable amount of time must be spent reviewing each task and planning assignments carefully in order to make sure all tasks work as a system. Judgmental decisions are constantly required.	
D. High variety and complexity Requires leading and coordinating of many tasks that are similar as well as some that are different in nature and that require highly trained and highly skilled employees. Necessitates a knowledge of all types of subordinate's work coupled with the ability to instruct and direct the total system efficiently. Much time will be spent on planning assignments and anticipating needs of the organization. Considerable judgment is needed to insure that all complex tasks are organized and made as streamlined as possible in order to maximize the organization's objectives.	

Management Planning

This factor refers to planning and scheduling. Take into consideration the complexity of the planning, whether the elements in the plan are related or unrelated and whether there are guidelines and precedents available to be followed. Consider how important the plan is to the entire institution, to what degree data must be brought in from various diverse sources, and how much interpretation of the data is required.

Fig. 12.30 Management Planning

Level		Points
A.	May involve planning and scheduling. This planning is based primarily on factual data and requires the use of prescribed methods or follows specific instruction. Precedents are readily available.	
B.	Planning involves using some background data and related facts and elements. Generally requires using well-standardized methods, guides, and procedures. Considerable precedent is available to use as a guide.	
C.	Planning involves utilizing considerable factual, background data; usually will include the necessity to consider some intangible, related elements. Usually guides and precedents are available, but may be required to select between clear-cut alternatives.	
D.	Planning involves the necessity to take into consideration and to rely on considerable intangible data. Diverse factual data that appears unrelated must be brought together and utilized. Standardized methods, procedures, and techniques are only a small part of the required planning. Little precedent is available. Limited interpretation of data is required as the basis for plans.	
E.	Planning is complex. Works with a number of diversified and unrelated, intangible facts and elements. Usually no precedent is available. Planning requires consideration of the institution's overall policies, rules and objectives. Requires the interpretation of data as a basis for making plans.	

Source: Courtesy of American Compensation Association, P.O. Box 1176, Scottsdale, Arizona, 85252.

Pressure

This factor concerns the pressure found in the position resulting from the necessity to make quick decisions, the speed with which the job incumbent must work to keep up with the normal flow, the level of concentration required, distractions from the scheduled routine, and the diversity of problems. The frequency of interruptions and the kinds of distractions should be taken into account.

Fig. 12.31 Pressure

Level		Points
A.	Little or no pressure to make rapid decisions. Work flow is normal. Task assignments are related. Interruptions and distractions are minimal or of little consequence.	
B.	Seldom must make rapid decisions. Attention to detail can be important; however, these tasks occupy less than 20% of the day. Interruptions and distractions are infrequent, but do affect job performance.	
C.	Occasionally must make rapid decisions. About 50% of the job is comprised of related tasks and the other half of unrelated tasks. Interruptions can occur about 40% of the time, and may significantly interfere with job performance. Work flow is considered above the typical level for these kinds of jobs.	
D.	Many decisions cannot be deferred. Work flow is high, and/ or of considerable variety in task assignments—many of which are unrelated. Interruptions are frequent and distracting. Work requires attention to details. Approximately 60% of the day work flow is heavy.	
E.	Decisions cannot be deferred. The work flow can be extremely heavy. Incumbent must pay close attention to subject matter at hand. Work includes a wide variety of unrelated tasks in a short period of time. There is a high frequency of interruptions that takes attention away from work at hand.	

Source: Courtesy of American Compensation Association, P.O. Box 1176, Scottsdale, Arizona, 85252.

Environment

This factor pertains to those environmental conditions in which the majority of duties are carried out such as whether much of the time of the employee is spent in a well-lighted and air-conditioned office or outside in uncontrollable weather. Environmental influences such as noise, which is created either by equipment or by students presenting their claim or grievances, should be analyzed since they too may affect the mental or physical well being of the employee. Potential safety hazards are also a part of this factor.

Fig. 12.32 Environment

Degree	Points
A. Works regularly under very desirable working conditions with very few or no disagreeable features. Performs work having little or no accident hazard. Injuries sustained would be minor.	
B. Inside and outside weather conditions, but employee not required to remain out in extreme weather. Employee may be exposed to moderate accident hazards and probable injuries would consist of minor cuts and bruises.	
C. Outside most of the time. Exposure to all types of weather conditions. May be frequently exposed to severe injuries resulting in lost time.	

Note: If an employee qualifies on either the environmental condition or the hazard for a degree level, he or she will qualify for that particular level. They *do not need to qualify on both* the environmental and the hazard part of the factor.

External Contacts

This factor refers to the degree to which the position involves responsibility for the maintenance of effective relationships with such persons as patients, vendors, government agents, and community members. It includes public and private agencies and companies as well as individuals. It takes into consideration the nature and the importance of the contacts inherent in the position.

Fig. 12.33 External Contacts

Level	Points
A. None, or contacts are limited to furnishing, obtaining, or exchanging well-established or repetitive, factual information according to standard procedures.	
B. Has contacts with vendors and/or consultants to maintain good working relationships, such as dealing with normal complaints, making preliminary agreements, minor adjustments to agreements, or expediting action to solve day-to-day operating problems. Tact and judgment are requirements in obtaining or giving information of a confidential nature.	
C. Has contacts with vendors and consultants of a serious or specialized nature. Resourcefulness is required to reach or adjust working agreements within departmental regulations, procedures, and operating needs.	
D. Occasional contacts of a difficult or advanced nature with influential management, association, or government representatives and committees. Discusses adjustments, agreements, or contracts that may affect several phases or operations using the organization's policies, objectives, and operating needs as a guide.	
E. Frequent contacts with community leaders, consultants, federal or state government officials, leading national associations, or foremost public officials. Makes decisions or initiates actions that may affect the entire organization using a broad knowledge and understanding of health-care–field trends and conditions, current and proposed top government policies and programs, and business conditions.	

Source: Courtesy of American Compensation Association, P.O. Box 1176, Scottsdale, Arizona, 85252.

Impact of Duties with Employees and Students

This factor covers the degree to which the position involves the responsibility for personally dealing with individuals within the organization but *outside the direct line of authority.* The nature of contacts involves tact, diplomacy, cooperation, and promotion, and serves as the basis for evaluation as well as the frequency with which such contacts must be made.

Fig. 12.34 Impact of Duties with Employees

Degrees	Points
A. The information is regularly interchanged to maintain work flow or to adjust working arrangements. Contacts may vary in frequency, but are not considered to be an important part of the job. When present, impact is not too great.	
B. Coordination, cooperation, or joint action are necessary in dealing with immediate management or individual problems of a serious or specialized nature. Such contacts tend to occur on a regular basis.	
C. Coordination, cooperation, or joint action are necessary if dealing with management or individual problems of a difficult or advanced nature. Organizational policies are usually available, but require interpretation if the internal contacts are to result in effective action. Such contacts tend to be regular and frequent.	
D. Coordination, cooperation, or joint action are necessary in dealing with management or individual matters of a difficult or controversial nature that may affect the relationship among the parties concerned and/or the financial well being of the department or unit. Contacts may be a major part of the job.	

Fig. 12.35 Numbers Supervised

Total number of employees supervised directly and indirectly	None	5 or less	6–14	15–30	31 and over
	0	4	8	12	16

Number of management employees supervised	None	2 or less	3–5	6 and over
	0	5	10	16

Level of supervision	None required	First level	Second level	Third level
	0	8	16	24

Levels of Supervision and Numbers Supervised

This factor covers the responsibilities for supervision (direct and indirect) of employees, including the level of those supervised and the size of the group supervised.

Level and Difficulty of Supervision

This factor refers to the supervision and control function. Supervision refers to the different degrees of supervision required in obtaining the maximum potential from each employee of the group.

Fig. 12.36 Supervision

Degrees	Points
A. No supervisory responsibilities. May direct the work of some employees, but works with, as well as guiding, other employees.	
B. Requires providing leadership to obtain the cooperation of others; directs the joint effort of others in controlling and administering the work of a small department where direct responsibility for the smooth operation of the department is inherent in the job and where the primary function is supervision including the selection and assignment of personnel, but where the procedures and methods are fairly well standardized.	
C. Requires the controlling and administering the work of varied work groups (departments) to obtain cooperation and maximization of the efforts and performance of the groups. The general supervision of a complex department where overall responsibility is partially delegated to unit supervisors.	
D. The major responsibility of jobs at this level is supervising and coordinating major and varied work groups and the coordination of work programs. The administration and coordination of a very large department or division. The job requires the establishment of standards, overall checking of progress, the formulation of policies, etc.	

Impact of Duties on Total University

This factor covers the amount to which the position affects the University as a whole. The influence and nature of the duties that affect the organizational climate and the operation of the University serve as the basis for the allocation of points.

Fig. 12.37 Impact of Duties

Degree	Points
A. Little or None Involves routine duties that have a minimum or no influence on the work flow or the organization. The duties have been standardized to some extent. Example: Supervisor of Grounds Maintenance	
B. Limited Involves duties that may have some influence on the work flow in the immediate department and the division. Example: Chief Accountant	
C. Moderate Involves duties that not only will influence the immediate department substantially, but also, will influence subsequent decisions, the department and the division. Decisions may occasionally affect many of the departments at the University. Example: Director of Purchasing	
D. Advanced Involves duties that affect serious or controversial matters that could greatly affect future organizational climate and work flow. The duties of this nature are highly significant and frequent. Duties deal with well-established policies and procedures. Demands quick, independent judgment to meet unexpected and/or serious developments. Decisions frequently affect entire organization. Example: Controller	

Review Questions

1. Why is it important that the job evaluation committee members be well qualified?

2. How can the quality of job evaluation ratings be improved?

3. Why is it impractical in most companies to assign seven degrees to the factor of work conditions?

4. In a weighted-in-points job evaluation program which is more important, a well-prepared evaluation manual or a very well-qualified evaluation committee? Explain.

5. What determines the number of degrees or levels into which each factor can be subdivided?

6. In industry today there is constant change. Why do you feel that a weighted-in-points job evaluation program can handle this situation?

Work Exercises

1. Write the definitions for each factor and each degree of the following factors.

   Job knowledge — 5 degrees
   Physical effort — 3 degrees
   Responsibility for equipment — 4 degrees
   Special training — 4 degrees

2. A company has chosen the following factors and degrees for the evaluation of their hourly paid personnel. They have chosen 800 points as the total number of points in the program. They have also assigned the following weights and numbers of degrees for each factor. You are given the assignment of allocating points to each degree for each factor. Prepare a chart similar to the one on page 182 and assign the respective point values for each block shown.

Factor	Weight (%) of the total	Degree				
Job knowledge	33	1	2	3	4	5
Complexity	25	1	2	3	4	5
Experience	19	1	2	3	4	
Work conditions	10	1	2	3		
Hazard	8	1	2	3		
Physical effort	5	1	2	3		

13

Establishing Rules for Evaluation

At this point in the job evaluation program a job description should have been written for each existing job. In Chapter 12 we weighted the factors, defined the various levels within a factor, and set up the point score for use in the evaluation. The next step is to establish rules for evaluating the jobs against the job evaluation manual that has been prepared. (A manual contains the job descriptions and the factor descriptions plus the rules for evaluating new jobs and re-evaluating revised jobs.)

The following are rules for evaluating. Each rule is stated followed, in parenthesis, by an interpretation of the rule or information about why the rule was included.

RULES FOR EVALUATING

A manual has been prepared to provide a means for placing jobs in the proper relationship, one with another. When a job is being evaluated, it is to be fitted into the proper level on each factor according to the definitions supplied for each level. (All job descriptions are to be reviewed against the factor definitions. Agreement must be reached by the committee to which level or degree that a job rates on each of the factors. By adding the score of all the factors, the total point score of the job is obtained.)

There shall be no midway points between levels. (There should not be any interpolation between levels. The committee must decide if a particular job rates, for example, at the third or fourth degree for a certain factor. They can not set the rating at a 3½ or 3¾; it must be established either at a 3 or a 4 but nowhere between the two *distinct* levels.)

When additional guide rules for the application of the manual to certain types of jobs are agreed upon, they are to be put in writing and sent to all holders of the manual. Otherwise, they are not in effect. (From time to time, rules may be developed for inserting new jobs or for re-evaluating existing jobs. If this should occur, a retyping should be done for the entire set of rules and be issued to all members of the job evaluation committee. To avoid embarrassment to all or part of the committee, no oral rules should be used. If the committee agrees that a new rule is needed or an existing rule should be altered, it should be reduced to writing. If rules are not in writing, it could be very difficult to process a grievance properly with an employee and/or a union.)

Job evaluations and descriptions, once agreed on, shall remain in effect until the job changes, at which time the description and evaluation shall be reviewed in their entirety. If there is a change in the actual content or requirements of any factor that effects the point values, a revised and corrected description and evaluation shall be issued. (Once each year, the chairman of the job evaluation committee should ask each supervisor to review the job descriptions for his or her particular department. If any major change in a job's content has been made, the job should be re-evaluated. The changing of a factor definition is even more serious, as all jobs should be reviewed on this factor to see if the rewriting of the definition changed the degree level for any job.)

The manual shall be used to *evaluate the job, not the person* performing it. (Occasionally raters will tend to evaluate how a particular employee is fulfilling the duties of the job. The rule states that only the job content is reviewed. Whether the person is an outstanding or inefficient worker should not be considered in the evaluation. Reviewing how well an employee performs is covered in Chapter 20.)

Duties not assigned or approved by management are not to be considered in evaluation. (Often an employee will independently perform a certain task that is not part of his job. It is hoped that this condition will be discovered when the supervisor reviews the job questionnaire of the employee. At that time the task can either be included in the job description or transferred to another employee in the department. This discovery of unauthorized work was described in Chapter 1 as being one of the advantages of installing a job evaluation program.)

The evaluation is to assume that a fair day's work is being done. Since every employee is paid to work a specified number of hours, an increase or decrease in the amount of work performed does not justify a re-evaluation of the job unless it changes the point value of the factors. (Employees are paid for the importance or difficulty of the job as compared to other jobs in the company. If additional work of the same general level is assigned to an employee this does not mean that the job should automatically receive more money. The same would be true in reverse if some tasks were taken away from the job. Jobs are evaluated by the way they compare to the factor definitions and not by whether the employee is actually working a full day.)

In evaluating each factor, consider the average requirements to do the job satisfactorily, and do not evaluate the job on exceptions to the average. Do not consider the job performance of specific individuals who are above or below average in their response to the job's requirements. (On some jobs, it may be difficult to separate the evaluation of the job tasks from that of the person performing the tasks. If the employee is not efficient on the job, it may appear that the job is rather difficult when this might not actually be the case. The opposite could also be true if an exceptional employee were assigned to the job; this condition might make the job seem easier than it really is. As stated, it is the duty of the committee to consider only the average requirements of the job.)

In evaluating each factor, care is to be taken that only one factor at a time is considered. For example, every occupation requiring extensive job knowledge does not necessarily impose a high responsibility or complexity. In evaluating the latter factor, therefore, care should be taken to consider it alone. (In reality, what this rule is trying to state is that there should not be any halo effect, prejudice, or bias carried over in evaluating the jobs on the various factors. Each factor should be evaluated on its own merit and not how the job "fits" on other factors.)

Job descriptions are to be sufficiently accurate to reveal those features of the job that determine its classification. At the same time, they are not intended to provide a complete listing of every individual feature of the job. If new duties, which may be assigned at any time, become a permanent feature of the work, the job should be restudied to see if the description or evaluation should be changed. (Keeping job descriptions up to date is a never-ending job. Updating a description is part of every supervisor's responsibility, but often the job changes or new equipment is brought into play and the updating of the description is overlooked. To guard against this, every job should be reviewed by each supervisor at least once in every 12 to 18 months. If a change has taken place, it should be made part of the description. If the change appears to be something of more than minor nature, the entire job should be re-evaluated to see if there was sufficient point change to warrant a change in pay grade.)

Classifying an existing job—Any employee and/or supervisor may request that a particular job be restudied. Requests should be made to the _____ (insert the title of the person at company in charge of the job evaluation program). She or he shall see that a corrected job description is prepared, call a meeting of the job evaluation committee, and they in turn shall re-evaluate the job. All existing jobs being re-evaluated must be processed through the job evaluation committee. Factors affected by the job change shall be re-evaluated and points assigned accordingly. If there is a point change, it shall replace the old point value for that factor and be used in figuring the total points for the job. If, in the total point value for the job, there is a point change that places the job in a different pay grade, the change shall be made at the beginning of the next pay period. There shall not be any retroactivity (back dating) on the assignment of a job to a pay grade.

Classifying a new job—In creating a new job, it will be necessary for the immediate supervisor to submit to _____ (the same title as mentioned above) a completed job questionnaire including the supervisor's evaluation. The head of the job evaluation committee, together with the supervisor, will then make a job analysis and prepare a job description for the job. A meeting will be called of the job evaluation committee and they will proceed with placing the new job in a grade in the following manner.

1. The job shall be compared, factor by factor, with the definitions in the manual and shall be assigned to the most suitable level on each factor. The job characteristic justifying its assignment to each level shall be written in the space provided. Where possible, these reasons are not to be copied from the general wording of the manual.

2. The job shall be entered on the factor comparison sheets and its rating on each factor compared with that of related jobs to be sure that it is in line.

3. The total rating for the new job shall be compared with that of the next highest and lowest existing jobs in the promotional line to see either that the job is correctly placed or if the promotional pattern needs revision.

4. The job title shall be reviewed and revised when necessary for accuracy and brevity.

5. The established procedure for making the job effective shall then be followed.

6. The entire procedure should be completed prior to submitting a requisition for transferring or hiring for a newly established position. In this manner, a proper wage rate is established *prior* to recruitment, which is necessary for proper placement.

7. All classifications for new jobs must be approved by the job evaluation committee.

Review Questions

1. Why is it not desirable to have midpoints between degrees? Example: a 3½ degree evaluation rather than a three *or* a four. Explain.

2. Why is it essential that rules for evaluating be in a written form?

3. Why is volume of work performed not a part of job evaluation?

4. How should a company compensate a person if he performs well above a fair day's work standard?

5. Why is it desirable to keep the name of the incumbent on the job away from the committee that is doing the evaluation?

6. Should the job evaluation manual ever be changed? What problems would occur if you did change certain parts of the manual?

7. Should employees receive a copy of the manual? If not, what should an employee receive? How would they go about learning how their job rates were determined?

8. Why is it necessary to review and/or change job specifications if the job description is rewritten?

9. Why is it necessary to have a supervisors' questionnaire accompanying each job questionnaire?

Work Exercise

1. List the items you feel should be in the job evaluation manual that would permit you to evaluate a new job.

14

Evaluating Jobs, Assigning Point Values, and Writing Job-Rating Specifications

So far we have been concerned with the work of preparing the manual for eventual evaluation of each job. We now are in a position to evaluate all of the jobs and to try to place each in its relative position to all the others in the company.

Each job should be compared, factor by factor, with the definitions in the manual and should be assigned to the most suitable level on each factor. Normally, the evaluator and/or committee takes four or five jobs at a time and evaluates each against one factor. Once the level has been decided for that factor for all the four or five jobs, then evaluation is started on a second factor. In this way, the evaluator gets accustomed to studying one factor at a time and can apply the same approach to the factor analysis to five jobs at a time before proceeding with a different factor.

When a decision has been made as to the correct level that a job rates on a particular factor, a written statement (job-rating specification) is recorded on the back of the job description. This specification shows why that job rated where it did on that factor. This will be discussed later in the chapter in regard to the method of writing and the use of this job specification.

In addition, a box score is kept for the tentative ratings for all the jobs. The following table (Fig. 14.1) shows a sample of jobs listed in the box score.

FACTORS

JOB TITLE	Job knowledge	Complexity	Interaction with others	Training time	Practice time	Hazard	General	Weather	Odors, fumes	Dirt	Noise	Direction of others	Physical effort	TOTAL POINT SCORE
						WORK CONDITIONS								
Yard maintenance	70	56	16	20	10	B3 10	12	F8	4	3	2	20	21	252
Secretary C	140	112	16	10	5	A1 3	4	0	0	0	0	20	7	317
Receptionist	140	112	48	20	10	A1 3	4	0	0	0	0	20	7	364
Clerk-typist	140	56	16	10	5	3	4	0	0	0	0	20	7	261
Accounting clerk				20	10	3	4	0	0	0	0	20	7	
Library clerk	140	112		20	10	A7 3	4	E1	0	0	0	20	7	
Shipping clerk	140	112	32	20	10	3	4	0	0	0	0	20	14	355
Booking clerk	140	112	64	30	10	B3 10	4	0	0	0	0	20	7	390
Mail clerk	140	112	32	20	15	3	B 8	E2 1	2	2	0	20	14	376

Fig. 14.1 Box Score

Job														Total
Printer B	140	112	32	30	15	15	8	0	6	5	10	20	14	407
Terminal operator B	140	140		20		3	8	0	0	0	10	20	7	
Key punch operator B	140	168	32	20	15	3	8	0	0	0	5	20	7	418
Driver	140	112	64	20	10	25	12	G6	4	2	5	20	14	434
Secretary B	210	168	64	30	10	3	4	0	0	0	0	20	7	516
Illustrator	280	168	16	20	10	3	4	0	0	0	0	20	7	528
Electronic technician B				20		B10	4	0	0	2	0	20	7	
Film inspector B	210	168	48	30	15	15	8	G3	2	0	5	40	14	558
Key punch operator A	210	168	48	30	10	3	4	0	0	0	0	20	7	
Secretary A	280	168	64	30	10	3	4	0	0	0	0	20	7	586
Remote job entry terminal operator	210	224	48	30	15	3	8	0	0	2	8	40	14	602
Film inspector A	210	224	32		15	5	4	0	2	0	2	80	14	
Terminal operator A	210	224	48	30	15	3	8	0	0	0	10	100	7	655
Photo technician	280	224	48	20	10	B5	8	0	4	2	0	20	7	628
Film librarian	280	224	64		10	3	4	0	0	0	0	80	7	
Lead clerk–business office				40		3	4	0	0	0	0	100	7	

As explained, this box score is a tentative rating, but the rating will become final once the end results are compared. The value of the box score approach is to recheck the work on all the jobs. The evaluator or committee is thus able to compare the level of each job on every factor. Example: If the degree level of job knowledge for a Shipping clerk was degree B, 140 points, and the level for Booking clerk was degree A, 70 points, the evaluation may be correct and could be defended against a grievance submitted by the Booking clerk. On the other hand, it may be incorrect and it might be wise to review why the Booking clerk received only degree A, 70 points. Another example might be on physical effort. If Secretary A, B, and C all received degree A, worth 7 points, for this factor, that might be considered accurate. However, if Secretary A and C only received 7 points and Secretary B received 14 points, a review should be made to be sure which evaluation is the correct and final one.

This box score has another purpose—it graphically points out which jobs and which factors have not yet been assigned point values. At times, when assigning point values to a particular factor, the committee comes to an impasse in that they cannot agree as to the correct level for a job on a particular factor. This is shown in the box score table by the unfilled squares of the jobs of Accounting clerk, Library clerk, Terminal operator B, Electronic technician B, Key punch operator A, Film inspector A, Film librarian, and Lead clerk. In this instance, somehow the committee is going to have to assign point values to the 18 individual factors assigned to these eight jobs. This is not an uncommon conclusion to a job evaluation program. In assigning the point values to jobs, most committees will, when an impasse occurs on a particular factor, bypass that factor for the time and return to it when all the jobs on which they can agree have been completed. This is where the evaluation stands on the box score table in Fig. 14.1. If a union is involved, these 18 undecided factors probably will be negotiated and some compromise made to get an agreement for the total point score of each. If no union is involved, the committee will try to settle their differences on the factors. If they are unsuccessful, then the decision for the point values for these factors probably will be referred to higher management for a decision. In either case, a written report is made concerning each disputed factor. In this way, if the job content changes in the future on one of the jobs in question, or if there is a grievance on one of the jobs, all of the necessary information on how the job was evaluated will be there to assist in making a decision. It is important to remember that a job evaluation program lasts for many years, and that no real problem may arise for 10 to 15 years. By this time, perhaps, many of the original committee are no longer with the company, or they just do not remember the details concerning how various jobs were slotted. In any case, a written report is good backup material for any job controversy involving the placing of point values to jobs.

WRITING JOB SPECIFICATIONS

After all the jobs have been reviewed on all factors and the results recorded in the box score, the job evaluation part of the total program is completed except for recording why each job was slotted in its respective degree level for each of the factors. The final phase of completing the job evaluation is writing the job-rating specifications.

The table in Fig. 14.2 shows the various items that might appear on the job specification. These, of course, only refer to the six factors as shown. Other factors would require different items.

The specification is in part a rewrite of the job description, listing the requirement of each of the factors rather than listing the duties. The specification is divided into sections paralleling the factors listed in the manual. In each section appears a statement of the job requirement of the job content of each factor. These are compared by the evaluator and/or committee with the manual. The most appropriate degree of each factor is selected for the job. In this way the degree definition that most nearly covers the job content of the factor is determined [1].

Figures 14.3 through 14.6 are examples of how job specifications are written. These examples also point out how, by using the degree definition, it is possible to grade several layers of skill for one job such as plumber, electrician, accounting clerk, etc.

1. Moore, F. C. and T. E. Hendrich. *Production Operations Management,* 7th ed. Homewood, Illinois: Richard D. Irwin Co., 1977.

Fig. 14.2 Items Appearing on Job Specifications

Mental requirements	Skill	Physical requirements
Kind and amount of special education	Kind of muscular coordination	Nature of physical effort
Kind of technical knowledge	Degree of proficiency	Steady or intermittent
Kind of work instruction provided	Precision required	Semi-automatic
written	Repetitive	Rest periods
oral	Varied	Good voice
Intelligence	Time experienced person to acquire acceptable proficiency	Minimum height
Mathematics used		Minimum age
Prepare reports		Maximum age
Fluency in speech		Sex
Monotony	Dexterity	Color
Distractions	fingers	Unusual strength
Meet emergencies	hands	hands
Read blue-prints	legs	arms
Personal qualities	Precision required	legs
Instruct others	Layout	back
Memory for _____	Set up	Endurance
Other	Templates	Neat appearance
	Jobs which train for	Keen hearing
	Jobs to which this one leads	Eyesight rating
	Good handwriting	Color discrimination
	Kind of sensory training	Percent standing
	sight	Percent sitting
	hearing	Percent walking
	smell	Percent other
	touch	Other
	taste	
	muscular	
	Other	

Source: Courtesy of the Bureau of Business Practice, 24 Rope Ferry Road, Waterford, Conn., 06385.

Responsibility	Working conditions	Heading and closing

For tools
  materials
  equipment
  methods
  records
  property
  money
  savings
  employee contacts
  public contacts
  for work of others
Other
	Place
	  outdoor
	  indoor
	  platform
	  overhead
	  underground
	  scaffold
	  pit
	  unlocalized
	Type
	  desk
	  bench
	  machine
	  counter
	Surroundings
	  clean
	  dirty
	  greasy
	  orderly
	Illumination
	  natural
	  artificial
	  glare
	Atmosphere
	  natural
	  ventilated
	  drafty
	  noxious gas
	  fumes, odors
	  dust
	  dry
	  humid
	  moist
		Title of form
		Title of position
		Alternate titles
		Department and loca-
		  tion or division
		Normal force
		Name of immediate
		  superior
		Duties
		Remarks
		Date
		Prepared by
		Approved by
		
		Hazards
		  fire
		  electricity
		  muscular strain
		  sight
		  heating
		  lungs
		  violence
		  hands
		  feet
		Gangwork
		Type of co-worker
		Crowded
		Regular working hours
		  From— to—
		Others

Fig. 14.3

JOB-RATING SPECIFICATION

JOB NUMBER: 0805   GRADE: 8

JOB TITLE: PLUMBER A   POINTS: 621

FACTOR*	SPECIFICATION†	EVALUATION Degree	EVALUATION Points
JOB KNOWLEDGE	Journeyman skill in the plumbing trade is required. *May work without direct supervision.* Plumbing codes and regulations have to be understood and followed to assure safe sound plumbing and correct installation. Able to perform all tasks assigned in the trade.	E	280
COMPLEXITY	Responsibility for the maintenance of existing *plumbing facilities* and systems and the *installation* of plumbing facilities in construction; makes sure frequently used plumbing *supplies* are *kept in stock.* Works in other areas as assigned.	E	160
PHYSICAL EFFORT	Much bending, stooping and straining. *Frequently lifts heavy objects.*	D	76
HAZARD	Minor cuts, bruises, and *muscle strains difficult* to avoid. Major infection may occur but possible to avoid by conscious safety precautions, clean up, and use of antiseptics.	C	48
RESPONSIBILITY FOR EQUIPMENT	By using *reasonable care* can prevent damage to equipment such as pipe threader, acetylene torch, electrical drills, etc.	B	22
WORKING CONDITIONS	Poor—Often exposed to *disagreeable weather* condition, *foul odors,* and sewage. Often works in mud.	D G H J K	16 7 4 6 2
TOTAL POINTS		—	621

*The information needed to complete this form is found in Chapter 10 (the job description for Plumber A) and the definitions for the six factors are found in Chapter 12.

†The part underlined in each factor specification is the main reason the rating is at the level designated.

Fig. 14.4

JOB-RATING SPECIFICATION

JOB NUMBER: 0605   GRADE: 6

JOB TITLE: PLUMBER B   POINTS: 533

		EVALUATION	
*FACTOR**	*SPECIFICATION†*	*Degree*	*Points*
JOB KNOWLEDGE	Must have *general knowledge* of the trade, being able to do many tasks with *general direction* and able to assist on other jobs with specific direction. Plumbing codes and regulations have to be understood and followed to assure safe and sound plumbing and correct installation.	D	224
COMPLEXITY	Responsible for the *preventive maintenance* of existing plumbing facilities and systems; *assists in the installation* of plumbing facilities in minor construction. Works in other areas as assigned.	D	128
PHYSICAL EFFORT	Much bending, stooping, and straining. *Frequently lifts heavy objects.*	D	76
HAZARD	Minor cuts, bruises, and *muscle strains* difficult to avoid. Major infection may occur, but possible to avoid by conscious safety precautions, clean up, and use of antiseptics.	C	48
RESPONSI-BILITY FOR EQUIPMENT	By using *reasonable care* can prevent damage to equipment such as pipe threader, acetylene torch, electric drills, etc.	B	22
WORKING CONDITIONS	Poor—Often exposed to *disagreeable weather* condition, *foul odors,* and sewage. Often works in mud.	D G H J K	16 7 4 6 2
TOTAL POINTS		—	533

*The information needed to complete this form is found on the job description for Plumber B in Chapter 10 and the definitions for the six factors are found in Chapter 12.

†The part underlined in each factor specification is the main reason the rating is at the level designated.

Fig. **14.5** Job Specification

Printer Operator*

FACTOR	Reason	SYMBOL	POINTS
Hazard	By exercising habitual care, minor cuts from corrugated board can be avoided.	B-1	130
Physical Effort	During the printing operation, repetitively lifts an average weight stack of corrugated blanks, accompanied by frequent bending alternating with lighter activities.	E	240
Responsibility for Materials	The possible causes of a material loss in corrugated blanks or printed shipping cases are easily recognized. By periodically checking a printed case for specification conformance, loss of material can be held to a low level.	B-1	130
Responsibility for Equipment	By using habitual care when mounting printing mats, damage to mats and other parts of the printer such as the analox, can be kept to a medium degree.	B-2	135
Responsibility for Safety of Others	May cause severe cuts and bruises to others when moving loaded pallets of printed cases, however, can be avoided by using habitual care.	B-2	135

Complexity

When mounting printing mats performs a series of operations during the opening and closing of the printer. Makes routine adjustments to correct for printing mat misalignment, lack of ink coverage, incorrect slotting, scoring and case dimensions and when changing case sizes. — D — 170

Job Knowledge

Must know case printing defects. Know how to operate the printer and make proper adjustments to correct printing defects and change case sizes. Must know how and where to put oil into the oil reservoir cups and to maintain mat inventory records. Directs the work of the Printer Helper. — D — 200

Job Conditions

Normal factory conditions. — 125

COND.	PROCESS HEAT/COLD & WEATHER	DIRT & GREASE	DAMPNESS	NOISE	MOTION	FUMES, DUST & ODORS
Degree	Nor.	Nor.	Nor.	Nor.	Nor.	Nor.
Percent						
Points	25	25	25	25	25	0

Total	1265

*This job specification is prepared for the job description on Printer Operator found in Chapter 4.

Fig. 14.6 Job Specification

Construction and Maintenance Electrician*

FACTOR / Reason	DEGREE	POINTS
Hazard Concentration and precaution necessary to avoid severe electric shocks, flashes, or explosions from live lines.	D-4	185
Physical Effort Lift heavy objects several times per day. Frequently climb ladders in wiring installations.	F	260
Responsibility for Materials Use judgment in connecting equipment or overloading protection devices to avoid burning out, necessitating repairs at high cost.	D-3	170
Responsibility for Equipment Lack of care may cause damage to electric drill, threaders, and pipe-bender, necessitating repairs at moderate cost.	B-2	135
Responsibility for Safety of Others Conscious alertness required to prevent possible lost time accident when working on electrical circuitry of equipment that others may operate.	C-3	155
Complexity Install all types of electrical equipment throughout the factory.	G	215
Job Knowledge Know electrical trade sufficiently well to do all types of installation work without specific instructions.	G	260

Job Conditions
Part time exposure to dirt and grease.

COND.	PROCESS HEAT/COLD AND WEATHER	DIRT AND GREASE	DAMPNESS	NOISE	MOTION	FUMES DUST AND ODORS	POINTS
Degree	Nor.	L-2	Nor.	Nor.	Nor.	Nor.	127
Percent		50%					
Points	25	27	25	25	0	25	

	Total	POINTS
	Total	1507

*This job specification was prepared from the job description of Construction and Maintenance Electrician found in Chapter 4.

Review Questions

1. What is the value of having a job specification sheet for each job?

2. Once job evaluation ratings have been agreed upon by management and employees, should they be subject to collective bargaining?

3. If the point value of a factor on a particular job is assigned through negotiations with the union, should there be a notation made and kept in the job evaluation manual? Explain.

4. Once the point value of a job has been set, what circumstances would justify a change of the rating?

5. Of what value, other than for use in job evaluation, is a job rating specification?

6. List and describe the steps necessary for establishing a point program of job evaluation.

7. If a job evaluation committee can not agree on the degree value of a particular factor, what is the best manner in assigning the point value on this job for this factor?

8. What is the value of preparing a box score as shown on page 190?

9. What advantages does the point plan of job evaluation have over the other plans that have been reviewed in this book?

10. A review has been made in this text explaining the four most used methods of doing a job evaluation program. For a company having 15 different jobs and 63 employees, which system would you choose? Why?

11. Same question as #10 except the company has 84 different jobs with 519 employees assigned to these jobs.

12. If the system used in question #10 is different than the one used in question #11 explain your reasoning.

13. Many managers feel that either of the analytical approaches for job evaluation is superior to either of the non-analytical methods. Do you agree? Defend your position. Under what circumstances would you choose one of the non-analytical methods?

Work Exercise

1. Prepare a job specification for the job of Printer operator. Review the job description in Chapter 4. Use the following factors described in Chapter 12: work conditions, job knowledge, complexity, physical effort, and hazard.

15

Establishing and Slotting Jobs in Pay Grades

Once the job evaluation is completed and the total point values have been established for each job, all jobs must be grouped into pay brackets or pay grades.

A list should be made of all the jobs in the program, starting with the job that has the fewest number of total points and the remainder of the jobs ranked by their point value in ascending order. Such a list from the box score of jobs found in Fig. 14.1 it would be as follows:

Yard maintenance	252	Mail clerk	376
Clerk–typist	261	Booking clerk	390
Secretary	317	Printer B	407
Shipping clerk	355	Key punch operator B	418
Receptionist	367	Accounting clerk	420*
Terminal operator B	367*	Film inspector B	432
Library clerk	369*	Driver	434

(Continued)

*These jobs did not have the total point scores in the comparison box score in Fig. 14.1. Through further work by the job evaluation committee, these jobs were ultimately placed with the total point scores as shown.

Secretary B	516	Terminal operator	628
Illustrator	528	Photo technician	649
Film inspector A	552*	Electronic technician B	649*
Key punch operator A	560*	Terminal operator A	655
Secretary A	586	Film librarian	692*
Remote job entry terminal operator	602	Lead clerk	748*

The point scores for all the jobs in the group range from 252 to 748. This makes a differential between the lowest job of Yard maintenance and the top job of Lead clerk of 496 points (748 − 252 = 496). A realistic view must be taken, at this point, in determining the number of pay grades to be established.

ESTABLISHING PAY GRADES

Selecting the number of pay grades to be established depends on several items.

1. The *point differential* between the bottom pay grade and the top pay grade.
2. The total *number of jobs* involved in the program.
3. The money differential between the bottom pay rate and the top pay rate.

Point Differential

Of the three items this is probably the most important. In the just-listed example there are 26 different jobs. Some of the jobs are separated only by two or three points. To have 26 pay grades for this company of 110 employees would be too cumbersome and would create too many grades, causing the money differential between pay grades to be too small. Job evaluation is a reasonably accurate method of establishing the level of pay for each job, but it can not differentiate so closely that one job is worth three cents or even five cents more per hour than another job. Thus it is necessary to group jobs with similar points into a pay grade. In this example, 26 pay grades were too many. What would happen if it were reduced to five?

If this were done, we would have the following point assignment:

Grade 1 — to 350
Grade 2 — 351–450
Grade 3 — 451–550
Grade 4 — 551–650
Grade 5 — over 650

By having such a large point differential (100) between pay grades, we would be grouping too many jobs in pay grades one and two. In addition, if the content of a job were substantially changed, the job probably would not get upgraded, since a 100-point differential between jobs is very high when there is only a maximum of 800 points in the program. Note—the total number of points in this particular program was decided when we multiplied the percentages by a number, in this case eight, as explained in Chapter 12.

One important aspect to look at when deciding points per each step in the pay grade rate scale is the amount of points allotted to the levels in the most important factor. In the six factors used as examples for explaining how to put a program together in Chapter 12, job knowledge rated 35% of the total points, and each level in this factor was 56 points higher than the preceding level. Consequently the point differential between pay grades probably should be somewhere between 55 and 70 points. This would only be true with the data we are using here. If there were 300 points in the total program and job knowledge had 35% of the total points, then a 20-point differential between pay grades would be more appropriate.

Number of Jobs in the Program

If a company had ten different jobs with 43 employees assigned to them, it certainly would not want ten pay grades, since some of the jobs might be very close in total points received with other jobs in the company. If two jobs were separated by only three or four points but one job received a higher pay grade because of receiving four more points, there probably would be friction between employees and the company. Consequently, with such a small number of jobs involved, probably four to six pay grades would divide the jobs adequately.

The Money Differential

If the lowest grade paid $3.25 an hour and the top grade paid $4.25 an hour, perhaps five pay grades would be sufficient. On the other hand, if the top grade paid $7.00 an hour, then 10 to 14 pay grades might divide the pay more equitably.

There is no foolproof method of determining the number of grades, but all three items discussed above have a bearing on the total number of grades to be established.

Effect of Unionization on the Number of Pay Grades

In reviewing many different union contracts in various industries, no real trend was uncovered as to the proper number of pay grades that should be established.

Table 15.1 shows the wide range in the number of grades that are used, as well as the wide variance in the difference in pay from the bottom grade to the top grade.

The data in Table 15.1 merely emphasizes that there is a wide variance in the number of pay grades in job evaluation programs. It appears that companies that are just now installing a program try to keep the number of pay grades under 15. Some unions, particularly those in the

Table 15.1
Pay Grades in Unionized Companies

Industry	Number of grades	Percent difference from grade one to the top grade
Mining	5	18
Food	15	69
Aluminum	28	45
Flooring	18	70
Oil	11	34
Chemical	20	42
Paper	10	131
Steel (hourly)	34	74
Steel (salaried)	16	73
Electrical	11	34

trucking and warehousing industry, often have fewer than five grades in their program.

PREPARING THE PAY GRADE TABLE

Preparing the pay grade table is relatively easy. The number of points for the bottom grade is established by using the number of points the lowest job receives. In our example, the Yard maintenance received 252 points. We could establish grade one with a point value of 0 to 300 points, 0 to 315 points, or 0 to 330 points. Any of the three might be appropriate; the one selected depends on the rest of the data. If the job next to Yard maintenance had 305 points, then it might be better to have jobs in grade one with point values from 0 to 315. In any case, the point value for grade one is established so that it will include the bottom job in point value.

The following three figures show how the starting point for grade one would affect the later slotting of all jobs. Table A in Fig. 15.1 has the lowest possible pay grades. Tables B and C are progressively higher.

In establishing pay grades, one starts with the bottom grade and assigns a point differential to be used between grades. It does not matter that some pay grades might not have any jobs assigned to them. The

Fig. 15.1
Tables Showing How Point Scores Are Established

Table A		Table B		Table C	
Grade	Points	Grade	Points	Grade	Points
1	to 300	1	to 315	1	to 330
2	301 to 355	2	316 to 369	2	331 to 382
3	356 to 410	3	370 to 423	3	383 to 434
4	411 to 465	4	424 to 477	4	435 to 486
5	466 to 520	5	478 to 531	5	487 to 538
6	521 to 575	6	532 to 585	6	539 to 590
7	576 to 630	7	586 to 639	7	591 to 642
8	631 to 685	8	640 to 693	8	643 to·694
9	686 to 740	9	694 to 747	9	695 to 746
10	741 on	10	748 on	10	747 on

grade is included so that other jobs higher in point value will be placed in still a higher grade. In this way the relative positions of all jobs in the program are established. By merely starting at a different level for grade one, some jobs would be assigned to a different pay grade. In evaluating the jobs and their respective point scores as listed in the beginning of this chapter, we found that certain jobs either advanced a grade or lost a grade depending on which table (starting point) was used (Fig. 15.2).

When in using Table C over one half of the number of jobs (14) were in the bottom three pay grades. Table B had 12 jobs in these same pay grades while Table A had only ten. If only eight grades were used, the assigning of jobs by point scores would of course be different than shown above. The starting point for grade one, the differential between grades and the number of grades used all affect the slotting of a particular job.

In Chapter 14 all jobs were evaluated and a total point value was established for each job. In this chapter, a set number of pay grades is being established, with each grade being allotted a certain number of points. The next step is the placement of the jobs into their respective

Fig. 15.2
Assigning Jobs by Point Score to Pay Grades
Using Tables A, B, or C From Fig. 15.1

	Number of jobs in pay grade		
Grade	Table A	Table B	Table C
1	2	2	3
2	2	5	5
3	6	5	6
4	4	2	0
5	1	2	2
6	3	2	3
7	3	3	2
8	3	4	4
9	1	0	0
10	1	1	1
Total	26	26	26

Fig. 15.3 Index of Jobs by Grades

Grade one
0101 Yard maintenance
0102 Laborer for all departments
0103 Custodian
0104 Typist
0105 Cook

Grade two
0201 Mail clerk
0202 Accounting clerk C
0203 Quality control inspector

Grade three
0301 Quality control technician
0302 Water treatment operator
0303 Terminal operator
0304 Key punch operator
0305 Secretary

Grade four
0401 Carpenter C*
0402 Pipefitter C
0403 Electrician C
0404 Auto mechanic C
0405 Plumber C
0406 Receiving clerk
0407 Cook

Grade five
0501 Secretary
0502 Accounting clerk B
0503 Fork lift operator
0504 Labeling machine operator
0505 Filling machine operator

Grade six
0601 Carpenter B
0602 Pipefitter B
0603 Electrician B
0604 Auto mechanic B
0605 Plumber B
0606 Shipping clerk–warehouseman
0607 Secretary

Grade seven
0701 †
0702

Grade eight
0801 Carpenter A
0802 Pipefitter A
0803 Electrician A
0804 Auto mechanic A
0805 Plumber A
0806 Accounting clerk A
0807 Secretary

*There are job descriptions written and job numbers assigned to the A, B, and C classifications for the trades. This does not mean necessarily that each of the job numbers has an employee assigned to it. The description and numbers are there if needed. A small plant may have only one or two employees working as carpenter, pipefitter, electrician, etc. Such an employee would be assigned to the job classification corresponding to what he is asked to do, taking into account his personal ability in that trade.

†No jobs were assigned to pay grade seven because no job fell in the point range for this grade.

pay grades and the preparation of a table showing an index of jobs by pay grades.

Figure 15.3 is an example of such an index for a listing of jobs for a company having both production and maintenance type employees.

The numbering of the job descriptions was explained in Chapter 10; however, to again emphasize the procedure, the first two digits indicate the pay grade to which the job is assigned, and the last two digits refer to a particular job in that grade. Example: If there were to be a new job rate placed into grade three, the number assigned would be 0306.

Review Questions

1. How are wage problems simplified by using pay grades?

2. How does the evaluation committee convert the point scores of an individual job to a dollar wage rate?

3. Why are pay grades used?

4. From an administrative point of view, how many pay grades are desirable for a company having 40 different jobs, one having 140 jobs, and a third having 240 different jobs? Explain why there is a difference between the number required for each size of the work force.

5. Is it desirable to establish a different rate of pay for each job, for each employee assigned to the same job? Why or why not? Explain.

6. How is the point score for pay grade one set?

7. How are the point scores set for the remaining pay grades in the wage structure?

8. What do the four digits represent in the number assigned to the job? Example: 0406 Receiving clerk.

9. How many grades should be established for a company having 81 employees assigned to 21 different jobs? The bottom job receives $3.40 an hour and the top paying job receives $4.75. Would the number of grades be different if the top paying job received $7.00 per hour? Explain.

Work Exercises

1. The following list indicates the total point scores for each of the jobs listed.

Heavy equipment operator	277	Electrician A	256
Operator chilling plant	217	Mail clerk	160
Custodian A	133	Roofer	185
Electrician B	221	Senior clerk	220
Secretary	183	Bus driver	253
Offset operator	197	Lead electrician	280
Assistant to manager of maintenance	235	Clerk–typist	135
Carpenter A	256	Head grounds keeper	227
Lead personnel-custodians	179	Clerk	155
Yard maintenance	112	Electrician C	184
Administrative clerk	239	Administrative secretary	253
		Carpenter C	183

These 23 jobs are all of the jobs listed for the 175 hourly paid employees of your company. Prepare two pay grade schedules.
a. One schedule with eight pay grades.
b. One schedule with seven pay grades.

Recommend to your management which schedule you prefer. Defend your choice.

2. Using the point scores for the pay grades prepared in work assignment number one, prepare an index of jobs for both wage structures (index to be similar to the one shown in Fig. 15.3). Evaluate the slotting of jobs under both structures: now recommend to your company which pay structure you prefer. Explain your reasons. If you changed the starting point for grade one for either of the schedules, could this affect your preference? Explain.

PART III

Wage and Salary Administration

16

Conducting An
Area Survey

In evaluating a company's compensation program, it is important not only to review wages being paid but also to review all the other economic benefits the employee receives. Any item that helps to make a company a good place for employment should be studied.

Although an area survey is not absolutely necessary, it does give the person preparing the job evaluation program some idea of where the company currently stands in the community in regard to the level of wages and fringe benefits being paid to employees.

In addition to wages, such things as life insurance, incentive payment, hospitalization and surgical insurance, pension programs, incentive plans, overtime pay, and shift differential pay all affect the employees' total pay and certainly should be taken into account when establishing the pay level for the company. Other items such as time off for vacations, holidays, death in the family, sick leave, etc., certainly add to the cost of doing business and also should be considered a part of the economic benefits the employee receives.

One way to gain information about a particular work location is to ask other companies in the area about their policies in regard to wages and fringe benefits. Most companies will cooperate if the information is kept confidential.

The procedure normally followed for getting an area survey questionnaire completed is:

1. The originating company completes the questionnaire for its own company and sends it to other companies in the area.

2. Enclosed with the questionnaire is a letter explaining the request for information and a blank questionnaire to be completed by the company and returned to the originator.

3. Also in the letter, the companies are told that the information will remain confidential and that all participating companies will get a summary of the survey when it is completed. The summary will be coded so that no participating company will know which company is which in the report.

4. Upon receipt of the completed questionnaires, a coded summary similar to Figs. 16.4 and 16.5 is compiled and sent to the participating companies.

An example of a brief area survey that might be used to gather information on wages, work policies and practices in the area is shown in Fig. 16.1.

In addition to a company's conducting its own area survey, it may also obtain wage information concerning a particular area through the use of information prepared by the Bureau of Labor Statistics.

Figure 16.2 lists the geographical areas where wage surveys are made periodically, by the Bureau of Labor Statistics. If someone wishes to receive a copy of a certain survey, he needs only to request one from the regional office that services his area. The listing shows over 120 geographical areas for which a wage survey is prepared each year. However, the time when such information is released may vary, depending upon the particular city being surveyed. All of this wage information plus much more concerning other aspects of employment can be found in the booklet entitled *Publications of the Bureau of Labor Statistics*. This pamphlet is published twice a year and may be requested from the national and/or regional office of the U.S. Department of Labor.

Figure 16.3 is the type of area survey material available from the Bureau of Labor Statistics. This report is from the February 1980 Baton Rouge, La. survey.

Fig. 16.1 Sample Area Survey

Area Survey

Name of Company _____ Name of Contact Person   Telephone #

Address _____ _____ _____

Number of Full Time Hourly Paid Male Employees _____ Female Employees _____

Current Pay Scale _____ Date rate became effective _____

Job Title	Hiring Rate or Probationary Rate	Top Rate	Number of Employees on this Job
Common labor			
Janitor			
Fork lift operator			
Warehouseman			
Mechanic A (top)			
Mechanic C			
Electrician A (top)			
Electrician C			

2. Pay for working overtime Saturdays, Sundays, Holidays, etc. Please show the premium rate paid for the following as St.T, 1½, 2, or 2½ times.

After 8 hours _____ On recognized Holiday _____ Saturday _____
After 40 hours _____   Sunday _____

3. Night Shift Bonus. (Shift Differential)

For Second Shift _____   For Third Shift _____

4. Report in Pay—(Amount of hours paid an employee for reporting to work and then sent home as there was no work available. _____ Hours pay.

Fig. 16.1 (continued)

5. Vacation Schedule

One week vacation pay after _____ years of service.

Two weeks vacation pay after _____ years of service.

Three weeks vacation pay after _____ years of service.

Four weeks vacation pay after _____ years of service.

Five weeks vacation pay after _____ years of service.

6. Number of paid holidays a year _____ . List them.

_____ _____ _____ _____

_____ _____ _____ _____

7. Do you have an incentive system? _____ If yes, what type of work is covered under the plan? _____

How is the incentive earned, by individuals, group, etc.? _____

What is the average incentive rate paid for all the employees on the incentive? _____

8. Probationary Period (Duration) _____

Is there a pay differential for the period? _____ If so—How much _____

Please explain briefly your company's benefits on the following items. Please include under items D, E, F, and G how these benefits are financed. Does the employee pay part of the Premium? If so, on what basis.

A. Funeral Leave _____

_____

_____

B. Jury Duty _____

_____

_____

C. Sick Leave _____

_____

_____

D. Life Insurance _____

_____

_____

E. Hospitalization and Surgical Insurance _____

_____

_____

F. Medical Insurance _____
_____
_____
_____

G. Pension Plan _____
_____
_____

Questions on the following items might also be included.

　　Rest periods per shift
　　Issuing of uniforms
　　Amount of time for changing clothes
　　Free meals for working overtime
　　Supplemental unemployment compensation
　　Pay for injury time at work
　　Pay for illness time at work

Fig. 16.2 Geographical Areas Surveyed Annually for Earnings. Plus Listing of U.S. Department of Labor National and Regional Offices.

National Office—U.S. Department of Labor, Bureau of Labor Statistics, Washington, D.C. 20212

Region #1 1603 JFK Federal Building, Government Center, Boston, Mass., 02203. Tel. 617-223-6771.
　　States of Connecticut, Maine, Massachusetts, New Hampshire, Rhode Island, Vermont

Boston, Mass.	Providence, Warwick, Pawtucket, R.I.
Fitchburg, Leominster, Mass.	Springfield, Mass.
Hartford, Conn.	Vermont (statewide)
New Hampshire (statewide)	Worcester, Mass.
New London, Norwich, Conn.—R.I.	

Region #2   Suite 3400, 1515 Broadway, New York, N.Y. 10036. Tel. 212-944-3121.
　　States of New Jersey, New York, Puerto Rico, Virgin Islands

Atlantic City, N.J.	Middlesex, Monmouth, Ocean cos., N.J.
New York City, N.Y.	Patterson, Clifton–Passaic, N.J.
Nassau, Suffolk, N.Y.	Poughkeepsie, N.Y.
Northern New York	Utica, Rome, N.Y.

Fig. 16.2 (continued)

Region #3   3535 Market Street, P.O. Box 13309, Philadelphia, Pa. 19101.
Tel. 215-596-1154.
  States of Delaware, Maryland, Pennsylvania, Virginia, Washington, D.C., West Virginia

Baltimore, Md.

Frederich, Hagerstown, Md.

Harrisburg, Lebanon, Chambersburg, Md. and Pa.

Lower Eastern Shore

Norfolk, Virginia Beach, Portsmouth, Va.

Richmond, Va.

Southwestern Virginia

Washington, D.C.

West Virginia (statewide)

Wilmington, Del.

Region #4   1371 Peachtree Street, N.E., Atlanta, Ga. 30309. Tel. 404-881-4418.
  States of Florida, Alabama, Georgia, Kentucky, Mississippi, North Carolina,
  South Carolina, Tennessee

Albany, Ga.

Asheville, N.C.

Atlanta, Ga.

Augusta, S.C.

Biloxi, Gulfport, Miss.

Birmingham, Ala.

Brunswick, Ga.

Charleston, S.C.

Chattanooga, Tenn.

Clarksville, Hopkinsville, Tenn.

Columbia, Ga.

Columbus, Ga.

Columbus, Miss.

Daytona Beach, Fla.

Dothan, Ala.

Fayetteville, N.C.

Fort Lauderdale, Fla.

Gainesville, Fla.

Greensboro, Winston-Salem, N.C.

Greenville, Spartanburg, S.C.

Goldsboro, N.C.

Lexington, Fayette, Ky.

Macon, Ga.

Meridian, Miss.

Miami, Fla.

Mobile, Pensacola, Ala., Fla.

Nashville, Tenn.

Orlando, Fla.

Raleigh, Durham, N.C.

Savannah, Ga.

Selma, Ala.

Tampa, Saint Petersburg, Fla.

Region #5   9th Floor, Federal Office Building, 230 S. Dearborn St., Chicago, Ill. 60604.
Tel. 312-353-1880.
  States of Illinois, Indiana, Michigan, Minnesota, Ohio, Wisconsin

Ann Arbor, Mich.

Battle Creek, Mich.

Canton, Ohio

Champaign, Urbana, Ill.

Chicago, Ill.

Cincinnati, Ohio

Cleveland, Ohio

Crane, Ind.

Decatur, Ill.

Duluth, Superior, Minn.

Fort Wayne, Ind.

Green Bay, Wis.

La Crosse, Sparta, Wis.

Lima, Ohio

Logansport, Peru, Ind.

Lorain, Elyria, Ohio

Madison, Wis.

Milwaukee, Wis.

Sandusky, Ohio

South Bend, Ind.

Springfield, Ill.

Toledo, Ohio

Region #6   2nd Floor, 555 Griffin Square Building, Dallas, Tx. 75202. Tel. 214-767-6971.
States of Arkansas, Louisiana, New Mexico, Oklahoma, Texas

Alexandria, La.
Austin, Tx.
Baton Rouge, La.
Beaumont, Port Arthur, Tx., La.
Corpus Christi, Tx.
El Paso, Las Cruces, Tx., N.M.
Fort Smith, Ark.
Laredo, Tx.
Lawton, Okla.
Houston, Tx.

McAllen, Edinburg, Brownsville,
  Harlingen, San Benito, Tx.
Oklahoma City, Okla.
Pine Bluff, Ark.
San Antonio, Tx.
Sherman, Denison, Tx.
Tulsa, Okla.
Waco, Killen, Tx.
Waterloo, Cedar Falls, Iowa
Wichita Falls, Lawton, Tx., Okla.

Region #7 and #8   911 Walnut St., Kansas City, Mo., 64106. Tel. 816-374-2480.
States of Colorado, Iowa, Kansas, Missouri, Nebraska, Montana, North Dakota, South
Dakota, Utah, Wyoming

Billings, Mont.
Cedar Rapids, Iowa
Colorado Springs, Colo.
Denver, Colo.
Des Moines, Iowa
Fort Riley, Junction City, Kans.
Grand Island, Hastings, Neb.
Kansas City, Mo., Kans.

Montana (statewide)
North Dakota (statewide)
Pueblo, Colo.
Salina, Kans.
South Dakota (statewide)
St. Louis, Mo.
Topeka, Kans.
Wichita, Kans.

Region #9 and #10   450 Golden Gate Ave., Box 36017, San Francisco, Cal. 94102
Tel. 415-556-4678.
States of Arizona, California, Hawaii, Nevada, Alaska, Idaho, Oregon, Washington

Alaska (statewide)
Bakersfield, Cal.
Bremerton, Wash.
Eugene, Springfield, Medford, Ore.
Fresno, Cal.
Los Angeles, Long Beach, Cal.
Oxnard, Ventura, Cal.
Phoenix, Ariz.
Portland, Ore.
Reno, Nev.
Riverside, San Bernardino, Cal.

Salinas, Seaside, Monterey, Cal.
San Diego, Cal.
San Francisco, Oakland, Cal.
San Jose, Cal.
Southern Idaho
Stockton, Cal.
Tacoma, Wash.
Tucson, Douglas, Ariz.
Vallejo, Fairfield, Napa, Cal.
Yakima, Richland, Kennewick,
  Pendleton, Wash., Ore.

Fig. 16.3
Hourly earnings[1] of office and plant workers in Baton Rouge, La., February 1980

Occupation	Number of workers			Hourly earnings (all workers)[2]			3.00 and under 3.40	3.40 — 3.80	3.80 — 4.20	4.20 — 4.60	4.60 — 5.00
	All	Men	Women	Mean	Median	Middle range					
Secretaries[2]	467	—	460	$6.36	$6.19	$4.90– $7.37	—	18	33	31	54
Secretaries, Class A	19	—	19	8.87	9.38	7.69– 10.33	—	—	—	—	—
Secretaries, Class B	93	—	93	6.28	6.34	5.18– 7.29	—	—	—	6	7
Secretaries, Class C	141	—	141	6.26	6.00	4.18– 8.07	—	17	24	9	13
Secretaries, Class D	108	—	108	6.53	6.64	4.90– 7.58	—	—	2	4	23
Secretaries, Class E	99	—	99	5.98	5.69	4.90– 6.53	—	1	6	12	10
Stenographers	118	1	117	6.48	6.20	5.49– 7.13	—	—	1	3	9
Stenographers, Senior	35	1	34	7.79	7.56	6.81– 8.94	—	—	—	—	—
Stenographers, General	83	—	83	5.92	5.75	5.32– 6.88	—	—	1	3	9
Typists	92	—	92	4.21	4.00	3.50– 4.89	7	35	12	8	12
Typists, Class A	21	—	21	4.54	4.90	4.03– 5.00	—	2	6	1	6
Typists, Class B	71	—	71	4.12	3.74	3.46– 4.59	7	33	6	7	6
File Clerks[2]	107	1	106	3.59	3.50	3.31– 3.71	39	44	16	1	6
File Clerks, Class B	71	—	71	3.70	3.65	3.46– 3.89	14	38	12	1	5
File Clerks, Class C	35	1	34	3.34	3.17	3.17– 3.50	25	6	4	—	—
Switchboard Operators	33	—	33	4.04	3.95	3.55– 4.21	2	11	11	4	1
Key Entry Operators	156	—	156	4.60	4.28	3.76– 4.90	—	41	28	22	29
Key Entry Operators, Class A	25	—	25	6.13	6.20	5.27– 6.50	—	—	—	1	4
Key Entry Operators, Class B	131	—	131	4.31	4.16	3.74– 4.65	—	41	28	21	25
Computer Operators	106	63	43	5.69	5.21	4.62– 6.30	—	4	4	18	16
Computer Operators, Class A	11	11	—	7.13	—	—	—	—	—	—	—
Computer Operators, Class B	67	37	30	5.77	5.15	4.75– 6.48	—	—	3	11	11
Computer Operators, Class C	28	15	13	4.93	4.79	4.37– 5.34	—	4	1	7	5
Peripheral Equipment Operators	38	19	19	3.86	3.88	3.74– 4.00	2	15	16	5	—
Drafters	204	163	41	7.52	7.25	6.25– 8.90	—	4	3	4	12
Drafters, Class A	66	62	4	9.24	8.97	7.99– 10.30	—	—	—	—	—
Drafters, Class B	84	75	9	7.34	7.25	6.93– 8.00	—	—	—	2	4
Drafters, Class C	43	20	23	6.06	6.15	5.60– 6.60	—	—	3	2	1
Drafters, Class D	11	6	5	4.29	—	—	—	4	—	—	7
Maintenance Carpenters	68	68	—	10.18	10.18	10.13– 10.43	—	—	—	—	—
Maintenance Electricians	425	423	2	10.23	10.13	10.02– 10.47	—	—	—	—	—
Maintenance Painters	97	97	—	10.16	10.18	10.00– 10.18	—	—	—	—	—
Maintenance Machinists	159	159	—	10.25	10.37	10.13– 10.37	—	—	—	—	—
Maintenance Mechanics (Machinery)	628	624	4	10.07	10.02	10.02– 10.18	—	—	—	—	—
Maintenance Mechanics (Motor Vehicles)	120	120	—	9.06	9.07	8.00– 10.18	—	—	—	—	—
Maintenance Pipefitters	396	392	4	10.20	10.13	10.13– 10.18	—	—	—	—	—
Stationery Engineers	52	52	—	9.63	10.02	9.99– 10.02	—	—	—	—	—
Truckdrivers[2][3]	808	797	—	6.13	5.75	4.90– 7.18	25	44	60	49	40
Light Truck	129	129	—	5.14	4.00	4.00– 5.75	5	16	46	14	—
Medium Truck	278	267	—	5.57	5.00	4.50– 5.62	20	28	14	30	35
Tractor-Trailer	184	184	—	6.59	6.00	5.62– 7.78	—	—	—	5	5
Material Handling Laborers	331	327	—	5.31	4.25	3.95– 5.50	15	12	120	40	22
Forklift Operators	151	151	—	5.54	5.62	4.90– 5.75	10	—	1	14	40
Guards	238	222	16	5.87	4.42	3.60– 9.10	22	56	34	14	7
Guards, Class A	70	68	2	9.08	9.10	9.10– 9.32	—	—	—	—	—
Guards, Class B	168	154	14	4.53	3.90	3.50– 4.56	22	56	34	14	7
Janitors, Porters, and Cleaners	1,578	781	793	3.44	3.10	3.10– 3.20	1,376	56	38	4	—

[1] Excludes premium pay for overtime and for work on weekends, holidays, and late shifts. Incentive payments, such as those resulting from piecework, production bonuses, and commission systems, are included in the wages reported; nonproduction bonuses are excluded. Cost-of-living allowances are considered as part of the workers' regular pay. Hourly earnings reported for salaried workers are derived from regular salaries divided by the number of workers. The median designates position—half of the workers receive the same or more and half receive the same or less than the rate shown. The middle range is defined by two rates of pay: a fourth of the

Number of workers receiving straight-time hourly earnings (in dollars) of —														
5.00 – 5.40	5.40 – 5.80	5.80 – 6.20	6.20 – 6.60	6.60 – 7.00	7.00 – 7.40	7.40 – 7.80	7.80 – 8.20	8.20 – 8.60	8.60 – 9.00	9.00 – 9.40	9.40 – 9.80	9.80 – 10.20	10.20 – 11.00	11.00 and over
35	27	36	36	39	42	31	15	8	9	15	12	8	15	3
—	—	—	—	3	—	5	1	—	—	3	—	2	5	—
14	9	7	9	12	14	10	2	1	1	1	—	—	—	—
3	3	5	8	9	11	2	2	5	6	5	6	4	6	3
9	—	10	6	12	13	9	7	2	2	2	2	1	4	—
9	14	12	11	3	4	5	3	—	—	4	4	1	—	—
13	25	7	5	10	22	8	3	2	2	2	3	3	—	—
1	3	—	1	6	1	8	3	2	2	2	3	3	—	—
12	22	7	4	4	21	—	—	—	—	—	—	—	—	—
12	—	1	2	3	—	—	—	—	—	—	—	—	—	—
6	—	—	—	—	—	—	—	—	—	—	—	—	—	—
6	—	1	2	3	—	—	—	—	—	—	—	—	—	—
1	—	—	—	—	—	—	—	—	—	—	—	—	—	—
1	—	—	—	—	—	—	—	—	—	—	—	—	—	—
—	—	—	—	—	—	—	—	—	—	—	—	—	—	—
2	1	1	—	—	—	—	—	—	—	—	—	—	—	—
9	5	4	8	6	—	1	1	—	1	—	—	1	—	—
3	—	4	7	3	—	1	—	1	—	1	—	—	—	—
6	5	—	1	3	—	1	—	—	—	—	—	—	—	—
21	12	3	11	5	—	2	—	3	—	—	3	—	1	3
2	3	1	—	1	—	1	—	1	—	—	1	—	—	1
13	8	1	9	4	—	—	—	2	—	—	2	—	1	2
6	1	1	2	—	1	—	—	—	—	—	—	—	—	—
—	—	—	—	—	—	—	—	—	—	—	—	—	—	—
2	8	17	8	25	31	11	14	5	13	13	8	6	10	10
—	—	—	—	5	5	3	8	2	11	5	1	6	10	10
—	3	4	4	10	26	8	5	1	2	8	7	—	—	—
2	5	13	4	10	—	—	1	2	—	—	—	—	—	—
—	—	—	—	—	—	—	—	—	—	—	—	—	—	—
—	—	—	—	—	2	—	—	—	—	—	—	43	23	—
—	—	—	—	—	1	—	—	—	—	1	12	209	202	—
—	—	—	—	—	—	—	—	—	—	—	—	78	19	—
—	—	—	—	—	—	—	—	—	—	—	—	75	84	—
—	—	—	—	1	—	1	2	—	6	5	19	467	127	—
—	1	—	1	1	3	4	45	—	1	14	—	30	20	—
—	—	—	—	—	—	4	—	—	—	—	—	342	54	—
—	1	—	2	1	—	4	—	—	—	—	—	36	8	—
65	126	18	14	139	78	85	2	—	—	22	7	—	34	—
10	10	2	2	2	1	3	—	—	—	18	—	—	—	—
32	57	6	2	—	6	20	—	—	—	4	—	—	24	—
21	58	10	1	1	11	62	—	—	—	—	—	—	10	—
—	40	2	—	—	—	—	80	—	—	—	—	—	—	—
—	59	7	—	4	—	8	2	—	—	—	—	6	—	—
8	2	4	5	—	—	—	—	—	20	55	11	—	—	—
—	—	1	3	—	—	—	—	—	—	55	11	—	—	—
8	2	3	2	—	—	—	—	—	20	—	—	—	—	—
2	33	5	1	—	—	22	—	41	—	—	—	—	—	—

workers earn the same or less than the lower of these rates and a fourth earn the same or more than the higher rate.

[2] Includes workers other than those presented separately.

[3] Includes all drivers regardless of size and type of truck operated.

After the questionnaires from the various companies in the area have been returned, it is necessary to compile the data to be able to compare your company with other companies in the community. Figures 16.4 and 16.5 are examples of a summary of an area survey.

The following points might help to interpret Fig. 16.4, the summary on wages being paid in the area.

1. In each block there are two numbers. The first number shown is the number of employees that particular company has assigned to the job. The second number is the current rate per hour now being paid.
   Example: Company A has 32 employees performing Common labor work and each employee is receiving $3.00 per hour.

2. For each job, a weighted average is also computed. For the Common-labor job, Company A is paying $3.00 an hour while Company G is paying $3.80 an hour. This raises a question of what should be a realistic figure to pay for a Common-labor job. The weighted average helps to set such a rate.

3. The form also shows where a particular company fits into the area wage structure for each job reviewed. An example is shown by using Company D and plotting its position for the jobs in question. On the Common-labor rate, Company D is at the median (midpoint), but for the jobs of Janitor, Mechanic A, and Electrician A, Company D is second from the bottom in a group of seven companies.

The following (Fig. 16.5) are examples of how the summary of an area survey is prepared. This summation is compiled by the originating company from the completed questionnaires that were returned. The originating company then assigns each participating company an identifying letter or number. When the summary is sent to the participants each company is told only which letter in the alphabet identifies their company.

Fig. 16.4

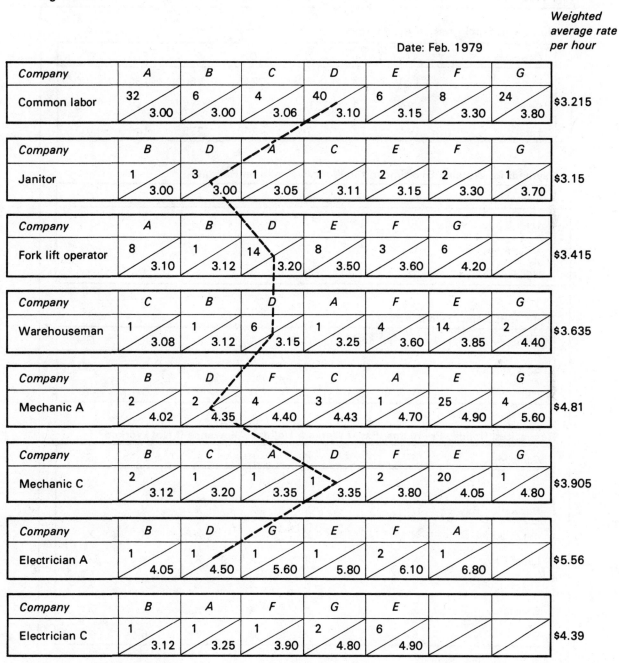

Weighted average rate per hour

Date: Feb. 1979

Company	A	B	C	D	E	F	G	
Common labor	32 / 3.00	6 / 3.00	4 / 3.06	40 / 3.10	6 / 3.15	8 / 3.30	24 / 3.80	$3.215

Company	B	D	A	C	E	F	G	
Janitor	1 / 3.00	3 / 3.00	1 / 3.05	1 / 3.11	2 / 3.15	2 / 3.30	1 / 3.70	$3.15

Company	A	B	D	E	F	G	
Fork lift operator	8 / 3.10	1 / 3.12	14 / 3.20	8 / 3.50	3 / 3.60	6 / 4.20	$3.415

Company	C	B	D	A	F	E	G	
Warehouseman	1 / 3.08	1 / 3.12	6 / 3.15	1 / 3.25	4 / 3.60	14 / 3.85	2 / 4.40	$3.635

Company	B	D	F	C	A	E	G	
Mechanic A	2 / 4.02	2 / 4.35	4 / 4.40	3 / 4.43	1 / 4.70	25 / 4.90	4 / 5.60	$4.81

Company	B	C	A	D	F	E	G	
Mechanic C	2 / 3.12	1 / 3.20	1 / 3.35	1 / 3.35	2 / 3.80	20 / 4.05	1 / 4.80	$3.905

Company	B	D	G	E	F	A	
Electrician A	1 / 4.05	1 / 4.50	1 / 5.60	1 / 5.80	2 / 6.10	1 / 6.80	$5.56

Company	B	A	F	G	E	
Electrician C	1 / 3.12	1 / 3.25	1 / 3.90	2 / 4.80	6 / 4.90	$4.39

Fig. 16.5 Area Survey Summary

Number of Employees on the Payroll

Company	A	B	C	D	E	F	G
Male	120	75	20	248	260	133	100
Female	24	2	54	0	15	13	2
Total	144	77	74	248	275	146	102

Payment for Working Overtime in the Workweek and on Holidays

Company	A	B	C	D	E	F	G
Over 8 hours worked	1	1	1½	1	1	1	1½
After 40 hours	1½	1½	1½	1½	1½	1½	1½
Holiday worked	2	2½	2	2	2	1½	2½

Night Shift Bonus Paid per Hour

Company	A	B	C	D	E	F	G
Second shift	0	0	.20	0	0	0	.08
Third shift	0	0	.30	0	0	0	.13

Recognized Holiday Premiums, Pay if Worked, Holiday Allowance if Not Worked

Company	A	B	C	D	E	F	G
New Year's	X		X	X	X	X	X
Decoration Day			X	X	X	X	
4th of July	X		X	X	X	X	X
Labor Day	X	X	X	X	X	X	X
Thanksgiving	X		X	X	X	X	X
Christmas	X	X	X	X	X	X	X
Total	5	2	7*	6	7†	6	9‡

*Also has Christmas Eve

†Also has Easter

‡Also has Good Friday, Christmas Eve, and New Year's Eve

Earning Requirements for Vacation (Years)

Company	A	B	C	D	E	F	G
1 week vac.	1	1	1	1	1	1	1
2 week vac.	5	3	3	3	2	2	3
3 week vac.	—	—	10	10	—	10	8
4 week vac.	—	—	—	—	—	20	15

Jury Duty, Funeral Leave, Report in Pay Review

Company	Jury duty	Funeral leave (days)	Report in pay (hours)
A	Difference between	2	4
B	8 hours base rate	3	4
C	and Jury Pay	4	4
D		3	4
E		2	5
F	Full pay plus jury pay	3	4
G	Difference (as above)	3 plus traveling time	4

Sick Leave Benefits

Company	Number of days	Number of days that can be accumulated
A	6 days/year	Up to 30
B	.6 days/month	Unlimited
C	1/2 day/month	Up to 50
D	6 days/year	Up to 30
E	8 days/year	Unlimited
F	.5 days/month	Up to 60
G	6 days/year	Up to 60

Probationary Period and Pay Differential for the Period

Company	Probationary period	Pay differential
A	60 work days	.10 less per hour
B	6 calendar months	.10 less, 1st three months
C	30 work days	None
D	90 calendar days	.08 less per hour
E	4 months	.10 less, 1st two months
F	60 work days	None
G	60 work days, non-skilled	.15 less, first 30 days
	6 months for "trades"	None

Fig. 16.5 (continued)

Clothes Change and Clean-up Pay, Rest Periods

Company	Clothes change and clean-up pay	Rest period
A	15 minute clean up for mechanics at end of shift	Not as such, relieved when necessary
B	Quit five minutes at end of shift	Not as such, relieved when necessary
C	Five minutes at beginning and end of shift.	15 minutes in AM and PM
D	None as such	Not as such, relieved when necessary
E	12 minutes	10 minute shut down of department in AM and PM
F	18 minutes (painters only)	Not as such
G	None as such, 10 minutes assumed	Not as such

Clothing Allowance and Laundry Review

Company	Type of uniform	Bought by company	Laundered by company	Garments per week
A	General	Yes (6 a year)	No	
B	Nurses only	Yes	Yes	3
C	General	Rented	Yes	3
D	None	None	None	
E	Employee paid 1.00 a week	None	No No	
F	Service men only	Yes	Yes	4
G	Print shop only	1/2 by company	No	

Review Questions

1. Why should a firm be interested in the actual rates being paid in the area? The average wage for each job?

2. If many conflicts occur between the evaluated and the area survey rates, what can or should be done?

3. Are employees likely to be more concerned with intercompany or intracompany pay inequities? Explain.

4. Why is it necessary to get so many types of data in the area survey? How can all this data be used?

5. In using area surveys, how can a fair comparison between rates be made when the jobs described are really not the same? The title may be the same, but the jobs do differ.

6. What are some shortcomings of using an area survey?

7. What difficulties might be encountered in obtaining an area survey?

Work Exercises

1. Prepare a list of what other sources of information, other than an area survey, may be used for obtaining information on the wage and fringe benefits being offered in one's area.

2. How can a company or governmental agency that specializes in a certain product or service conduct an area survey when its skilled employees have no direct counterpart in the area?

3. List the topics that should be covered in an area survey questionnaire and explain why each is important.

4. Assume that you are the Personnel Manager for Company D in the area survey shown in Figs. 16.4 and 16.5. It is now time to give management your recommendations for improvements of the *total*

employee benefits. You have the equivalent of 7 percent of the cost of wages to spend. Prepare a list, in the order of their importance, as to what you would recommend to change. What percentage of the total increase would you give to each of the benefits being improved?

17

Establishing a Wage Structure

Basically, Chapters 1 through 15 explained how to establish a job evaluation system; Chapters 16 through 19 deal with the administration of wages for the program. The first part of wage administration, after the area survey, is the establishment of the monetary rate per hour for a pay grade. This is the wage rate per hour, or in the case of salaried employees, the salary per month that a job is worth to the company. To establish this base rate, several factors are taken into account.

1. The company's philosophy on wages and/or salaries
2. The company's present rate of pay
3. The wage level and fringe benefits being paid in the area where the company is located
4. The company's ability to pay (profitability)

The Company's Philosophy on Wages and/or Salaries

The philosophy concerning payment of employees varies greatly between firms. Many factors or conditions affect the thinking of management. For example:

1. In some geographic areas, the base for salaries for non-exempt office employees, if they are not unionized, might be determined simply by the going rate of pay necessary to attract people in the locality. A company in a small town in South Carolina might be able to get office help by recruiting the housewives in the area at a much lower rate of pay than a similar size firm might have to pay in Detroit, Michigan.

2. This rate of pay might be relatively lower for a given level of skill than for an equivalent job in another company that has its rate established through union negotiations.

3. How unionized is the industry in which the company is operating? How large is the company in the industry? If it is very small compared to the leaders of the industry, the national union may not be too anxious to try to organize it. On the other hand, if it is a large plant, the union may be very interested in seeing that the plant is unionized. The level of pay is an important issue when discussing the pros and cons of unionization, both from the union's and from the company's point of view. If a company is trying to forestall unionization, what they are willing to pay probably will be higher than if the threat of unionization were not there.

4. How unionized is the local geographic area in which the company is located? If highly unionized, this would affect the general thinking of management concerning the payment of employees and the fringe benefits they are offering to their employees.

5. Is the company in a highly profitable industry, one in which the future also looks very good, or is just the opposite true? Either view makes an imprint on management's decisions.

6. What percentage is the labor cost compared to the total cost of operating the company? If low, the desire to pay high wages may be high, but if labor costs are a high percentage of total cost, then of course the general philosophy probably will change.

7. Are the majority of jobs skilled or is the work force made up mainly of easy-to-replace, low-paying jobs? This could also affect the thinking on the base rates in the wage structure.

8. Is there regularity of employment or are the jobs seasonal? Both types of employment have a bearing on the philosophy of management.

9. If the jobs to be evaluated are highly technical or professional, then a company may be competing for labor in a national market and be

forced to pay higher salaries than if the jobs were such that they could be filled from local sources.

Perhaps no one item of the above tends to mold management's philosophy concerning the setting of the base rate. One company, because of certain conditions, may have an entirely different point of view than another company located just across the street. It is important that top management set the general guide lines in the very beginning in establishing a formal job evaluation program.

The Company's Present Rate of Pay

In many cases a formal job evaluation program replaces an existing plan that is based primarily on each employee's personal rate. Under the new program, a rate is assigned to a job and any employee working on this job is paid this rate. It is important to review the wages currently being paid under the personal rate approach to wage administration. This can be done by plotting the current rates on a scatter diagram as shown in Fig. 17.1.

Fig. 17.1 Plotting of Jobs on Scatter Diagram with a Freehand Drawing of the Wage Line (Data taken from the jobs listed in Chapter 15, and Table A, Figure 15.1.)

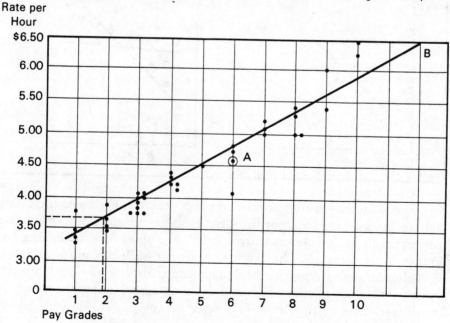

To make such a diagram, it is necessary to relate only two figures for each employee—the present rate per hour and the pay grade to which each job is assigned. The payroll department can verify each employee's pay rate, and the new job evaluation program determines the point score for each job (Chapter 15). For example, if an employee currently is receiving $4.60 an hour and his job is rated at grade six, the dot marked A in Fig. 17.1 would identify him. Other personal rates would be plotted in a similar manner.

When all of the employees' rates have been recorded on the diagram, a wage curve can be drawn through the data (see the wage curve line marked B in Fig. 17.1). For the inexperienced evaluator, the line can be drawn through the middle of the data showing the average rates per hour being paid for each pay grade. Figure 17.2(a) is an example of drawing the line that *best fits* the distribution of the jobs to the pay grades. As you can see, the solid wage regression line (sometimes erroneously called a trend line) in Fig. 17.2(b) does divide the jobs reasonably even, but it is not a good fit. The broken line for (b) would be an acceptable wage regression line for the data.

Fig. 17.2 Drawing Wage Regression Lines through Raw Data

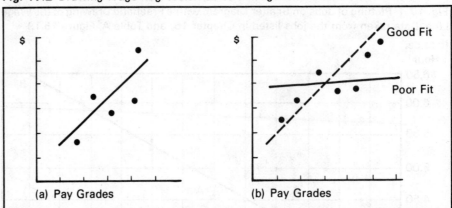

(a) Pay Grades   (b) Pay Grades

The wage curve that is decided upon provides the basis for establishing the average rate per hour for each pay grade. Point scores are converted to pay grades as shown in the examples on establishing pay grades in Chapter 15. The rate per hour for each pay grade is determined by drawing a perpendicular line up from the pay grade until it intersects the wage curve line, and drawing a horizontal line to where it intersects the vertical axis. This point on the pay scale would be the tentative amount set for the pay grade. For example, in the scatter diagram in Fig. 17.1 pay grade two would receive $3.70 an hour (point score 301 to 355 on Table A, Fig. 15.2; see the dotted lines on the scatter diagram in Fig. 17.1).

The wage curve can actually be computed by using the least-squares method of computing a line of regression. Linear regression least-squares method of estimating the trend of current wage rates provides a more accurate guide than the averaging method mentioned above. The least-squares method minimizes the sum of the squares of the distance between each observation and the line itself. The line formed is the best fit in that it is the only line that can minimize these vertical distances. An appendix has been added at the end of the chapter to explain how to compute a wage curve.

Area Wage Level and Fringe Benefits Being Paid

In many respects, these data may establish the rate for the bottom and top of the pay scale. If the prevailing rate for common labor in the community is $3.20 an hour, then it is almost imperative that your grade one pays approximately $3.20. Otherwise, the recruiting and retention of good employees will be difficult. The same is true for the top rate in the pay grade scale. If an experienced electrician is earning $6.75 an hour, it is not realistic to expect to hire a qualified, experienced electrician for $6.00.

By evaluating the summary of the area survey, Figs. 16.4 and 16.5, realistic rates can be established.

It is not difficult to meet the top pay grade rate, because the total cost for this grade is not excessive. The top grades normally constitute less than 5% of the total work force. This number will vary from company to company, however, depending on the types of skills required for producing the product or service.

Ability to Pay (Profitability)

In the end, the ability to pay dictates the wages offered. If the firm is a reasonably profitable one, then the old personal rates and the information taken from the area survey will help decide the bottom and top grade rate. If the company is not profitable, then the company will establish a lower pay scale and encounter difficulties in recruiting and retaining good employees.

By comparing the wage curve of the existing system (personal rates as shown in the scatter diagram in Fig. 17.1) and the results of the area survey, Fig. 16.4, we can establish the pay rates for the bottom and top pay grades.

If the company is just beginning operations, the area survey and information received from the State Employment Office would serve as a guide in establishing the rates.

ESTABLISHING PAY GRADES

From the information presented on the scatter diagram and the area survey, the bottom pay grade should be approximately $3.18 and the top grade rate $6.05. (The rate for Electrician A in the area survey is partially distorted because two of the seven companies in the survey had very low rates for this job, thus pulling the average rate down, Fig. 16.4.)

If the rate paid for grade one is $3.18 and the rate for the top grade is $6.05, there is a rate differential of $2.87 between the two grades; this is the amount of money to be distributed among the other pay grades in the system. The assignment of the pay grade rates can be done in a variety of ways, but there are two common ways.

Equal Pay Differential between Pay Grades

If the goal is to have the same amount of money between pay grades one and two, two and three, three and four, etc., then one needs only to divide the money that separates the bottom and top pay grades by a number one less than the number of pay grades desired to establish the rate differential. In the example given, a differential of $2.87 exists between the bottom rate and the top rate ($6.05 minus $3.18 equals $2.87). If eight pay grades are desired with an equal differential between the grades, divide $2.87 by seven (one less than the total number of pay grades). If ten pay grades are wanted, then $2.87 would be divided by nine. The results of these computations and the assigning of money to the pay grades are shown in pay schedules A and B in Fig. 17.3.

Progressive Differential between Pay Grades

A second approach, and the one the author prefers, makes it possible to pay high wages for the upper grades without very much in added cost.

Fig. 17.3
Computing Pay Grades with the Same Differential

A		B	
Eight pay grades with same differential		Ten pay grades with same differential	
$\dfrac{.41}{7\,\overline{)2.87}}$		$\dfrac{.32}{9\,\overline{)2.87}}$	
Pay grade	Rate	Pay grade	Rate
1	$3.18 .41	1	$3.18 .32
2	3.59 .41	2	3.50 .32
3	4.00 .41	3	3.82 .32
4	4.41 .41	4	4.14 .32
5	4.82 .41	5	4.46 .32
6	5.23 .41	6	4.78 .32
7	5.64 .41	7	5.10 .32
8	6.05	8	5.42 .32
		9	5.74 .32
		10	6.06*

*One cent over the $6.05 desired. This however is very little added cost, since it means only 8 cents a day more (for an 8-hour day) for a very few employees.

It covers a large differential between the bottom and top pay grades with a lower number of total pay grades. A final recommendation for a progressive pay structure is that it can keep the total cost down. In most wage structures of eight grades, 40 to 60 percent of all employees are in the bottom two or three grades. Thus, the total cost per operating hour for these grades is high. In a progressive differential approach to money distribution, the differential in the lower grades is always less than in the equal differential system. Compare the pay rate for grades one, two, and three in pay schedules A and B under the equal differential approach and the same pay rate in schedules C, D, E, F, and G in Fig. 17.4 using the progressive differential approach.

To arrive at the rate scale desired, one approaches the task in a trial-and-error method. Such an approach will show which pay rate system best fits what the company is trying to accomplish in the distribution of money and in establishing the proper number of pay grades in the system. The pay schedules in Fig. 17.4 are examples of the trial-and-error approach.

Schedule C has a $3.18 grade-one starting point with a 25-cent differential between grades one and two and a 5-cent increasing differential for the remaining grades. However grade eight did not reach the desired $6.05 mark.

Schedule D with the same starting point, uses a 26-cent differential between grades one and two and a 5-cent increasing differential for the remaining grades. Schedule D reaches the desired grade eight rate of $6.05.

Schedules E, F, and G are trial-and-error approaches to see which starting differential, plus a 10-cent increasing differential, will reach

Fig. 17.4
Pay Schedules with Progressive Differentials

Grade	C Rate	D Rate	E Rate	F Rate	G Rate
1	3.18	3.18	3.18	3.18	3.18
	.25	.26	.25	.21	.23
2	3.43	3.44	3.43	3.39	3.41
	.30	.31	.35	.31	.33
3	3.73	3.75	3.78	3.70	3.74
	.35	.36	.45	.41	.43
4	4.08	4.11	4.23	4.11	4.17
	.40	.41	.55	.51	.53
5	4.48	4.52	4.78	4.62	4.70
	.45	.46	.65	.61	.63
6	4.93	4.98	5.43	5.23	5.33
	.50	.51	.75	.71	.73
7	5.43	5.49	6.18	5.94	6.06
	.55	.56			
8	5.98	6.05			

$6.05 in seven pay grades (one less grade than in schedules A, B, C, and D). Schedule E went over the $6.05, but schedule F did not reach that desired level. Schedule G meets the desired goal of approximately $6.05.

Pay schedules A, B, D, and G all would be acceptable as the proper pay structure. Many other schedules could be constructed to fit the company's particular need. The pay schedule selected depends on whether one wants equal or progressive differentials and how many pay grades are desired.

As was shown in Fig. 15.1 the number of pay grades varies from as low as five in the mining industry to a high of 34 in the steel industry. Choosing the right number for your particular company basically depends on two factors.

1. The pay differential between the bottom grade and the top grade: if the differential is $1.20 fewer grades would be desirable than if the differential were $4.80.
2. The total number of jobs being evaluated: if only 12 jobs were involved there probably would be a need of fewer pay levels than if there were 105 jobs involved.

These two points were covered earlier in Chapter 15.

Once the basic pay schedule is chosen, a decision should be made whether the company wants to have a single rate structure, or a dual or a triple rate structure. Many companies establish a hiring rate, sometimes called a probationary rate, which is below the regular rate for the job. Once an employee completes the probationary period, he or she is automatically promoted to the regular rate for the job. Some companies have only a single rate structure, but every new employee is employed at the pay scale one grade lower than the job. At the end of the probationary period, the pay is automatically adjusted to the proper pay grade rate. In such companies, a "hiring rate" is set for grade one, and the employees' pay is adjusted to the regular rate for grade one after completion of the probationary period.

Figure 17.5 shows a dual rate structure whereby an employee is hired in at a probationary rate and then automatically is promoted to the base rate for the job.

In Fig. 17.5 the differential between the probationary rate and the base rate was arbitrarily set at six percent. There is no set rule about setting the width or range of the rate. Usually for hourly paid em-

Fig. 17.5
Wage Rate Structure for N. Bartley Manufacturing Co. Effective 11-1-81

Grade	Probationary rate	Base rate
1	$3.70	$3.92
2	3.92	4.15
3	4.15	4.40
4	4.40	4.66
5	4.66	4.94
6	4.94	5.24
7	5.24	5.55
8	5.55	5.88

ployees the range is between five and eight percent, with six being the most popular. For management positions the range is usually between ten and twelve percent per grade. The time element for promotion to the base rate varies according to the type of work being performed. If the work is easily learned, then usually the time period is the same for all grades. If however, there are many pay grades and the learning time varies, then the time element for the middle- and top-rated jobs might be extended. The following time table (Fig. 17.6) is an example of what one company installed for its automatic-promotion time schedule.

Some companies want to be sure they have a certain number of observations of an individual before he or she is allowed to become a regular employee. For this purpose, the company substitutes a certain

Fig. 17.6 Time Schedule for Promotion to the Base Rate

Employee is automatically promoted to the base rate of his grade in accordance with the following time schedule.	
Grades 1, 2, 3	At the beginning of the pay week following the completion of three (3) calendar months worked.
Grades 4, 5, 6	At the beginning of the pay week following the completion of six (6) calendar months worked.
Grades 7, 8, 9	At the beginning of the pay week following the completion of nine (9) calendar months worked.

number of days worked for the three, six, or nine calendar months as shown in the time schedule above. This is a more accurate approach to a time schedule; however, it does require keeping attendance records during the probationary period. For example, if an employee is assigned overtime work on Saturdays or Sundays he or she would earn regular status earlier than someone who had been hired on the same day but who did not get weekend overtime assignments. The opposite would be true if the employee were absent during the probationary period.

Another company may want three rate schedules for its system: a probationary rate, the regular rate, and a third rate called "merit" rate. With a triple rate structure, the employee is automatically increased to the regular rate upon completing the probationary period, but the employee can be raised to the merit raise only through the recommendation of the supervisor.

Most unions are against merit rating programs as part of the pay process, the problem being that it is most difficult to select properly the criteria against which the employee is rated. Even if this is properly done it is equally difficult to define or judge what is an outstanding performance on the job. If the merit rate is for truly outstanding performance, then it should only be used for that. Only a small percentage of the work force (10 to 20 percent) should qualify to receive this pay level. How to evaluate employees for merit rating is further discussed in Chapter 20.

Overlapping Pay Grades

Under this approach to wage administration, an upper and lower limit of each pay grade is set. The overlap means that the highest pay rate in a pay grade is above the minimum of the rate set for the next higher pay grade. In all cases the overlap involves at least one grade, and in some cases in the top grades the overlap could involve several grades. The overlapping program may be established in one of two ways.

Setting Limit Lines   Figure 17.7 shows limit lines for setting wage rates. The limits were arbitrarily set, for explanatory purposes, at five percent at grade one and at twelve percent at grade eight. Under this program, the center line is drawn using the midpoints of each pay grade. This establishes the average rate or midpoint for the pay grade. The percent spread from the lower to the upper grades varies in proportion to the type of work being performed and the amount of variation that

Fig. 17.7 Limit Lines for Setting Wage Rates

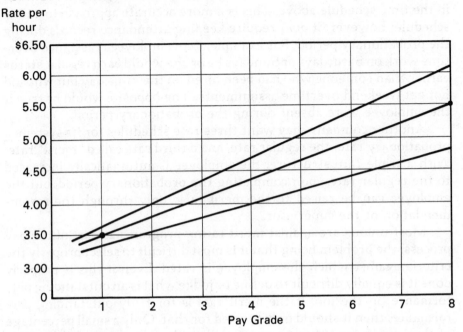

can be expected in the performance of the employees in the top pay grades. These percent variations may extend from five to twenty percent on hourly paid jobs and even higher for non-exempt office jobs. On jobs where individual initiative and talent can make a large difference in how the job is being performed larger percent variances can be used. Of course when this occurs, the overlap on the top grades will be greater.

Box Approach for Setting Wage Rates   The box approach sets the upper and lower limits by using either the midpoints of the area survey, the midpoint of the pay grade, or a combination of the two to establish what the committee feels is the average rate for the job. The percent spread is determined in the same manner as was explained in the limit line approach (Fig. 17.8).

This approach is more widely accepted by the employees because it graphically displays the information in a way that the employee can readily understand.

The wage structures in Fig. 17.9 show how wage schedule D could

Fig. 17.8 Box Approach for Wage Structure*

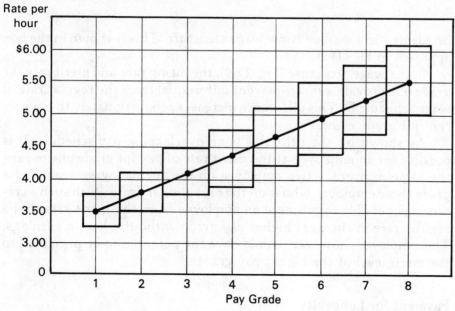

*Data taken from Fig. 17.9.

Fig. 17.9
Overlapping Wage Structure

Pay grade	Hiring rate or probationary rate	Regular rate taken from wage structure D	Merit rate	
1	$2.97	$3.18	$3.44	
	.21	.26	.31	differential
2	3.18	3.44	3.75	
	.26	.31	.36	
3	3.44	3.75	4.11	
	.31	.36	.41	
4	3.75	4.11	4.52	
	.36	.41	.46	
5	4.11	4.52	4.98	
	.41	.46	.51	
6	4.52	4.98	5.49	
	.46	.51	.56	
7	4.98	5.49	6.05	
	.51	.56	.61	
8	5.49	6.05	6.61	

be adapted to a dual or triple wage structure. This is shown in the box approach in Fig. 17.8.

In the wage structure (Fig. 17.9), the hiring rate and merit rate for grade one provide a seven-percent differential from the regular rate in wage schedule D. This difference increases proportionately to ten percent for grade eight.

As shown by the title, this is an overlapping pay schedule. It is possible for an employee at the merit rate of pay for grade one to earn the same as a grade two employee on the regular wage scale and a grade three employee who is on the probationary rate. With such a system it is possible to promote an employee from the merit rate to the regular rate in the next higher pay grade without a loss in earnings. This employee, however, would have the potential to be promoted to the merit level of the higher pay grade.

Payment for Longevity

Some managers want to pay additional compensation for length of service, but this is one policy on compensation that the author cannot recommend. Longevity pay is not a good motivator. In fact, in many cases it causes deterioration in the work and of the morale of employees who have less time in service. These employees feel that the older-in-service employee gets more pay for doing the same or, in some cases, less work than the newer, younger employee.

If a bonus for longevity seems appropriate, it can best be granted in benefits other than in the rate of pay. Most companies deal with this problem by granting additional benefits in the following personnel practices:

1. Additional service time earns more credits for such fringe benefits as pension, vacation time, and sick leave.
2. Continuous service is used as a factor in deciding among employees which employee is eligible for benefits such as promotions, transfers, vacation time preference, shift preference, and job preference.

If, however, a company does desire to install, in addition to its base pay structure, a longevity compensation program, it is not very difficult to place such a plan into effect. It may be done in the following manner.

1. Determine how many steps are desired in the plan (6, 7, 8, etc.).
2. Decide what increment, over the base rate, should be paid for each step (3%, 4%, 5%, etc.).
3. Set a length of time that should elapse between moving from one step to the next (12 months, 18 months, 24 months, etc.).

After these three decisions have been made, a table like the one shown in Fig. 17.10 is computed. This particular table is based on a

Fig. 17.10

Grade		Base rate	Steps in Grade					
			A	B	C	D	E	F
1	H*	3.18	3.34	3.50	3.655	3.815	3.975	4.13
	M†	551	579	607	634	661	702	737
2	H	3.44	3.61	3.780	3.955	4.13	4.30	4.47
	M	596	626	655	686	716	745	775
3	H	3.75	3.94	4.125	4.31	4.50	4.69	4.875
	M	650	683	715	747	780	813	445
4	H	4.11	4.315	4.52	4.725	4.93	5.14	5.34
	M	712	748	783	819	854	891	925
5	H	4.52	4.745	4.97	5.20	5.425	5.65	5.875
	M	783	822	861	901	940	979	1018
6	H	4.98	5.23	5.48	5.725	5.98	6.225	6.475
	M	863	906	950	992	1036	1079	1122
7	H	5.49	5.765	6.04	6.315	6.59	6.86	7.135
	M	951	999	1046	1094	1142	1189	1236
8	H	6.05	6.35	6.655	6.96	7.26	7.56	7.865
	M	1048	1100	1153	1206	1258	1310	1363

*H = Hourly rate

†M = Monthly rate equivalent

progressive 5% increase over the base rate. Step A for grade 1 is 5% greater than $3.18, step B is 10% greater, step C is 15% greater, etc. The table was established by using the pay grade and wage structure as shown in schedule D in Fig. 17.4.

In this system the hourly rate is based on a 5% progressive increment over the base rate. All rates are rounded to the nearest half-cent. The monthly rate is computed by multiplying the hourly rate by 173.3 rounded to the nearest dollar. Length of time between increases in grade is one year. All increases are formulated on one-year increments based on the anniversary date the employee first received the base rate.

Many deviations may be made from the above stated rules. One example: The program might include ten steps, but the increment between steps be reduced to three percent rather than five percent. In addition, the length of time between increases could be reduced to a period less than 12 months.

There is no set rule concerning time in pay grade. At one time the federal government had a ten-step wage progression scale that had the following time schedule.

one year to advance from step 1 to 2; from 2 to 3; from 3 to 4

two years to advance from step 4 to 5; from 5 to 6; from 6 to 7

three years to advance from step 7 to 8; from 8 to 9; from 9 to 10

A TOTAL WAGE AND SALARY STRUCTURE FOR A COMPANY

So far, the discussion on wage structures has centered on establishing a wage structure for a particular group of employees—production, hourly paid employees, non-exempt office employees, or management and professional employees. It has been said repeatedly that it is not practical to evaluate hourly production jobs or office-type jobs using the same evaluation program as is being used for management positions. The same method of evaluation may be used, but particularly when using an analytical method to evaluate, different factors or classifications should be used. Regardless of the method used, it is possible to end up with two or three different pay grade structures:

one for production, hourly paid employees

one for non-exempt office employees

one for management and professional employees

How then are these two or three wage structures tied together as a single wage structure for the entire company? The answer is that in most cases they *are not tied together* and each is handled on its own individual merit and facts concerning the group involved.

Production Employees   Often these jobs are assigned to a single rate structure and a range of rates is not used. Since 20 percent of all production jobs are on some type of incentive system, a single rate structure best adapts to an easy computation of pay for this group. In addition, a high percentage of the employees in manufacturing sections are unionized and the wage structure is decided through the process of collective bargaining. Consequently, management does not have complete authority over how the wage structure is set.

Non-Exempt Office Employees   Since these jobs can vary greatly with the type of work being performed in comparison to the work performed by production employees, a different set of factors should be used in evaluating the jobs. This then may create a greater or smaller number of pay grades, or the number of dollars assigned to each grade could be affected. In the production-type work there might be nine pay grades, but in the office-type work there may be only six or seven pay grades. Both the number of grades and the differential between grades would warrant constructing a different wage structure.

If the production employees were unionized and the office employees were not, the company would definitely want a distinct difference between the two groups of employees. On the other hand, if the office force were unionized, particularly if they were unionized by the same union that was representing the production employee, the wage structure probably would be very similar to the one used by the production employees. In some cases it may be identical. Unionization of both the production and the office personnel by the same union in the steel industry creates just such a condition.

Management and Professional Employees   Since the evaluating of these jobs encompasses entirely different factors than either of the other two groups and since the talent and experience of the individual may make a difference in how the job is performed, these positions are usually in a wage structure by themselves. Generally speaking, the rate ranges are used, and the minimum and maximum levels in the higher grades can go as high as 35 to 40 percent. This allows many steps or levels within a pay grade. It also allows for individual differences by the managers and gives the responsibility to management of properly regarding a manager for doing exceptional work.

In some companies the bottom grade in the management pay scale may be slightly lower than the very top grade jobs on the hourly paid or non-exempt paid salary payroll. This is usually the pay for the first line supervisor's position who is very close in pay to the very high skilled personnel on the hourly payroll. Once the supervisor is promoted, however, the pay differential widens quickly.

The following three wage structures (Fig. 17.11) might be the complete wage and salary structures used by a medium-size company. Small companies would probably have only two, one for the employees and one for management.

Fig. 17.11 Three Wage Schedules within a Company

Grade	Production employees*	Non-exempt office employees	Management and professional employees
1	$ 800 month	$ 800 to 835	$1000 to 1200
2	835 "	830 to 870	1125 to 1325
3	870 "	860 to 905	1250 to 1475
4	905 "	890 to 940	1375 to 1650
5	940 "	920 to 975	1500 to 1850
6	975 "	950 to 1010	1625 to 2075
7	1010 "	980 to 1045	
8	1045 "	1010 to 1070	
	A $35.00 straight grade differential with a single rate	A rate range starting with a 4% variance in grade 1 and a 7% variance in grade 8	Only 6-grade rate range varies from 20% in grade 1 to 28% in grade 6

*Hourly rates are converted to salary equivalent for comparison purposes.

Necessity for Maintaining Distinct Wage Administration for Different Types of Employees

What are the alternatives for an employee who becomes disenchanted with the company? He or she probably can do one of the following four things:

1. quit

2. make trouble at the job by becoming a problem employee

3. join or try to organize a union

4. deteriorate on the job doing enough only to get by but not so little that he requires discipline or risks being discharged

None of the above is a desirable alternative for proper wage administration. I agree with Dr. F. Herzberg that money is not a true motivator but that it is the number one maintenance factor. If the proper level of wages or salary is not paid for a particular job or a particular group of employees, those employees affected will become upset and may react in one of the ways listed above.

The following article appeared on page one of the June 23, 1980 edition of the *Wall Street Journal* [1].

White-Collar Blues

Middle-Rank Workers Often Find Pay Gains Trailing Subordinates'

Many Actually Earn Less; Recession Worsens Gap As Merit Increases Fade

'Like Meat in a Sandwich'

By KATHRYN CHRISTENSEN
Staff Reporter of THE WALL STREET JOURNAL

Late last March, a month after Teamsters members working in Honeywell Inc.'s Twin Cities operations won a 13% pay increase, 650 angry Honeywell engineers and technicians crowded into a hotel on the outskirts of Minneapolis. Riled because the Teamsters' raise far exceeded their own record of increases in the 7% range, the professionals eagerly signed cards demanding their own bargaining group.

"Considering what we contribute to the company and what they do, there's no logical reason why their pay is progressing faster than ours," Michael Lebowsky, a mechanical engineer, grumbled recently. "They don't work any harder, and they aren't any smarter than we are."

Elsewhere, similar frustration is building up. In San Diego, for example, a superintendent at a Solar Turbines International plant concedes that of the 40 supervisors under him, at least 15 earn less than many of their subordinates. Many companies must arm-twist workers into accepting promotions or cajole supervisors out of transferring back to the nonmanagement world of fewer responsibilities and paid overtime.

This is only one-sixth of the total article, but it points out to management several things to be remembered:

1. It is necessary to have more than one wage schedule in a company in order to pay properly the various types of employees (hourly, office, and management).
2. It is also extremely important that no one wage structure be allowed to get out of line with the other structures within the company.

If a company has properly installed wage structures and they are systematically reviewed and updated, the employees will certainly have less reason to become upset with that company's wage policies.

Appendix—How to Calculate A Line of Regression

The first step in computing the wage curve is to prepare a table divided into four columns.

Column 1	Column 2	Column 3	Column 4
y	x	x^2	xy
The current pay rate for each employee listed in pay grade order (column 2) is placed in this column	A list of each employee by pay grade. Start with grade one	Each figure in column 2 squared x^2	Column one times column two x times y

Table 17.A1 reflects the data of the 26 jobs listed in Table A in Fig. 15.3. The rates per hour were obtained from the payroll department for each of the 40 employees working on these 26 different jobs. These values will enable you to determine the value of a and b in order to compute the equation of the regression line ($y = a + bx$).

Once the summation of column y, x, x^2 and xy is obtained it is merely a matter of substituting the total of these four columns into the following equation to find the slope of the line.

$$b = \frac{\sum xy - \left[\frac{(\sum x)(\sum y)}{n}\right]}{\sum x^2 - \left[\frac{(\sum x)^2}{n}\right]} = \frac{177.05 - \left[\frac{(180 \times 177.05)}{40}\right]}{1156 - \left[\frac{(180)^2}{40}\right]} = \frac{113.43}{346} = 0.3278$$

Once the value of b is determined, it is an easy matter to find the value of a to be used in the least-squares equation. By substituting the value of b into the equation $y = na + bx$, we have

$$177.05 = 40a + (0.3278 \times 180),$$
$$177.05 - 59 = 40a,$$
$$2.951 = a.$$

Table 17.A1
Plotting Money and Pay Grades for Least-Squares Equation

y	x	x^2	xy
$ 3.25	1	1	$ 3.25
3.80	1	1	3.80
3.45	1	1	3.45
3.50	1	1	3.50
3.50	2	4	7.00
3.40	2	4	6.80
3.90	2	4	7.80
3.70	2	4	7.40
3.90	3	9	11.70
4.00	3	9	12.00
4.05	3	9	12.15
3.95	3	9	11.85
3.85	3	9	11.55
3.85	3	9	11.55
3.85	3	9	11.55
4.10	3	9	12.30
4.00	3	9	12.00
4.15	4	16	16.60
4.25	4	16	17.00
4.30	4	16	17.20
4.20	4	16	16.80
4.40	4	16	17.60
4.10	4	16	16.40
4.65	5	25	23.25
4.50	5	25	22.50
4.10	6	36	24.60
4.60	6	36	27.60
4.75	6	36	28.50
4.80	6	36	28.80
5.10	7	49	35.70
5.00	7	49	35.00
5.25	7	49	36.75

5.30	8	64	42.40
5.00	8	64	40.00
5.40	8	64	43.20
5.00	8	64	40.00
5.40	9	81	48.60
6.00	9	81	54.00
6.25	10	100	62.50
6.50	10	100	65.50
*$177.05	180	1156	$910.15

*These total figures are used in the equation to compute the line of regression. Since there are 40 entries in the x column (column 2), the number of employees, n, involved is 40.

All of the information needed to finalize the regression line is now available. As stated above, the general equation for a line is $y = a + bx$. The value of b has been determined as 0.3278 and the value of a is 2.951. By plugging these values into the following table, we can obtain the final figures for computing the line (Table 17.A2).

The figures in the last column of Table 17.A2 are the individual rates per hour for each of the pay grades. Plotted on a graph these data would result in Fig. 17.A1.

The example given is an illustration of one procedure for determining the wage slope. The following equation is a second approach for determining the value of a and b. In this approach the equations are worked simultaneously:

$$\Sigma y = na + b\Sigma x,$$
$$\Sigma xy = a\Sigma x + b\Sigma x^2,$$

where

Σx is the sum of the number of jobs being performed   (180)

Σy is the sum of the individual pay rates   (177.05)

n is the number of employees involved   (40)

Σxy is the summation of the xy column   (910.15)

Σx^2 is the adding of the figures in the x^2 column   (1156)

Table 17.A2
Value of _a_ Plus Value of (_b_ times _x_) equals _y_

Value of a	+	Value of b	×	Pay grade (x = value of regression line)	bx	=	y = value of the regression line
2.951	+	0.3278	×	1	0.3278	=	3.278
2.951	+	0.3278	×	2	0.6556	=	3.606
2.951	+	0.3278	×	3	0.9834	=	3.934
2.951	+	0.3278	×	4	1.3148	=	4.266
2.951	+	0.3278	×	5	1.6390	=	4.590
2.951	+	0.3278	×	6	1.9668	=	4.918
2.951	+	0.3278	×	7	2.2946	=	5.246
2.951	+	0.3278	×	8	2.6224	=	5.573
2.951	+	0.3278	×	9	2.9502	=	5.901
2.951	+	0.3278	×	10	3.2780	=	6.229

By substituting the above values into the equation, we obtain:

$$177.05 = 40a + 180b, \tag{1}$$
$$910.15 = 180a + 1156b \tag{2}$$

We eliminate a by multiplying Eq. (1) by 4.5 and subtracting it from Eq. (2):

$$
\begin{array}{rcl}
910.15 & = & 180a + 1156b \\
-796.72 & = & 180a + 810b \\
\hline
113.43 & = & 346b \\
0.3278 & = & b
\end{array}
$$

Substituting the value for b in the equation $y = na + bx$, we have:

$$177.05 = 40a + [0.3278 \times 180],$$
$$177.05 = 40a + 59,$$
$$177.05 - 59 = 40a,$$
$$2.951 = a$$

Fig. 17.A1 Calculated Wage Regression Line

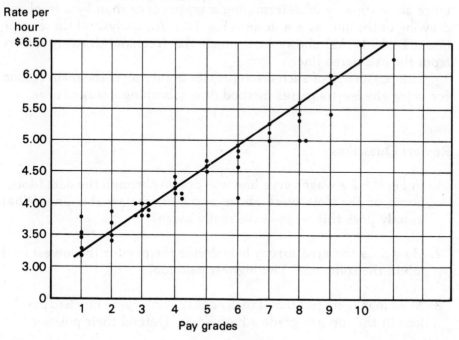

Table 17.A3
Comparison of Calculated Wage Line and a Wage
Line Drawn through the Data

Pay grade	Value of each pay grade calculated by least-squares method	Value as determined by freehand drawing of line through data
1	$3.28	$3.45
2	3.605	3.70
3	3.93	4.00
4	4.265	4.25
5	4.59	4.53
6	4.92	4.82
7	5.245	5.10
8	5.57	5.35
9	5.90	5.65
10	6.23	5.90

Use of the calculated wage curve shown in Fig. 17.A1 is a much more accurate way of determining a wage curve than by a freehand drawing of the line, as was done in Fig. 17.1. An analysis of these wage lines (Table 17.A3) shows how much the freehand drawing differs from the calculated line.

The possibility of such discrepancies occurring is the main reason for using the least-squares method of establishing a wage curve.

Review Questions

1. In Fig. 17.1 a wage curve line was drawn through the data (dots). Some of the dots were above and some below this line. What exactly does this wage curve really mean?

2. How does the area survey help decide the pay for the lowest paid job in the company? The highest paid job?

3. Most managers feel that it really does not cost very much to pay the jobs in the top pay grade a high wage. Defend their position.

4. If you are not in a high-paying industry, is it important to conduct an area survey? Explain.

5. Some managers feel earnings are more important than base wage rates. How would this thinking affect your decision about installing a job evaluation program?

6. Should compensation be based mainly on equity or contribution? Explain the reasons for your selection.

7. Which of the following rate increases would you recommend to be used in your company? Give reasons for your recommendation.
   a. automatic progression to the top rate
   b. merit progression to the top rate
   c. combination of a and b

8. If employees performing the same job vary in their performance, how can you justify paying them all the same rate of pay?

9. How important is "overlap" in a wage structure? To be meaningful, how large should the increment be between the steps within the pay grade?

10. If a company has ten pay grades and also has a policy of automatic progression from the probationary rate to the regular base rate, should the time in grade to earn the increase be the same for the bottom grades, the midgrades, and the top grades? Defend your position.

11. The wage structure is the main reason why a company installed a job evaluation program. How does the company's policy on compensation affect the wage structure?

12. In a weighted-in-points approach to job evaluation, each point is worth the same. This being true, defend the position of establishing a wage structure with a progressive increment.

13. What problem is the longevity wage structure designed to solve? Is it a good solution? What other ways may a company use to solve this problem?

14. Unions are basically against wage structures that include a rate based on merit. Why do you think they take this stand?

15. Your wage structure has a wage rate based on merit. You have just learned that one of your better employees will leave if he is not increased to this level. Should you promote this employee to this rate? What criteria would you use to justify your actions?

16. What are the advantages of an overlapping wage structure? The disadvantages?

Work Exercises

1. The bottom grade pays $3.45 an hour. The top grade pays $6.80. Construct a wage structure with nine pay grades with an even increment between the grades.

2. With the same pay for grade one and grade nine as shown in Work Exercise #1, construct a wage structure with nine grades using a progressive increment between grades.

3. Using either the wage structure prepared for Work Exercise #1 or #2, prepare a three-level overlapping wage structure. In grade one, use a six-percent differential between the three levels.

4. The jobs listed below have been evaluated and assigned to the pay grades shown.
   a. Plot the rates on a scatter diagram.
   b. Hand draw a wage line through the data.
   c. Compute a wage regression line using the least-squares method as explained in the appendix at the end of the chapter.
   d. Compare the wage rates for the pay grades between the rates that were calculated and those that were hand drawn (b versus c above).

Pay grade	Title of job	Rate per hour
1	Yard maintenance	$3.25
4	Mail clerk	4.20
8	Printer A	6.30
8	Accounting clerk	6.10
10	Electronic technician A	7.00
3	Key punch operator B	4.00
5	Key punch operator A	4.40
2	Clerk–typist	3.80
9	Research analyst A	6.60
7	Fork lift operator A	5.50
6	Secretary	5.00

18

Adjustments to the Wage Structure, Individual Adjustments Within the Rate Range, and Salary Management

ADJUSTMENTS TO THE WAGE STRUCTURE

When a company's compensation program is on a personal basis adjustment to each employee's rate is made in a variety of ways. Some companies adjust the wage rate for all employees at a specified time, but the amount of increase can vary for employees performing the same work. Other companies not only adjust the amount of the increase for each employee, but also adjust the time between raises. These latter companies make rate changes for part of their payroll each month. Under this program, the person adjusting the wages takes into consideration the time between increases as well as the amount of increase for each individual on the payroll.

The latter approach, of course, leads to greater discrepancies in the wage structure. Some employees might receive a $40.00 a month increase in 12 months from their last increase, while other employees performing the same work might only receive a $35.00 increase and have waited 15 months from their last increase. Under this system, there is little uniformity in either the amount of the raise or the length of time between increases. Each employee is evaluated on an individual basis and paid accordingly.

With a formal wage administration program for hourly paid personnel, the administration of wages, as described above, is no longer feasible. Under a formalized program, several rules are placed into effect.

1. An adjustment to the total wage schedule should be made effective at a specific time. Example: Wages being paid to *all hourly paid* employees will be increased for all hours worked, starting at 12:01 AM on December 1, 1980.

2. A percentage increase will be granted equally to *all pay grades.* To maintain a proper wage structure, all rates should be rounded to the nearest half-cent. It is imperative that only percentage increases be granted in the future. If an across-the-board increase (each pay grade getting the same amount of increase) is effected, it will narrow the differentials between the various grades.

When the job evaluation is first established, if the bottom and top rates are properly set, the pay relationship between grade one and eight should be maintained. Using wage schedule D in Fig. 17.4 as an example, a 90 percent differential exists between grade one and grade eight. By granting only percentage increases this differential will be maintained.

Figure 18.1 shows the difference between granting a percentage increase and an across-the-board increase. By granting a percentage increase, several benefits accrue to the company.

1. The differential between grade one and the top grade (grade eight) is maintained.

2. The company is able to attract and retain skilled employees because their pay is keeping pace with comparable jobs in the community. The cost to the company is the same whether the increase is in the form of an across-the-board increase or a percentage one. Why not apply the money where it will make the operation more effective?

3. The cost per operating hour for the lower grades would be less under a percentage increase. These grades usually have a very large percent of the work force assigned to them.

Cost-of-Living Adjustment

Many companies, particularly unionized plants, incorporate into their compensation program a cost-of-living adjustment (COLA). Here, too,

Fig. 18.1
Comparing Wage Schedule D—Across-the-Board Increase
and a Percentage Increase

Pay grade	Rate schedule	6% increase rounded to nearest ½ cent	New rate with 6% increase	A 27-cent across-the-board increse	New rate under across-the-board increase
1	3.18	.19	3.37	.27	3.45
	.26		.275†		.26
2	3.44	.205	3.645	.27	3.71
	.31		.33		.31
3	3.75	.225	3.975	.27	4.02
	.36		.38		.36
4	4.11	.245	4.355	.27	4.38
	.41		.435		.41
5	4.52	.27	4.79	.27	4.79
	.46		.49		.46
6	4.98	.30	5.28	.27	5.25
	.51		.54		.51
7	5.49	.33	5.82	.27	5.76
	.56		.59		.56
8	6.05*	.36	6.41*	.27	6.32‡

*The differential between grades one and eight has been maintained at 90 percent—that is, grade eight is 90 percent larger than grade one.

†The differential between grades has increased also by six percent. .06 of 26 cents is .015. Adding .26 and .015 equals .275.

‡The differential between grades one and eight has shrunk to 83 percent.

the adjustment should be made to the master wage schedule on a percentage basis. This is necessary if the original increment between jobs is to be maintained.

Example: Many labor agreements specify that when the cost of living index changes the wage rate should be changed accordingly. For instance, if the Consumer Price Index goes from 184.6 to 186.1, this is a gain of 1.5 index points for this particular time period. The adjustment in the wage schedule can be made in one of two ways.

1. Grant a percentage increase based on the change in the Consumer Price Index. Since the CPI increased from 184.6 to 186.1, this is an increase of 0.0081 percent. Each pay grade would be increased by

this amount. In referring to the wage rate in Fig. 18.1, this would mean an increase of 25 cents for pay grade one at $3.18 and a 5-cent increase for grade eight at the $6.05 rate. The increment between the pay grades has been maintained.

2. Write a policy or negotiate with the union a clause that states that for every .5 of one index point change, a one-cent adjustment will be made to each pay grade. (.5 was arbitrarily chosen as an example—this could be .2, .3, .4, etc. or whatever level that is negotiated with the union). In the example given, this would result in a three-cent across-the-board increase (a three-cent increase to each pay grade: 1.5 change in index points divided by .5 = 3 cents).

As stated earlier, an across-the-board increase will narrow the increment between the pay grades.

Record Keeping

In addition to adjusting the hourly pay grade each company should maintain good records on the payment of all fringe benefits. Knowing the "total" cost of having an employee on the payroll is essential if a company is to properly manage the total compensation of their employees. Figure 18.2 shows a summary of the cost of the fringe benefits for a company for a one year period.

By completing the survey of fringe benefit costs each year a company will be able to determine the total cost of "labor" as well as being able to compare one year with a previous year's costs. By having this completed form, the company also will be able to calculate additional new costs for any of the fringe benefits. The previous year's expenditures indicate the level that the existing benefits already cost.

Salary Administration of Rate Ranges

In Chapter 17 examples were given on using the overlapping wage structure. This type of structure is used quite frequently in payment of office employees and is used nearly 100 percent in compensating management employees. Figures 18.3 and 18.4 display an overlapping salary schedule. The overlapping is brought about by having a salary range in each pay grade. The midpoint is considered the proper value for the job. The minimum and maximum rates are used to allow placing an inexperienced employee on the job and to allow him or her to "grow"

Fig. 18.2
Cost of Fringe Benefits

Survey of Fringe Benefit Costs — Hourly Employees	Instructions: Prepare 8 copies

Location _____ Calendar year _____

1. Gross payroll (total earnings of all hourly employees prior to deductions, including vacation and holiday pay) $ _____

2. Total hours worked (include vacation and holiday hours paid for) _____

3. Average hourly earnings (item (1) divided by item (2)) $ _____

4. Average number of employees (add number of employees who worked or received pay in payroll period ending nearest 15th of each month of year and divide by 12) _____

		Total $ cost	*$/hr
5.	Total vacation manhours paid for and taken _____		
5A.	Total vacation manhours paid for and not taken _____		
6.	Total holiday manhours paid for but not worked _____		
7.	Night turn bonus manhours paid for _____		
8.	Overtime premium — daily and weekly		
	Holiday		
9.	Retirement (company contributions to trust fund)		
10.	Group insurance (company contributions for life, hospitalization, surgical, etc., including company cost for dependent coverage)		
11.	Old age and survivors insurance (company contribution only)		
12.	Unemployment compensation (company contribution only)		
13.	Sick and accident payments		
14.	Workmen's compensation		
15.	Funeral leave pay		
16.	Military duty pay		
17.	Jury duty pay		

Fig. 18.2 (continued)

18.	Company picnic or recreation			
19.	Christmas presents			
20.	Service awards			
21.	Free meal allowance			
22.	Clothing expense			
23.	Medical services			
24.	Gloves			
25.	Cafeteria losses			
	Other			
	Total			

*Dollars per hr. is calculated by dividing total dollars paid for specific benefit by total hrs. worked by hourly employees (Item Distribution and Retention: copies 1 through 5 — to Industrial Relations, H.O. Copy 1 — retain permanent; copies 2 through 5 — (3 yrs.); Copy 6 — to Factory Manager (3 yrs.-s); Copy 7 — to Regional Manager (3 yrs.-s); Copy 8 — retain (3 yrs.-s).

Fig. 18.3
Salary Structure with Grade One Starting at Midpoint of 1000 Dollars with a $500-Increment between Midpoints

Grade	Minimum rate	Midpoint	Maximum rate
1	800	1000	1200
2	1200	1500	1800
3	1600	2000	2400
4	2000	2500	3000
5	2400	3000	3600
6	2800	3500	4200
7	3200	4000	4800
8	3600	4500	5400

Fig. 18.4
Salary Structure with Grade One Starting at Midpoint of 1000 Dollars with a $400-Increment between Midpoints

Grade	Minimum rate	Midpoint	Maximum rate
1	800	1000	1200
2	1120	1400	1680
3	1440	1800	2160
4	1760	2200	2640
5	2080	2600	3120
6	2400	3000	3600
7	2680	3400	4120
8	3040	3800	4560
9	3360	4200	5040
10	3680	4600	5520

and thus receive more money. Figure 18.3 shows a midpoint with a 500-dollar increment between midpoints. Figure 18.4 starts at the same level of 1000 dollars, but has only a 400-dollar increment between midpoints. This latter approach, of course, requires more grades to arrive at the same maximum salary level for the top grade. Both approaches show a 20 percent range above and below the midpoint.

There is no set policy for establishing a salary range for each grade. If too small a differential is used, such as eight percent, then the experienced employee would not be making much more than the beginner. On the other hand if 22 to 30 percent were used, the starting rate would be too far below the midpoint (the proposed true value for the job) and conversely the company may end up paying too many employees considerably above the midpoint of the job merely because there was no personnel turnover and no one was transferred from the job. Somewhere between 14 and 20 percent above and below the midpoint is a realistic figure for a salary range. Figure 18.5 depicts the salary ranges as set forth in the table in Fig. 18.3.

Why have ranges? Why not pay a specific salary for any given job? In many respects this is exactly what happens when establishing a single rate schedule for hourly paid jobs. For instance, an hourly paid

Fig. 18.5 Salary Schedule with Ranges

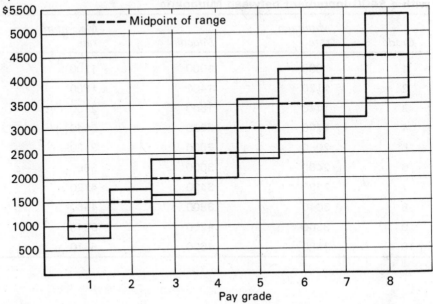

fork-lift operator may receive $4.75 per hour and any employee as-signed to the job, once he or she has completed the probationary or learning period, would receive this amount. If the company had 17 fork-lift operators, all regular operators would receive the $4.75 per hour. This job can be learned in the matter of several weeks or months and additional time on the job will not make the operator that much better. This same rationale, however, is not applicable to many office and managerial type positions. The skill requirement for the job and the complexity of the job may vary greatly. A good example would be a draftsperson. The skill and experience the employee has in drafting will help decide his or her worth to the company. On management positions the need for a salary range is even more pronounced. In fact, it is essen-tial to have salary ranges. For example let us assume that the following facts (Fig. 18.6) apply to four supervisors in pay grade three in Fig. 18.5.

One might ask the question, "What is the worth of an inexperi-enced supervisor?" In the Fig. 18.6, the company is paying Em-ployee D the minimum salary for the job, 400 dollars below the mid-

Fig. 18.6
Listing of Employees' Salaries in Pay Grade Three

Maximum rate	$2400		
		Employee A	$2338
		Employee B	$2126
Midpoint	$2000		
		Employee C	$1760
Minimum rate	$1600	Employee D	$1600

point. Employee C has received a ten percent raise above the starting rate. He or she presumably has been on this job at least a year. Employee B has received several increases and probably has been on this job for several years. Employee A, for a variety of reasons, is practically at the maximum rate and probably will not receive any additional raises other than a general adjustment to the salary schedule. The value of the four supervisors to the company can vary greatly because of their background and experience, thus explaining the need for paying different amounts and having salary ranges for office and managerial employees. Please note that the salary increment in assigning the salary for the four supervisors in Fig. 18.6 was ten percent. This percentage was used only to show an example. There is no set rule on the amount of granting increases within a salary range.

GRANTING INCREASES OTHER THAN A GENERAL INCREASE TO THE SALARY STRUCTURE

There are many reasons other than the general adjustment to the salary schedule for an employee to merit an increase. Perhaps the two most common factors used for recommending increases are for performing outstanding work (merit) or for receiving a more difficult job assignment (promotion). Other reasons for increases are: length of service (longevity), transfer to another locality, reevaluation of the job, temporary assignment that involves different duties, and additional responsibilities and upgrading in a particular job ladder (planned progression for a certain position, i.e., class C inspector to class B to class A).

Merit Increase

When does an employee deserve more salary for doing the job he or she has been assigned to do? This is a very difficult question to answer. Management usually relies on several factors in determining the amount and the timing of the increase.

1. How did the employee fare in the last performance appraisal? Some companies prepare a table, as shown in Fig. 18.7, stipulating the percentage of increase that would be acceptable by the wage and salary administrator. This information guides the manager in submitting requests for merit increases for employees. Figure 18.7 is an example of such a policy.

    The table in Fig. 18.7 applies if all merit increases are to be granted at the same time each year, but it does not give any guidance as to when to submit an increase if a company has a policy of allowing salary adjustments to be made at the beginning of any month during the year. Figure 18.8 is an example of a policy that suggests when to give an increase and for how much.

2. Figure 18.8 leads into the second factor of determining the amount and timing for the increase. How long has it been since the last increase or since the date of employment if this is the employee's first increase with the company?

3. What is the employee's position in the salary range for that particular job? (This is outlined in the example given in Fig. 18.6.)

Fig. 18.7
Percentage Recommendation for Merit Increases

Rating on the last performance appraisal	Percent of increase to be recommended
Fails to meet minimum requirements	0
Meets minimum requirements	4–5
Meets normal requirements	6–8
Exceeds normal requirements	8–10
Far exceeds normal requirements	10–13

If an increase other than suggested above is to be recommended, it should first be discussed with the wage and salary administrator prior to submitting the increase for consideration.

Fig. 18.8
Time in Rate and Percentage Recommendations for Exempt Salaried Employees

EXEMPT EMPLOYEES
100% Midpoint

PERFORMANCE MEASURED AGAINST EXPECTATIONS: / Salary is a % of midpoint:	Below minimum	First quartile	Second quartile	Third quartile	Top quartile	Over maximum
Far exceeds	3 months 10–13%	6–9 months 10–13%	9–12 months 10–13%	9–12 months 10–13%	9–12 months 10–13%	Special consideration on incumbency basis
Exceeds	3 months 8–10%	6–9 months 8–10%	9–12 months 8–10%	9–12 months 8–10%	9–12 months 8–10%	Same as above
Meets standard	3 months 6–8%	9–12 months 6–8%	12–15 months 6–8%	12–15 months 6–8%	15–18 months 6–8%	Note 3
Needs improvement in some areas	3 months 5% Note 1	9–12 months 5% Note 2	12–15 months 5% Note 2	Note 3	Note 3	Note 3

1. If progress is satisfactory, as in the case of a new incumbent. Otherwise 4 to 6 months or re-consider choice of incumbent.

2. If progress is satisfactory as in the case of a new incumbent. Otherwise no review until progress is noted.

3. No review.

4. What is the market competition for this particular skill? Occasionally, because of market conditions, an increase is given merely to keep an employee from being hired by another company.

Promotion (Temporary and Permanent)

Temporary Promotions   Many managers do not feel that a salaried employee should receive additional money for "filling in" for someone who is on vacation or is ill. They contend that this is part of the job and a good learning experience for the employee in becoming qualified for a permanent promotion. Some companies pay a one-time bonus of an indefinite amount not tied to any salary structure; others give a temporary adjustment in salary to the person while on the job. Often this is done when it is known that the assignment is going to be for a number of months, as in the case of a prolonged illness of the person being replaced. Another approach by some companies is to grant an increase earlier than the salary schedule calls for and then to inform the employee that the increase came earlier than usual because of his "filling in" on other assignments.

Permanent Promotions   When a company has a formal job evaluation program and an employee is promoted from Job A to Job B, which is in a different pay grade, there is no question that the employee is entitled to an increase in salary. Usually, with the overlapping pay structure the employee is promoted, at least, to the minimum rate for the new pay grade. If the employee is making more than the minimum rate of the new pay grade, then the increase is fitted into the salary range of the new pay grade. Extreme care should be taken not to offend employees already in the pay grade. This can best be explained by referring to Fig. 18.5. How would Employee C feel if a new inexperienced supervisor were assigned a salary of $1980 just because the previous nonsupervisory position paid $1800 per month? Such considerations must be taken into account when making promotions.

When a company does not have a formal job evaluation program and does not really have a definite job description, the question then becomes whether the reassignment of job responsibilities warrants being called a promotion. There is no clear-cut formula to be used in making this evaluation. One thing is certain—all companies should have some written guidelines or rules established concerning what should occur when a true promotion takes place. Some factors that might be incorporated into the guidelines would be:

1. The promoted employee should never be required to take a cut in pay.
2. The salary for the promoted employee should be increased, at least, to the minimum rate of the new job.
3. The new rate for the promoted employee should not exceed the maximum for the range of the new pay grade.
4. Some ruling should be established that the promotion increase was in addition to any merit increase due. In other words, a company should not make a promotion at the same time a merit increase is given and call the salary change a promotion increase.

Longevity Increase

As stated earlier in the text, the author does not recommend an increase merely because an employee has many years of service with the company, but if it is given, the adjustment should be added on to the basic salary. The table in Fig. 17.10 reflects a method of paying for service (longevity) for hourly paid employees. This type of wage structure is used in many governmental agencies. By adding on as a type of bonus the longevity adjustment the basic salary remains at the proper level. This allows the company to compare one employee's rate with another's. It also is a better figure to use when an employee who has little service with the company begins comparing his salary with that of someone who is assigned to the same job but who has many more years of service.

Transfer to a New Locality Increase

In recent years, certain cities of the country have become very expensive places in which to live; New York City is a prime example. The August 18th, 1980 issue of *Time* magazine states that a two-bedroom apartment in Manhattan rents for $1500 a month [1]. How would this one item affect the transfer of an employee from a small town in Iowa

---

1. Roger Roseblatt (Reported by Peter Stoler). New York, New York, It's a . . . . *Time, August 18, 1980.*

to New York City? Does the company adjust the basic salary for the excessive living costs when the employee is transferred to New York? If so, what happens to the salary of an employee transferred from New York City to Iowa? Is it immediately adjusted downward? Many companies will give a promotional increase, but also give a *separate* housing allowance, parking allowance, etc., which can be adjusted if the employee is later transferred out of a high cost area. There is no established way of handling abnormal adjustment in salary, but a basic principle is that the adjustment should not be part of the basic salary. A similar adjustment must be made when an employee who has been working abroad is transferred back to the United States. Here, too, care should have been taken when the employee was given an assignment outside of the country that an understanding was reached on what would occur when the overseas duty was completed.

Reevaluation of Existing Job's Increase

When there is a formal job evaluation program in existence, the reevaluating of an existing job can be done with a minimum amount of effort. The job is reevaluated in accordance with the rules for the evaluation program and the job is slotted in the proper pay grade according to its number of evaluation points. If the result of the evaluation is an increase in grade, usually the incumbent is placed at least at the minimum rate for the new pay grade. There may be times when the incumbent is a long-term employee or one who has been doing very good work and the pay adjustment might be to the same position in relation to the midpoint of the new pay grade as it was in relation to the midpoint of the old pay grade. Another factor to be considered is how the insertion of the reevaluated job in the new pay grade will affect the other employees already in the pay grade. A questionable placement can make one employee satisfied but may perhaps make eight or ten other employees dissatisfied. Most companies do not pay retroactive salary adjustments because it is very difficult to determine exactly when the important and meaningful changes took place. If management notices the change quickly retroactive salary adjustment is not a problem, since the pay change would occur also very near to the time the change took place.

The problem on reevaluation arises when there is no formal evaluation program in the company. What were the previous duties? How have the duties changed? Is the change significant? These questions are difficult to answer. Without written job descriptions and a written program or guidelines to evaluate jobs, it is very difficult to place a value on the old job, as well as to try to set a value on the new one. Often, under this method, the *job* is not being evaluated, but rather a personal rate had been set for the *employee* on the job. This is especially true in very small companies when the management personnel are assigned a myriad of duties. In some cases, one person might be in charge of the office, the personnel department, and the shipping department. What should happen if that individual also is assigned the duties of overseeing the receiving department? The new duties would be very similar to the duties of the shipping department, and in some companies the same hourly paid employees might be doing both tasks— shipping and receiving. Is there a promotion? The employee is certainly doing more work and having more responsibility.

In practice, unless there is a very significant change, not too many management jobs are reevaluated. Once a particular job is upgraded, other employees tend to become dissatisfied with the placement of their particular job. Reevaluation of a job is supposed to correct inequities of that job and not to create unrest within the department.

If a job is re-evaluated and the new evaluation places the job in a lower pay grade, the usual custom is to "red circle" the rate of the employee on the job so that when he leaves this job, the new employee assigned to the job is paid the re-evaluated lower rate.

Progression Increases

On some technical and professional jobs, the employee may be hired as a beginner and then progress through a class C, class B, and class A grade of that trade or skill. This type of assignment was covered in Chapter 10 on how to write job descriptions when a progression in a skill is used. It is not an easy task to differentiate the following items in this type of promotion:

1. What tasks are assigned to a class C technician and what additional tasks are required to place the job in the class B level?
2. What is the capability of each of the technicians on this job skill?
3. When is an employee capable of doing a higher level job?
4. What percentage of an employee's time should be on the higher level work? In other words, if he or she were qualified to do more

highly skilled work but the work that was available required only 12 percent of the time during the work week, should the wages be upgraded for that employee?

The principle of progression within a certain skill is sound, but applying it to the work force has its problems. Many companies rely exclusively on the passage of time (so many months on class C, class B work, etc.) to set the pay level for the employee. If there is very little turnover on the job, the employees will be upgraded just by the passage of time, but this does not necessarily mean that they all will be qualified for the top-skill rate. Some companies, to prevent this very thing from occurring have set up a quota system allowing only so many A's, B's, C's, etc. to be on the payroll. If the quota for the number of A's is eight employees and there are already eight A's presently working, then no B's will be upgraded until a true vacancy exists.

Processing an Increase in Salary

Regardless of the reason for the increase, all salary increases should be put in writing showing the facts concerning the increase and having the form approved by the proper persons involved. Figure 18.9 is an example of such a form.

SALARY MANAGEMENT AND CONTROL

Many companies prefer to hire new employees at a rate close to the minimum rate for the job because they feel that this is the rate that is proper for the new, inexperienced employee. The remainder of the salary in the rate range is considered by management as a reward for doing exceptional work. Of course, if the new employee has experience in the field, the salary is negotiated with him or her for proper placement in the salary range of the pay grade.

Many companies also stipulate that no employee should be hired above the midpoint of the grade. If for some particular reason the supervisor wishes to hire the person at a rate above this point, it is necessary for him or her to obtain prior approval from the wage and salary administrator. This rule is essential in enforcing uniform hiring practices in a large company.

Fig. 18.9
Recommendation for a Salary Increase

RECOMMENDATION OF SALARY OR WAGE CHANGE	Name	
	Date Employed	Age

Division	Department

Present or New Position (Title)

Former Position (Title) (Complete only if change has occurred since last adjustment)

A M O U N T	Recommended $ per mo. $ per yr.	[ ] Exempt [ ] Non-exempt	Date Effective
	Present $ per mo. $ per yr.	[ ] Exempt [ ] Non-exempt	Date Effective
	Previous $ per mo. $ per yr.	[ ] Exempt [ ] Non-exempt	Date Effective

Reason for Recommendation	Transfer	Promotion	Merit	Reevaluation	Other (Explain)

Recommendation is [ ] is not [ ] provided for in budget	Date for which budgeted	% of Increase

R E M A R K S	Complete this section for promotions and exceptions to budget.

A P P R O V A L S	Originator Date	Line Management Date	Line Management Date
	Divisional Vice President	Director of Personnel Date	

INSTRUCTIONS
Prepare 3 Copies. Forward Copies 1 and 2 for approvals according to procedure. Retain Copy 3. Copy 2, when returned approved, is your authority to notify employee of salary change (retain Copy 2).

The policy in effect on hiring influences what policy a company will establish for granting merit increases. If the hiring rate of a particular company is above average for the area, then it may not grant merit increases as quickly as some company whose hiring rate is below the area average. In a well-organized systematic approach to merit increase, all increases to the operations cost should be budgeted. This necessitates the planning or scheduling of merit increases within the department and/or company. These merit increases are in addition to the regular adjustments to the basic salary structure. Figure 18.10 is an example of a budget for one department of a company.

In conjunction with a budgeting program, a company should also make periodic analysis of the comparison of the salaries being paid versus the midpoint of the various pay grades. This ratio tells how close the company is paying to the midpoint of the range. For instance, if the percentage ratio is .95, then the company total salary structure is five percent less than the midpoint of all the grades. This ratio, of course, could vary in each pay grade. For example: If a ratio were to be computed on the four supervisors listed in pay grade three as shown in Fig. 18.6, it would be computed as follows.

> Salaries of four supervisors — $2338, 2126, 1760, and 1600. Total salaries $7824.
>
> Weighted mean — $7824 divided by 4 = $1956.
>
> Midpoint of grade three = $2000.
>
> Ratio — $1956 divided by $2000 = .978.

In other words, the average salary for the four supervisors was 97.8 percent of the midpoint for grade three, the midpoint being considered as the "true" value for the job. In this example the ratio is below 100, which means that all the employees in grade three average less than the midpoint of the grade. If the ratio were 108, then the actual salaries would be eight percent higher than the midpoint. By analyzing the various ratios, it allows a company to be aware of where it stands in regard to the midpoint of each pay grade and the total salary structure. Ratios can be computed on:

1. Actual salaries paid versus the midpoint for all the pay grades.
2. Actual salaries paid versus the midpoint of each pay grade.
3. Actual salaries paid versus the midpoint for a particular job such as lawyer, engineer, purchasing agent, etc.

Fig. 18.10
Budget for a Department

N. Bartley Manufacturing Company
Accounting Department
Salary Budget — 1980

Employee name	Annual salary	Jan	Feb	Mar	April	May	June	July	Aug	Sept	Oct	Nov	Dec
Kelly McDermott	10,800	900	900	900	900	900	1025*	1025	1025	1025	1025	1025	1025
Juan Gonzalez	14,040	1170	1170	1170	1170†								
New employee						915	915	915	915	915	915	1000‡	1000
Jennifer Pietrini	9300	775	775	775	840†	840	840	840	840	840	840	840	840
Karie McDermott	9600	800	800	800	800	800	800	875‡	875	875	875	875	875
Deborah Pietrini	9000	750	750	750	750	810‡	810	810	810	810	810	810	810
Kenneth Wade	15,000	1250	1250	1250	1250	1250	1250	1250	1250	1350‡	1350	1350	1350
Total	67,740	5645	5645	5645	5710	5515	5640	5715	5715	5815	5815	5900	5900

Monthly Salary

*Promotion
†Retirement
‡Merit increase

A company's compensation program may have a very good comparison record for ratio number one above, but could have localized trouble spots in certain pay grades or on certain jobs. By making these various comparisons, the management is better able to properly manage the compensation program.

After making an analysis, what does it really mean if your company's ratio for ratio number one above is below 100? On the surface, this could indicate that some of the following conditions might exist:

1. Recent expansion of jobs in the company—many new employees at the beginning rates.
2. High turnover of personnel creating the necessity for new employees who will also receive the lower beginning rates.
3. The company's hiring and retaining of employees without having to pay high rates.
4. The company's midpoints are set too high for the area.
5. The computing of the ratios might be at the wrong time of the year. If a general wage increase was made to the wage structure, then the ratios would probably be less than 100. However, if no general increase had been made, then perhaps the percentage figure might be over 100.

Control of Salaries Being Paid

One of the prime essentials of control of salaries is that there should be a separate salary curve for each group of employees (non-exempt, exempt, and executive). Figure 18.11 depicts the general approach to the three different structures. With such a salary structure, the company can attack the various problems that affect these three types of employees. It is important to note however, that management must take into consideration the other two salary curves when it is making an adjustment to one of the three curves. There are several criteria that can be used to judge whether a company's salary structure and management is right. These are:

1. Is it able to attract a highly qualified applicant?
2. Can the company retain good workers?
3. Is the cost of labor reasonable for the particular company and industry? Some companies make monthly and/or quarterly reports on labor costs by using such reports as ratio of salary cost as a per-

Fig. 18.11 Separate Salary Scales

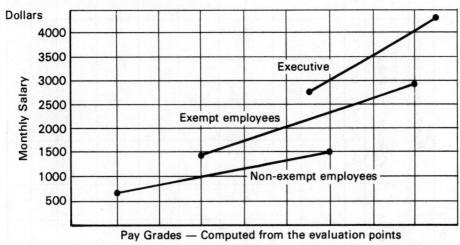

Pay Grades — Computed from the evaluation points

cent of sales, or by merely keeping a record of the number of employees in each category of employment. Figure 18.12 is an example. Firms with an Affirmative Action program are already keeping
records similar to this report.

This type of record not only makes it possible to keep track of the
total number on the payroll, but it also gives a good review of your
status and trends in the hiring of minorities and females.

Some other companies control the number on the payroll and the
amount being paid with a different approach. Figure 18.13 is an
example.

This report is used primarily for a manufacturing unit, and so
attempts to consider productivity as well as labor costs. However, the
form may be adapted to fit any type of business. The items to be
changed would be the categories listed under production at the top of
the form.

Other Items to be Updated Periodically by the
Wage and Salary Administrator

As we know, nothing in business remains status quo. The employees,
the work, and the business environment are constantly changing;
therefore, it is necessary for management to keep abreast of what is

Fig. 18.12
Number on Payroll by Job Categories, Sex, and Minority Grouping

	Total employees in establishment			Minority group employees							
				Black		Oriental		American Indian		Spanish surname	
Job categories	Total employees including minorities	Total male including minorities	Total female including minorities	M	F	M	F	M	F	M	F
Officials and Managers											
Professionals											
Technicians											
Sales workers											
Office and Clerical											
Craftsmen (skilled)											
Operatives (semi-skilled)											
Laborers (unskilled)											
Service workers											
Total											

Fig. 18.13
Monthly Statistical Analysis

Monthly statistical analysis	Month of _____ 19 ___		Location _____		
	Current month	Previous month	Accumulative fiscal year to date		Increase or decrease
			Current year	Last year	
Production					
A. Cases					
B. Tons					
C. Tons shipped					
Labor hours and productivity					
A. Direct labor hours					
B. Indirect labor hours					
C. Total hours worked					
Payroll & personnel					
A. Employees–hourly					
B. Employees–salary					
C. Employees–total					
D. Payroll–hourly					
E. Payroll–salary					
F. Payroll–total					

happening by reviewing company policies and establishing follow-up procedures:

1. To train supervisors so as to be sure they are capable of doing a quality job of performance appraisal of each employee.

2. To establish procedures when employees are to be evaluated and against what criteria.

3. To evaluate the training needs for each of the employees, and to supervise that the training received by each employee is recorded in the employee's personnel folder.

4. To evaluate the type and number of written grievances received by the company, particularly noting those grievances that involved compensation to the employee in the form of wages and/or of fringe benefits that involved pay such as overtime, holiday allowance, premium pay, etc.

5. To review all jobs to see if some of the jobs have changed substantially enough that they would warrant a change in pay.

6. To review the number of employees who are at the top of their respective rate range. Each employee in this category should be studied and consideration be given for a possible transfer to a more highly graded position.

7. To review the use of the computer in regard to recording information on employees. Those companies that have access to computers should attempt to obtain individual as well as composite information on all fringe benefits that the employee receives. This record would give the historical and financial data on each of the fringe benefits. Such information could then be compared to the area practice.

8. Other items involving pay for the employees that should be periodically reviewed are: incentive pay, payment for overtime, payment for premium time worked, pay received as holiday allowance, shift differential, probationary rate, rate paid to handicapped employees, number of days held back before an employee receives pay, and the payment of first line supervisors (some first line supervisors receive less pay than the top hourly employee reporting to them. Should the company consider paying these supervisors extra for working overtime?).

All of the items in number 8 affect the total pay of the employee. They also add to the total cost of the price of labor. By changing the base rate, many of the items in number 8 also are affected and "creep" can enter the compensation picture. "Creep" is a hidden increase in costs. The word derives from the fact that some costs directly related to wages can increase even though no direct adjustment has been made to that item. A good example is the cost of granting overtime. If an employee was receiving $5.00 per hour and he worked overtime, the overtime rate at time and one-half would be $7.50. If, however, the employee received a 50-cent per hour increase his new rate would be $5.50 an hour, but the overtime rate would be $8.25. No adjustment was made to the overtime as it is still time and one-half, but the cost of the overtime is now 75 cents more per hour even though the base rate was increased only 50 cents. Other examples of "creep" are:

1. If the base rate of a certain grade is increased by 10 cents, the overtime rate would be increased by 15 cents.
2. The cost for granting holidays would be higher as the cost of the labor rate increases so does the cost of granting time off with pay. There would be an increase cost in holiday allowance even though no new holidays were granted.
3. If the shift differential rate was a percent of the basic rate, and the basic rate was increased, then the shift differential would increase.

Compensation for Executives

Because of the complexity and the many ramifications of this topic, it is being rather briefly covered in this text. Since complete books are written on this subject merely assigning a chapter or two to the topic cannot review it adequately. However, these two points should be kept in mind when evaluating pay for top executives: (1) the executives' basic pay should be in the top grades of the regular salary schedule for the management personnel, and (2) additional compensation in the form of additional money and/or other fringe benefits should be integrated into a separate compensation program for executives.

Satisfying these criteria is difficult. Below are some of the questions that have to be answered when designing a compensation program for executives.

1. What is the *current* tax ruling on this type of compensation?
2. Who is eligible for coverage under the program? What levels of management are eligible?
3. What percentage of bonus should be paid at what level?
4. What is the best way to evaluate the performance of the executive? Can changing conditions in the industry, the economy, etc. affect how the manager succeeds?
5. What is the formula for computing the award?
6. How will the award affect the company's and the employee's taxes?
7. How does the supply and demand of a particular type of manager (marketing, research, engineer, etc.) affect the program?
8. Does the geographic location of the firm affect the program?
9. Is the market value of the job today taken into consideration when planning the program? What is in the program to allow for a change in the market value of a particular type of job?

When these questions have been answered satisfactorily, then decisions must be made on what extra compensation or benefits should be granted. The following is just a partial list of programs that are used by companies to grant extra benefits (compensation) to their executives.

stock options
non-qualified stock options
deferred compensation
pensions
classic performance shares
book value plans
sales bonus
estate building
individualized compensation package
future service contracts
psychic income

In addition to the above, *very liberal coverage* on the following fringe benefits may also be granted. Here again, granting of the benefits must come under the *current* ruling of the tax laws.

hospitalization and surgical insurance

medical insurance

long-term disability

life insurance

travel accident insurance

travel and living allowance

overseas allowance

housing allowance

automobile subsidy

Because of the complexity of first establishing a company program and then selecting the proper methods of compensation (money, fringe benefits, or a combination), very careful study should be made before installing any program. The program *must be designed to fit the particular current needs of the company.* Texts are written exclusively on management compensation. A suggested reading list is given.

Suggested Readings

Burgess, Leonard. *Top Executive Pay Package.* New York: Free Press, 1963.

Crystal, Graef S. *Executive Compensation.* New York: Amacon, 1978.

Henrici, Stanley. *Salary Management for the Non-Specialist.* New York: Amacon, 1980.

Marshall, Don R. *Successful Techniques for Solving Employee Compensation Problems.* New York: John Wiley, 1978.

McBeath, George and D. N. Rands. *Salary Administration.* London: Business Books Limited, 1974.

McCaffery, Robert. *Management Employee Benefits Programs.* New York: American Management Association, 1972.

Moore, Russell F. *Compensating Executive Worth.* New York: American Management Association, 1968.

Roberts, David. *Executive Compensation*. Glencoe, Ill.: Free Press, 1959.

Sibson, Robert E. *Compensation*. New York: Amacon, 1974.

Review Questions

1. What are the advantages and disadvantages of tying the Consumer Price Index into a wage structure?

2. Should a general wage increase be placed into effect for all employees at the same time? Explain. What advantages would there be to granting certain segments of the work force an increase at a different time?

3. Discuss the use of the principle of supply and demand as it pertains to granting percentage increases to a wage structure.

4. What is the advantage of having salary ranges for managerial positions?

5. Why do most companies have a single rate structure for hourly paid jobs rather than a salary range approach to compensation?

6. In today's business world, why is it good business to keep track of types of employees as shown in Fig. 18.6?

7. Same question as the one above, but using Fig. 18.13.

8. Explain the benefits that can be derived from knowing the information found in the Survey of Fringe Benefit Costs, Fig. 18.2?

9. What is the difference between wage and salary administration and the management of compensation of a company?

10. Why is it important to have three separate salary scales (Fig. 18.11) in a medium size and a large company?

Work Exercises

1. Company A has the following pay grade wage rates.

Pay grade	Rate
1	$3.30
2	3.50
3	3.72
4	3.96
5	4.22
6	4.50
7	4.80
8	5.12
9	5.46
10	5.82

   Prepare a notice for the bulletin board showing a new seven-cent across-the-board pay increase.

2. Prepare a letter to the home for your employees announcing a new pay increase. The increase is for five percent. Use the base rate as shown in work exercise #1 for your present wage rate.

3. The Consumer Price Index in a six-month period changed from 184.1 to 187.3. Compute the rate of increase that would be given if the factor used was one cent for each .3 change in index points, for each .4 change in index points, and for each .5 change in index points.

4. The union at your company has asked for a 25-cent across-the-board increase. This increase is the equivalent of a seven-percent increase. Other companies in the area have recently granted pay increases. After conducting an area survey, plot the results of the survey, the 25-cent across-the-board adjustment, and the equivalent seven-percent wage curves. Make your recommendations to top management as to what you think should be the new wage increase. List reasons to back up your recommendation.

5. Prepare an eight-grade salary table similar to Fig. 18.4 with $800 as the midpoint of grade one. Also use sixteen percent as the minimum and maximum level for each pay grade.

6. Prepare a pictorial display similar to Fig. 18.5 using the figures as computed in work exercise #5.

7. The employees in pay grade seven in Fig. 18.4 receive the following salaries: $2700, 2800, 3000, 3500, 3700, and 4000. Compute a ratio for the actual salaries paid versus the midpoint for the grade.

8. The ratio in the #7 work exercise shows that the employees are not averaging the midpoint for this pay grade. List five items that might be the cause of this so-called underpayment.

19

Reevaluating Present Jobs, Slotting New Jobs, and Red Circle Rates

As with all things in business, changes occur, and they in turn influence employees' compensation, i.e., new equipment is purchased, new processes are placed into operation, new products are produced, etc. Such changes generate changes in the content and duties of a job that can affect the employee's level of pay. To anticipate this possibility of change, procedures should be established for reevaluating existing jobs and slotting new ones. The rules that follow might be adapted to fit each company's implementation of jobs into the program.

RECLASSIFYING AN EXISTING JOB

Any employee and/or supervisor may request that a particular job be restudied. Requests should be made to the person in charge of the job evaluation program. He or she shall see that a revised job description is prepared, and when the company is using the weighted-in-points evaluation program, the following procedures shall be instituted:

1. A job evaluation committee will convene on a specific date for the purpose of reevaluating the job. If no committee exists, then the person in charge of the program would perform this task.

2. Evaluate the factors affected by the job change and assign points accordingly.

3. If the changes in the job content effect a point change on any particular factor, the new points will replace the old point value for that factor and be used in computing the total points for the job.

4. If, in the total point value for the job, there is a point change that moves the job into a different pay grade, the change should be made at the beginning of the next pay period. The assignment of a job to a new pay grade should not be retroactive.

5. A new job specification should be prepared to accompany the new job description.

6. The reevaluated job and job number should be inserted into the index of jobs by pay grade.

In reevaluating jobs under the ranking, job classification, or factor-comparison method of evaluating, the same steps as were used for the original evaluation should be followed.

CLASSIFYING A NEW JOB

In creating a new job, it will be the responsibility of the supervisor and the head of the job evaluation program to complete a job questionnaire regarding the tasks the job will require. They will then prepare a job description and proceed to evaluate the job by using the following steps. (If a job evaluation committee exists, the committee will follow this same procedure.)

Using a weighted-in-points system:

1. The job shall be compared, factor by factor, with the definitions in the manual and shall be assigned to the most suitable level on each factor. The job characteristic justifying its assignment to each level shall be written in the space provided. Where possible, these reasons are not to be copied from the general wording of the manual.

2. The job shall be entered on a factor-comparison chart (see Fig. 14.1) and its rating on each factor compared with that of related jobs to be sure that the rating is in line.

3. The total rating for the new job shall be compared with that of the next highest and lowest existing jobs in the promotional line to

verify that the job is correctly placed or the promotional pattern needs revision.

4. The job title shall be reviewed and revised when necessary for accuracy and brevity.

5. The established procedure for placing the job into effect shall then be followed.

6. All of the above should be completed prior to submitting a requisition for transferring or hiring for a newly established position. Thus, prior to recruitment, a proper wage rate is established.

7. All classifications for new jobs must be approved before being placed in the authorized list of jobs recognized for payment.

When classifying a new job using a ranking, job classification, or factor-comparison plan the same procedure is used as was used originally in establishing the program. See Chapters 3, 4, and 5.

RED CIRCLE RATES

When a formal job evaluation program replaces a compensation program where the employees have been paid on a personal rate basis, it is inevitable that some employees are assigned to a job in a pay grade with lower compensation than the employee is currently receiving. (All employees receiving less than the new rate for the job are automatically increased to the new rate.) If the job is evaluated at grade four, which is rated at $4.11 per hour, but the employee on the job is currently receiving $4.41, or $.30 more per hour than the job is rated, how should an adjustment be made? Usually, one of four things occurs.

1. Every effort is made to transfer this person, who is assigned a red circle rate to a higher rated job whose pay rate is equal to the old personal rate.

2. The red circle-rate employee is paid a lump sum amount (usually the amount is determined by multiplying the cents per hour differential between the personal rate and the evaluated rate by a set number of hours—either 1000 or 2000 hours, depending upon the length of service of the employee). Usually, a red circle-rate employee has many years of service. Because of this longevity his personal rate is higher than that of other employees. Rather than taking several years to bring the personal rate in line with the eval-

uated rate, the employee is paid a lump sum and goes immediately to the lower evaluated rate. For example, if an employee's personal rate is $5.00 per hour, and the newly evaluated rate is $4.85 per hour, the company may give him a check for $150.00 (1000 hours × 15 cents) and immediately assign him the new rate of $4.85.

3. No immediate change is made to the rate, but each time an adjustment is made to the wage schedule in the future, the employee on a red circle rate would not receive the full increase. For example, if the wage schedule were increased six percent, the employee on a red circle rate may receive only three percent. In this way, over a period of several wage adjustments, the employee on a red circle rate would ultimately be brought into line with the regular pay schedule.

4. No attempt is made to bring the red circle rate into line with the regular pay structure. When the employee leaves the job, the new employee receives the regular pay rate.

Review Questions

1. Why is the maintenance of a job evaluation program just as important as the original installation of the plan?

2. How can failure to keep job descriptions current result in poor employee relations, labor turnover, and written grievances?

3. Select one of the four listed solutions for doing away with red circle rates and defend it.

4. How substantial a change must come about before a job should be reevaluated?

5. Should a job be reevaluated when it changes, or should the entire system be updated once a year? Explain.

6. Defend the position that jobs when reevaluated deserve an upgrading, that the rate of pay increase is not made retroactive to the employee. Some companies put a restriction on retroactive pay, such as that it is not to exceed one month. Defend this approach.

7. What are the advantages and disadvantages of each of the four approaches to solve the red circle-rate problem?

8. What criteria would you use in selecting one approach over another in selecting the solution for a red circle rate?

Work Exercise

1. Your company has just completed a job evaluation program. Of 119 total employees, 12 employees are receiving more on their current personal rate than the rate proposed under the new pay grade schedule. All 12 are red circle employees. Five of the 12 have been with the company less than two years and the maximum out-of-line rate for the group is 11 cents per hour. The other seven employees are long service employees; one has been employed for over 30 years. The overpayment for this group ranges from 5 to 43 cents per hour.

   Prepare a recommendation to top management stating which of the four solutions or combination of the four solutions to the red circle rate should be used.

   Prepare a recommendation to top management stating which of the four solutions or combination of the four solutions for correction of red circle rate should be used.

   What other factors might sway your decision on how to handle one or all of the red circle-rate employees?

How Employee Performance Appraisal Programs Blend with the Program

As explained earlier, a job evaluation program shows the relationship between jobs in the company and is designed to establish correct wage differentials between these jobs. This differential is based on an average or acceptable performance by all employees. What about an employee on the job who performs the work in an outstanding manner?

Some managers feel that the job evaluation program already takes into consideration the work being done by an exceptional employee. They contend that the evaluated rate was established fairly, and that, with any system of payment (excluding the personal rate approach), a company could have several employees doing the same job with varying degrees of efficiency. They believe evaluating these degrees adequately and fairly is too difficult. These managers state that the outstanding worker will be recognized and will be considered for promotion to other jobs in the program when a vacancy occurs.

Others feel that some attempt should be made to try to compensate the *outstanding* worker on the *present* job. A wage structure entitled merit rate was shown in Chapter 17 explaining how this can be implemented. In this particular approach to compensation, three wage rates were established.

1. A "hiring" rate, or rate paid during the probationary period.
2. The regular rate for the job—the wages paid after completion of the probationary period.
3. The merit rate—a rate established for compensating the few employees on the payroll who do outstanding work.

The following wage structure (Fig. 20.1) is a reproduction of the first four grades in the wage structure showing a merit rate in Fig. 17.9.

The main question concerning the merit rate approach is "How does one promote an employee to this level in an objective and equitable manner without making other employees dissatisfied and without raising the question of favoritism being used for promotional purposes?"

Most union leaders are opposed to the merit rate wage structure, because they feel it reverts to a personal rate approach, which implies that favoritism may be used by some supervisors. But if a company desires a merit rating program, such an objection can be overcome by judging all employees in the company by the same criteria. This evaluation is done at the same time throughout the company (once a year), and all merit raises are placed into effect at that time.

In establishing a performance appraisal program companies often have two distinct programs. One program for the hourly paid employees and other non-exempt employees, and a different one for management and professional employees.

Fig. 20.1

Pay grade	Hiring rate	Regular rate	Merit rate
1	2.97	3.18	3.44
2	3.18	3.44	3.75
3	3.44	3.75	4.11
4	3.75	4.11	4.52

ESTABLISHING A MERIT RATING PLAN FOR HOURLY PAID AND OTHER NON-EXEMPT EMPLOYEES

An evaluation of an employee's performance must be understandable to the employee involved as well as to other employees in the department. This is not to imply that the evaluation is not held in confidence between the supervisor and the employee. However, if an employee ultimately receives a merit increase, others in the department will probably learn about the increase. Therefore, all merit increases should be defensible against complaints, or under a union agreement, against grievances from the following three areas.

1. From other employees in the same level of pay grade that did not get an increase.
2. From employees in the level of pay grade that the employee getting an increase is joining. Their feelings are that if this employee rates a promotion, then they certainly rate one too because they are superior to that employee in achievement.
3. From employees in the level directly under the employee who is getting the merit increase. Their feelings are that if a certain employee received a merit increase, then their performance is good enough to merit an increase at least to the level of pay grade that the other employee is leaving.

In other words, employees below the pay level, of the same pay level, and one step ahead in pay level are all conscious of the granting of merit increases. Therefore, a careful and thoughtful approach should be made on the personal evaluation of all employees that are being considered for merit increases.

Unfortunately, most personal evaluations or performance appraisals are more subjective than objective in nature. In attempting to be more objective, evaluation forms have been established for evaluating an employee's performance. These evaluations, to be meaningful, should be both valid and reliable. To be valid, the factors should accurately evaluate the performance of the employee. To be reliable, the evaluation process should produce similar results no matter who, within reason, made the evaluation. Example: If three supervisors of different levels of management made a personal evaluation of an employee, each of the evaluation results should be similar to the other two. If this did not occur, either the evaluators did not truly know enough about the employee to evaluate properly or the evaluation process was not reliable.

Validity

Choosing the factors is, of course, an essential part of the evaluation program. As in job evaluation, different factors should be used when evaluating what contributes to outstanding performance of different types of work. Factors that might be proper for evaluating production and office work might be chosen from those listed below. As stated before, the selection of the proper factors for evaluating outstanding performance for a particular group of jobs will either make or not make the evaluation valid.

Volume of work	Safety record
Quality of work	Job attitude
Interest	Maintaining customer relations
Initiative	Adaptability
Job knowledge	Training of others
Cooperation	Technical knowledge
Job experience	Responsibility
Contacts with others	Mechanical skill
Judgment	Aptitude for learning
Work habits	Potential leadership
Dependability	

The number of factors used in any one evaluation program varies from a low of approximately six to a high of ten or twelve. There is not a set number to be established. The factors used should be essential for evaluating the performance of the employee.

Reliability

Too often the reliability of the evaluation comes under criticism not only because of the factors that were chosen but also because of the way the evaluation was conducted.

This can best be understood by looking at the various formats now in existence. In this way each approach to evaluation can be studied and considered.

Rating of 1 to 10 or 1 to 15   In using words such as fair, good, very good, etc., there is a considerable range in the results when several persons are doing the evaluation. One supervisor's standard might be higher than another's, and so that supervisor would rate the employee lower. Whenever several different persons evaluate the same employee this is bound to happen. Another disadvantage in using this approach is that if a supervisor should be transferred to another department, the successor may evaluate the employee much higher or lower, depending on his or her understanding of what fair, good, very good, etc., mean. This tends to make this approach to evaluation not very reliable.

Fig. 20.2

Rate on factors below	Unsatis- factory		Fair		Good		Very good		Excep- tional	
A. QUALITY OF WORK: volume of work regularly produced, speed and consistency of output.	1 2 3		4 5 6		7 8 9		10 11 12		13 14 15	

Some rating forms use the following terms.

improvement required—does not meet work standards

poor—meets some work standards

satisfactory—meets most work standards

very satisfactory—meets all work standards

outstanding—exceeds work standards

The same criticism exists: if there is not a clearcut understanding of what the standard is for each factor, it will not be possible to rate the employee properly.

Percentage Standing in the Work Force   With this method each employee is evaluated by her supervisor in how she stands (expressed in percent) in regard to others in the department and/or company.

The principle involved is good in that only those who rate, on most of the factors used, in the top 25 or top ten percent of the department

Fig. 20.3

Factor	No basis for judgment	Below average	Average	Good	Very good	Outstanding	Truly excellent
		lowest 40%	middle 20%	next 15%	next highest 15%	highest 10%	
Leadership ability							

will be considered for a merit rating increase. The fallacy in the approach is trying to state what criteria were used for making such a judgment. It is difficult to defend a position that employee A rated in the outstanding (top 10%) category and employee B was in the very good classification (75 to 89 percent range).

Four-Step Evaluation Using General Terms   The general terms fair, good, excellent, and outstanding, as defined here are used for the third method.

Fair—performance below normal expectation. Less than completely satisfactory. Improvement effort called for.

Good—fully qualified and doing satisfactory work.

Excellent—above average performance. Ability, diligence and sustained effort producing consistently excellent achievement.

Outstanding—distinguished performance is obvious to all. Excellent ability and aggressive execution of responsibilities producing superior results.

Fig. 20.4

Factor	Fair	Good	Excellent	Outstanding
Work quantity— Are work quantity standards accomplished? How does employee respond to peak loads and deadlines?				

The same criticism of the 1 to 15 scale rating applies to this method of evaluation. Even with the definitions above there is no objective way to defend an evaluation that an employee is rated at the third level—good—rather than at the second level—excellent. What do the terms really mean and how could several supervisors evaluating the same employee agree on their evaluation?

Four-Step Evaluation Using General Terms in Addition to Numbers   The same comments apply to the four-step method of evaluation (Fig. 20.5) as were stated for the rating scale and general terms. In addition, this approach places a numerical value on the evaluation. There is nothing wrong with placing numerical values on the various factors, but it does add another dimension to the evaluation. Who decides and in what manner is the "weight" of each factor established? In the example given, the factor personality carries one-sixth the weight of mechanical skill, and this factor is two-thirds of the weight of the factor quality of work. How is this decision made? Defend it to an employee who did not fare well in the factor quality of work. He might contend that his rating was fair but that he was penalized too heavily in that factor as the factor rating (weight) was too high.

Fig. 20.5

Factor	Poor	Fair	Good	Excellent
Personality—courtesy, ability to meet people, and general conduct.	5	10	15	20
Mechanical skill—knowledge to use the equipment required for the job.	30	60	90	120
Quality of work—ability to perform duties neatly and accurately according to prescribed methods.	45	90	135	189

Forced-Choice Method: Using Sentences to Describe the Level of the Factor   Under this method a brief description of the factor is given. In addition to this, each level is described by sentences showing what the committee had in mind when they were establishing the program. The example given in Fig. 20.6 illustrates the approach.

Fig. 20.6
Forced-Choice Appraisal

Factor	A-1 A-2	A-3 A-4	A-5 A-6	A-7 A-8
Quantity—The amount of work the employee performs.	Output frequently below the required amount.	Employee turns out the required amount of work but seldom more.	Employee usually does more than is expected. Is fast.	Output is unusually high. Is exceptionally fast.

For reliability purposes this approach appears to be the best of the five methods described. The evaluator must make a choice as to which level of description most closely fits the employee. There is no interpolation between grades. The employee either fits in the second or the third level. Once the evaluator has decided which level, the selection can be refined by evaluating whether the employee just barely made that level or was very close to fitting the sentence description for the next level. Figure 20.7 is a complete example of a forced-choice personal appraisal form.

Fig. 20.7
Employee Rating Report

EMPLOYEE RATING REPORT

NAME _____   DATE _____

JOB TITLE _____   JOB NUMBER _____

RATED BY _____   APPROVED BY _____

         30 days ( )   90 days ( )
         60 days ( )   _____ days ( )
         Annual ( )   Merit ( )

INSTRUCTIONS TO THE RATER

Each employee's ability and fitness in present position or for promotion may be appraised with a reasonable degree of accuracy and uniformity through this rating report. The rating requires the appraisal of an employee in terms of ACTUAL PERFORMANCE. It is essential, therefore, that snap judgment be replaced by careful analysis. Please follow these instructions carefully:

1. Complete in triplicate — one copy for employee, one for supervisor, and one for Personnel Office.

2. Use your own independent judgment.

3. Disregard your *general* impression of the employee and concentrate on *one factor at a time.*

4. Study carefully the definition given for each factor and the specification for each degree.

5. When rating an employee call to mind instances that are typical of his work and way of acting. Do not be influenced by unusual cases which are not typical.

6. Make your rating with the utmost care and thought; be sure that it represents a fair opinion. DO NOT ALLOW PERSONAL FEELINGS TO GOVERN YOUR RATING.

7. After you have rated the employee on all factors, write under the heading *"General Comments"* any additional information about the employee which you feel has not been covered by the rating report, but which is essential to a fair appraisal.

8. Read all the specifications for Factor No. 1. After you have determined which specifications most nearly fit the employee, place an "X" in that square. Repeat for each factor.

9. When completed, discuss the rating with your division director and obtain his/her signature.

10. Discuss the "Rating" with the employee involved, seeking ways to improve the areas which might need improving.

Factor	A-1 ☐	A-2 ☐	A-3 ☐	A-4 ☐	A-5 ☐	A-6 ☐	A-7 ☐	A-8 ☐
Quantity— The amount of work the employee performs.	Output frequently below the required amount.		Employee turns out the required amount of work. but seldom more.		Employee usually does more than is expected. Is fast.		Output is unusually high. Is exceptionally fast.	

Fig. 20.7 (continued)

Factor	B-1 ☐	B-2 ☐	B-3 ☐	B-4 ☐	B-4 ☐	B-6 ☐	B-7 ☐	B-8 ☐
Quality—How well an employee does in meeting the quality standards for the job.	Employee's work only gets by. Often makes mistakes.		Work is usually passable. I must sometimes tell him/her to do a better job.		Usually does a good job. Seldom makes errors.		Consistently does an excellent job. Errors are rare.	
	C-1 ☐	C-2 ☐	C-3 ☐	C-4 ☐	C-5 ☐	C-6 ☐	C-7 ☐	C-8 ☐
Job Experience or Knowledge— The background knowledge or degree of skill one has for a particular job.	Has voids in basic knowledge and skills of job.		Has satisfactory knowledge and skill for routine phases of job.		Has a good knowledge and skill in all phases of job.		Has exceptional understanding and skill in all phases of job.	
	D-1 ☐	D-2 ☐	D-3 ☐	D-4 ☐	D-5 ☐	D-6 ☐	D-7 ☐	D-8 ☐
Responsibility— Worthy of a supervisor's trust in carrying out assigned or delegated task.	Cannot be depended upon. Avoids responsibilities.		Unwilling to accept additional responsibilities without protest.		Willing to accept additional responsibilities.		Seeks additional responsibilities.	
	E-1 ☐	E-2 ☐	E-3 ☐	E-4 ☐	E-5 ☐	E-6 ☐	E-7 ☐	E-8 ☐
Judgment— The ability to make reasonable decisions.	Conclusions are often faulty.		Often makes decisions without considering all alternatives.		Action generally based on good reasonings.		Outstanding ability to reach sound and logical conclusions.	
	F-1 ☐	F-2 ☐	F-3 ☐	F-4 ☐	F-5 ☐	F-6 ☐	F-7 ☐	F-8 ☐
Initiative— Being capable of starting or performing a job without prompting or prodding.	Needs considerable supervision.		Normal supervision required but is not a self starter (routine worker).		Does work on own initiative.		Always finds extra work to do or additional tasks sought, is highly ingenious.	

Interest for work—Desire or interest in wanting to do good work.	G-1 ☐	G-2 ☐	G-3 ☐	G-4 ☐	G-5 ☐	G-6 ☐	G-7 ☐	G-8 ☐
	Shows little or no interest.		Passive acceptance—rarely shows enthusiasm.		Has some interest, but enthusiasm is not sustained.		Exhibits great enthusiasm and interest in phases of work.	
Cooperation— One's ability to work in harmony with other people toward a common goal.	H-1 ☐	H-2 ☐	H-3 ☐	H-4 ☐	H-5 ☐	H-6 ☐	H-7 ☐	H-8 ☐
	Resents direction—causes friction in the department.		Causes no friction, but makes no group contribution.		Works well with others.		Goes all out to cooperate with co-workers and management.	
Contacts— Ability to deal with others both inside and outside the department in a friendly and diplomatic manner.	I-1 ☐	I-2 ☐	I-3 ☐	I-4 ☐	I-5 ☐	I-6 ☐	I-7 ☐	I-8 ☐
	Is abrupt, undiplomatic and/ or resentful.		Is mechanical and sometimes resentful.		Is business-like.		Is most pleasing and considerate.	

General comments:

Is job description current (   ) or need revision (   )?

Performance objectives:

A meeting with the employee was held on _____
to discuss this evaluation. A plan of action was established outlining ways to overcome the deficiencies.

Recommendations:

Supervisor _____ Date _____

Supervisor's immediate superior _____ Date _____ .

Copies: Employee
          Supervisor's File
          Supervisor's Superior

ESTABLISHING A MERIT RATING PLAN
FOR MANAGEMENT POSITIONS

Some companies use the same general structure of evaluation for managers as was just explained for the non-exempt jobs. The factors to be selected are all important in making a good evaluation on how a manager is performing. Figure 20.8 is an example of forced-choice factor descriptions used by the military.

Other factors usable for management evaluation are:

reasoning ability	employee development
creative intelligence	knowledge of work
motivation	organizing
judgment	cost management
leadership ability	job accomplishment
organizing ability	analytic ability
human relations	effectiveness in dealing
perseverance	with people
training of others	planning
originality	ability to accept and
effectiveness of communication	profit by criticism
skills	cooperation
industry	decision making
maturity	indepencence of thought
interest	writing ability
delegation ability	controlling

The number of factors used in any one evaluation program varies from a low of approximately six to a high of ten or twelve. There is not a set number to be established. The factors used should be essential for evaluating the performance of the manager. A complete battery designed for a particular department or company could be prepared for evaluating the work performance for the managers involved. Such an evaluation, if properly done, overcomes to some degree the criticism of favoritism in promoting an employee to the merit rate level.

The format in Fig. 20.8 would be acceptable for use by many companies. The factors, or the instructions used, could be changed, however, to meet the specific needs for a particular company. The important thing is that all employees in the system be evaluated against the same factors and that an interview is held with each employee to discuss his or her status.

Although the forced-choice appraisal system is used for management positions, the trend has been away from this approach to one of meeting set goals or objectives. With this approach, objectives are either mutually set by the supervisor and the employee (Management by Objectives) or goals are placed in effect by the supervisor and the employee is judged on performance against these goals. Those who do well are given merit increases.

The remainder of the chapter discusses the use of the theory of Management by Objectives (MBO) as a program for the evaluation of employee performance. This program or a variation of it is a widely used method of management for evaluating how an employee is performing.

To best understand how we can use MBO as a tool for evaluation,

Fig. 20.8
(Source: U.S. Air Force.)

EXECUTIVE MANAGEMENT

| NOT / OBSERVED | ☐ Is a poor organizer Does not really make effective use of materiel or manpower | ☐ Maintains ordinary efficiency of operation Control could be improved | ☐ Gives economy of operation careful attention Makes wise use of manpower and materiel | ☐ Maintains effective economy Carefully weighs cost against expected results | ☐ Highly skilled in balancing cost against results to obtain optimum effectiveness |

LEADERSHIP

| NOT / OBSERVED | ☐ Often weak in command situations At times unable to exert control | ☐ Normally develops fairly adequate control and teamwork | ☐ Consistently a good leader Commands respect of his subordinates | ☐ Exceptional skill in directing others to great effort | ☐ Leadership qualities reflect potential for highest level |

EXECUTIVE JUDGMENT

| NOT / OBSERVED | ☐ Decisions and recommendations are sometimes unsound or ineffective | ☐ His judgment is usually sound and reasonable with occasional errors | ☐ Displays good judgment resulting from sound evaluation He is effective | ☐ An exceptionally sound, logical thinker in situations which occur on his job | ☐ Has a knack for arriving at the right decision, even on highly complex matters |

we first should have an understanding of what MBO really is. From the author's point of view, MBO is all of the following:

1. It is a *planning* device to evaluate what should be done in the future.
2. It is the *setting of goals,* whether long-term or short-term, in a logical, systematic manner.
3. It is a *communicating device* designed for tremendous improvement in the communication process, particularly in upward communications.
4. It is a *motivation tool* because the key to the program is to obtain the *participation* of all employees in working toward goals that have been *mutually* established by the employee and the superior.
5. It is a different approach to *how to direct* the work in accomplishing these goals. This includes a more realistic approach being taken by management in the establishing of the goals and the directing of the work to attain these goals. There is a trend away from autocratic management by all supervisors in the company.
6. It is a *control* measure used by management to *evaluate* how an employee is performing in relation to the goals that were mutually established.

The way MBO is used varies from company to company. Two important aspects of any approach to MBO are that top management must be behind the project and that all management employees should be schooled on how to implement and use the program.

It is virtually impossible to cover all the techniques of Management by Objectives in a part of a chapter. A company that wishes to use this approach should review several ways in order to find the way most suitable for its own particular needs. For that reason, we have included at the end of this chapter a reading list of books that were written exclusively on the subject Management by Objectives.

Example 1   This approach (Fig. 20.9) to MBO basically requires four things to be done.

1. The supervisor reviews each individual employee's job description and records on an appraisal form (Fig. 20.9b) the major tasks of the job. The supervisor also lists on the appraisal form any other points that he or she or the boss thinks should be covered, such as improved housekeeping, safety, cost consciousness, etc.

2. The supervisor th⋯ ⋯ the employee is performing these ⋯ in the right hand margin of the for⋯ ⋯ode to be used for recording in the ⋯

   a. far exceeds ⋯
   b. exceeds norr⋯
   c. meets norm⋯
   d. meets minir⋯
   e. fails to mee⋯

3. The tasks or a⋯ ⋯t receive a high rating are listed in th⋯ ⋯ment Plan (Fig. 20.9c). Not having li⋯ ⋯erformed well does not mean that th⋯ ⋯em with the employee. For two rea⋯ ⋯he employee be compli- mented on t⋯ ⋯g in above-average man- ner. One re⋯ ⋯e employee to continue to perform w⋯ ⋯is to show the employee that good ⋯ ⋯ated so that he or she will accept con⋯ ⋯that may not be going very well. As ⋯ ⋯ployees, it is important to attack th⋯ ⋯ve that area rather than to attack th⋯ ⋯ the interview is to motivate the emp⋯ ⋯mechanism.

   Un⋯ ⋯y item can be placed on the Improv⋯ ⋯he general manager or some other ⋯ ⋯a whole division, department, or seg⋯ ⋯improve a certain function in that a⋯ ⋯area would have that particular item ⋯ ⋯plan form. A reduction in qual- ity c⋯ ⋯st-time accidents might be as- sign⋯ ⋯ area.

4. The⋯ ⋯ee discuss the evaluation and mu⋯ ⋯als or objectives that will improve the⋯ ⋯ee, and four of the improvement pl⋯ ⋯upervisor and the employee. The su⋯ ⋯he performance of the employee, g⋯ ⋯he is able to give to help him meet h⋯ ⋯ent is shown, the employee may at ⋯ ⋯erit increase.

Figures 20.9 (a, b, c) are examples of forms used by one company in their appraisal program for management by objectives. Of course, no program is placed into effect without the proper training of the supervisors on how to do the evaluating properly. A uniform approach is essential if a program is to be a success.

Fig. 20.9(a)

INSTRUCTIONS FOR APPRAISING

Forms P5 and P7 are designed to provide for the systematic appraisal and documentation of job performance for each employee under your supervision. Appraisals are to be conducted annually although a pronounced change in performance on the part of any individual should be so noted at the time it occurs and an employee appraisal be submitted.

The Appraisal consists of:
1. A review and evaluation of each part of the individual's job duties in relation to expected standards, results and goals.
2. Determining areas of strength which can be expanded upon.
3. Reviewing areas where improvement is desired and developing specific plans for increasing his effectiveness.

STEP I — Using the job description as a basis for the discussion, review each phase of his responsibilities. List and write on Form P5 the items which you feel are *most* important. Record your comments regarding performance on eight of the items. Such statements should refer to the success with which each responsibility has been handled. Refer to specific examples concerning which you are both aware. His level of performance measured against expected standards should be communicated to him in accordance with the degree of acceptability and listed in the column on the right using the following code.
1. Far Exceeds Normal Requirements
2. Exceeds Normal Requirements
3. Meets Normal Requirements
4. Meets Minimum Requirements
5. Fails to Meet Minimum Requirements

STEP II — Complete Column One on the Improvement Plan, Form P7.

STEP III — Together with the employee, review the targets and objectives you expect him to achieve in the coming period.

Fill in answers to Columns 2—3—4—and 5 on Form P7.
Consider his recommendations with your own. Objectives which are mutually acceptable become commitments and the extent to which they have been achieved form the basis of the next appraisal.

USE OF FORMS AFTER APPRAISAL

The goals of the appraisal program are two fold.
1. To improve the efficiency of the work of the employee.
2. To give a tool to the Salary Committee to help determine which employees should receive a "merit increase."

To accomplish #1, both forms and the interview should be completed as shown above, discussed with the supervisors, immediate superior and then used in the department for follow-up purposes and a basis for starting the procedure for the next appraisal period.

To accomplish #2—an additional copy of Form P5 should be prepared and forwarded to the Personnel Administrator for his review and filing in the employee's folder. This form together with Form P1 (Recommendation for Salary Change) will be forwarded to the Salary Committee for their consideration for a "merit increase."

(NOTE—Employee appraisal is to be completed each year for submission to the Personnel Division on August 1st.)

Fig. 20.9(b)
Form P5

Name of Employee Appraised	Job Number	Date

Job Title	Employment Date	Rating Scale
		1. Far Exceeds Normal Requirements 2. Exceeds Normal Requirements
Rating Period From to		3. Meets Normal Requirements 4. Meets Minimum Requirements 5. Fails to Meet Minimum Requirements

Make additional comments to explain your over all performance rating. Any unusual circumstances which may have affected performance should be noted here.

APPRAISAL OF INDIVIDUAL TASKS	RATING
Use backside of page if more space is needed.	

Fig. 20.9(c)
Form P7

Date of Meeting _____

IMPROVEMENT PLAN

1	2	3	4	5
AREAS IN WHICH IMPROVEMENT IS DESIRED	What Will Be Done	By Whom	When	Notes on Follow-Up

Action To Be Taken

Example 2 Forms used by a company for Management by Objectives (Fig. 20.10 a, b, c, d).

Fig. 20.10(a)

Employee Name (Last, First and Initial)		Employee Serial	
Position Title	Position Code — 4 Digit	Date Assigned Present Position	
Date Assigned To This Appraiser	Date of Performance Plan	Date of Performance Evaluation	
Location		Office or Dept. Number	Division

Fig. 20.10(b)

PERFORMANCE PLANNING

RESPONSIBILITIES (Key words to describe the major elements of this employee's job.)	PERFORMANCE FACTORS AND/OR RESULTS TO BE ACHIEVED (A more specific statement of the employee's key responsibilities and/or goals employee can reasonably be expected to achieve in the coming period.)	RELATIVE IMPORTANCE

CHANGES IN PERFORMANCE PLAN (May be recorded anytime during the appraisal period.)

OPTIONAL ADDITIONAL PLANS (Where considered appropriate by manager and employee.)

Fig. 20.10(c)

PERFORMANCE EVALUATION

ACTUAL ACHIEVEMENTS	LEVEL OF ACHIEVEMENT	Far Exceeded	Consistently Exceeded	Exceeded	Consistently Met	Did Not Meet
ADDITIONAL SIGNIFICANT ACCOMPLISHMENTS						

CONTINUING RESPONSIBILITIES

(Responsibilities, not covered at left, to be considered only when they have had a *significant* positive or negative effect on the overall performance.)

_____

_____

_____

_____

RELATIONSHIPS WITH OTHERS (JOB RELATED)

(*Significant* positive or negative influence this employee has had on the *performance* of other IBM employees.)

_____

_____

_____

_____

OVERALL RATING

(Considering all factors, check the definition which best describes this employee's overall performance during the past period.

Satisfactory

☐ Results achieved *far exceeded* the requirements of the job *in all areas.*

☐ Results achieved *consistently exceeded* the requirements of the job *in all key areas.*

☐ Results achieved *consistently met* the requirements of the job *and exceeded the requirements in many areas.*

☐ Results achieved *consistently met* the requirements of the job.

Unsatisfactory

☐ Results achieved *did not meet* the requirements of the job.

Fig. 20.10(d)

COUNSELING SUMMARY

Employee Strengths	Suggested Improvements
1. _____	1. _____
2. _____	2. _____
3. _____	3. _____

Significant Interview Comments

(Record here only those additional significant items brought up during the discussion by either you or the employee which are not recorded elsewhere in this document.)

_____
_____
_____
_____
_____
_____
_____
_____
_____
_____

Manager's Signature	Print Name	Date of Interview

Employee Review

Optional Comments: If the employee wishes to do so, any comments concerning the performance plan or evaluation (for example, agreement or disagreement) may be indicated in the space provided below.

_____
_____
_____
_____
_____

I have reviewed this document and discussed the contents with my manager. My signature means that I have been advised of my performance status and does not necessarily imply that I agree with this evaluation.

Employee's Signature	Date

Management Review

Optional Comments _____
_____
_____
_____
_____
_____

Reviewer's Signature	Print Name	Date

Example 3 Forms used by the Morton Salt Company in their evaluation program (Fig. 20.11 a, b, c) [1].

Fig. 20.11(a)

**PERFORMANCE PLAN
AND REVIEW**

MORTON SALT
DIVISION OF MORTON NORWICH

			EXEMPT ☐ NON EXEMPT ☐
EMPLOYEE'S NAME	JOB TITLE		SALARY GRADE _____ SALARY RANGE
LOCATION DEPARTMENT	DATE OF HIRE	TYPE	QUARTERLY ☐ SEMI-ANNUAL ☐ ANNUAL ☐
REVIEW COMPLETED BY DATE	DATE OF LAST REVIEW		

A. PERFORMANCE OBJECTIVES	PRIORITY	RATING	COMMENTS ON RATINGS

PRIORITY KEY: A = CRITICAL JOB REQUIREMENT
B = JOB GROWTH REQUIREMENT
C = JOB ENHANCEMENT

RATING KEY: 1 = OUTSTANDING—CLEARLY EXCEEDED ALL REQUIREMENTS
2 = COMMENDABLE—EXCEEDED MOST REQUIREMENTS
3 = SATISFACTORY—MET OBJECTIVE
4 = THRESHOLD—PARTIALLY MET OBJECTIVE
5 = UNSATISFACTORY—FAILED TO MEET OBJECTIVE

1. Courtesy of Morton Salt, a Division of MortonNorwich.

Fig. 20.11(b)

B. DEVELOPMENT PLAN

    1. MAJOR STRENGTHS List the job-related skills, knowledge and abilities which tend to enhance this employee's performance most significantly.

2. DEVELOPMENT AREAS	ACTION PLAN	PRIORITY	PROGRAM EVALUATION

PRIORITY KEY: A = CRITICAL TO CURRENT JOB PERFORMANCE
                       B = NECESSARY FOR JOB GROWTH
                       C = NECESSARY FOR CAREER DEVELOPMENT

Fig. 20.11(c)

C. SUMMARY

    1. TREND SINCE LAST PERFORMANCE REVIEW:

    Overall performance rating _____

---

    2. EMPLOYEE COMMENTS: If the employee wishes to do so, any comments concerning the performance review and development plan may be indicated in the space provided below.

    I have reviewed this document and discussed the contents with my manager. My signature means that I have been advised of my performance status and does not necessarily imply that I agree with this evaluation.

    Employee's Signature _____ Date _____

---

    3. REVIEWING MANAGER'S COMMENTS:

    Reviewer's Signature _____ Date _____

Suggested Readings

Albrecht, Karl. *Successful Management by Objectives, An Action Manual.* Englewood Cliffs, N.J.: Prentice Hall, 1978.

Albrecht, Karl G. *Management By Objectives, 1.* Englewood Cliffs, N.J.: Prentice Hall, 1978.

Carroll, S. J. and H. L. Tosi. *Management by Objectives Application and Research 1.* New York: MacMillan, 1973.

Marrow, Alfred J. *Management by Participation.* New York: Harper and Row, 1967.

McConkey, Dale. *How to Manage by Results.* New York: Amacom, 1976.

McConkey, Dale. *MBO For Non-Profit Organization.* New York: Amacom, 1975.

McGregor, Douglas. *Leadership and Motivation.* Cambridge, Mass.: MIT Press, 1966.

Odirone, George S. *Training by Objectives: Economic Approach to Management Training.* New York: MacMillan, 1970.

Odirone, George S. *Management by Objectives.* New York: Pitman, 1972.

Raia, Anthony P. *Managing by Objectives.* Glenview, Ill.: Scott, Foresman, 1974.

Review Questions

1. Explain why general terms such as poor, fair, good, does not meet standard, meets standard, and exceeds standard are not sufficient descriptions of identifying an employee's position on a factor for personal appraisal.

2. Explain why the factor used for evaluating production employees' performances should not be the same as the factors used for evaluating the work of management personnel.

3. Define validity. How does this differ from reliability when applied to evaluating the performance of an employee?

4. How is the number of factors to be used in a performance appraisal program established for production employees? For management employees? What number of factors should be used? Explain.

5. Justify to the union the company's insistence on establishing a level of pay based on merit.

6. What are the advantages of having a "merit" level of pay? The disadvantages?

7. What advantages and disadvantages can you list in having more than one level of merit pay rates?

8. Are there any advantages in separating merit and economic increases in informing employees of the pay change? Explain.

9. After an economic raise has been given to all pay grades, when should merit raises be placed into effect? If merit raises are based on performance, shouldn't they be granted each month regardless of what else might be occurring? Defend the position that an employee received an economic rate adjustment and a merit increase at the same time.

10. What is the advantage of using a MBO approach for management evaluation rather than comparing the manager to a factor description as shown in Fig. 20.7?

11. If economic conditions change drastically this could affect how a manager meets objectives. What happens to the items listed on the Improvement Plan if such should occur?

Work Exercise

1. Prepare a factor definition for the factor of work habits. After completing this definition, prepare the four-level descriptions for the factor. The format to be used is similar to the factor on quantity in Fig. 20.6.

21

Conclusion

Questions relating to the amount and type of work an individual should perform and the amount of wages that should be received reflect the source of most employees' gripes and grievances [1]. A job evaluation program provides a planned approach to wage management that is fair and equitable to the employee.

It is imperative that all management personnel support the program, and the more employee involvement in establishing the program the more acceptable it will be to those employees. The employees being evaluated should always be involved in the program development and implementation.

There are at least four different approaches to a job evaluation program for hourly paid employees.

1. ranking
2. job classification
3. factor comparison
4. weighted in points

1. Lytle, C. W. *Job Evaluation Methods.* New York: The Ronald Press Company, 1954.

Which one of these management should select for a particular company depends on the number of different jobs involved, the complexity of these jobs, and the technical manpower available for installing the program.

For a very small company, the author recommends the ranking method using the paired comparison with numbers as outlined in Chapter 3 (Fig. 3.3). For the more complex system, the weighted-in-points method is preferred for the following reasons.

1. The system is free of any bias. A review is made of a job description and this analysis is evaluated against the factors chosen for the program. It is a review of a job, not of the person on the job. In a large company, the committee does not even know the employee working on the job.
2. All jobs are evaluated against the factors chosen and receive a number of points determined by the job's ranking on those factors.
3. The factors are weighted according to their importance, and those jobs that rank high on an important factor (one with a high percentage of the total points) receive more money, reflecting fairly the high value of that factor and that job.
4. It is easy to reclassify an existing job and to "slot" a new job.
5. It is more scientific and more equitable than the other methods and, with the exception of the ranking system, is easier to understand.
6. It is the job evaluation system most used in business today.

Although the weighted-in-points method is mainly used to evaluate jobs of hourly workers, the program will work equally well for evaluating management positions. The selection of the proper factors is the most important point to remember when using a weighted-in-points system for these employees. If the factors are properly chosen, the approach will be successful.

The program is adaptable to a variety of businesses in both the private and public sector and has been successful in evaluating maintenance, service, and clerical employees for a university, a manufacturing plant, a city, and a chain of grocery stores, to name only a few. The same general approach is used in each program, but the significant differences remain the selection and the weighting of the factors.

Regardless of the job evaluation system chosen for implementation, the steps needed to install the system are identical through the first seven. These are:

1. Getting top management behind the program.
2. Announcing and selling the program to all the supervisors and the employees.
3. Updating the organizational structure of the company.
4. Assigning duties to each area or department.
5. Completing a job questionnaire for each job.
6. Having each supervisor review the questionnaires in his or her department.
7. Preparing a job description for each job.

Once these seven steps have been taken, the next task to be undertaken depends on the system of job evaluation that was chosen. The procedures or steps to be taken to complete the job evaluation part of the program vary for all four of the methods discussed in the book. No two of the four methods are alike. They each strive to arrange the jobs involved in a ranking hierarchy, ranging from the job that is the least important or demanding to the job that is the most important or demanding. Once this task is completed, the job evaluation part of the program is done.

The remaining task is the administration of the wages or salaries in the program. Detailed information of the wage administration was covered in Chapters 16 through 20.

After the job evaluation and the wage administration parts have been done, the entire program is complete. However, some managers want, as part of their compensation plan, a merit rate. Because of this Chapter 20 was added to the book. This chapter deals with appraising the employee on the job and how that employee may be rewarded in a fair and uniform manner if he or she is doing outstanding work. Putting these three items together—job evaluation, wage administration, and pay for outstanding work—completes the project for compensating the employee. Of course there are many other fringe benefits that enter the compensation area, but as explained earlier in the book, these are very complex and are not part of the basic job evaluation program.

Glossary

Across-the-board increase   A wage increase whereby each pay grade receives the same amount of increase. Example: An eight-cent per hour increase will be granted to each pay rate effective Feb. 1, 1981.

Area survey   A review made of the wages paid, fringe benefits offered, and working conditions for all of the companies in a particular geographic area.

Benchmark job   A well-known job in the company where there is no disagreement on the price or wage set for the job. Other jobs in the company can be compared against it to ascertain if the job is better than or worse than the benchmark job on any factor.

Box score   A table, similar to the one in Fig. 14.1, that illustrates comparison between the point values of all of the jobs in the program.

Compression   When the earnings of a subordinate are very close to the rate being paid the supervisor. The differential has been compressed.

Differential   The difference in money and/or points in a pay grade scale. Example: Pay grade one pays $4.00 an hour and pay grade two pays $4.17, the differential is 17 cents.

Equal increment   A set amount of points or money between factors or pay grades, such as 10-20-30-40; all have an increment of 10. (See Table A, Fig. 17.3.)

Exempt employee   An employee usually paid by the month who does not receive extra pay for working overtime. The Fair Labor Standards Act determines who is eligible to receive overtime pay. Exempt employees have three classifications: professional (lawyer); administrative (administrative assistant to the president); and executive (supervisor).

Factor   The job characteristic that contributes to producing a result; the features of a job that are important to the success of the job; the basic part of the job evaluation manual against which all jobs will be compared, such as job knowledge, complexity, work conditions, physical effort, etc.

Factor comparison   A method of job evaluation whereby all jobs in this program are ranked in importance on a particular factor. Once ranked, each job is assigned a monetary value for that factor. A summation of the values of each factor designates the total value of the job.

Increment   *See* Differential.

Index of jobs   The listing of jobs into their respective pay grades. A type of a table of contents showing which job is in which pay grade.

Interpolation   Interpolation is the assigning of point values between the degrees already established for the factors. Example: If Degree B was established at 50 points and Degree C was set at 76, interpolation would involve setting a numerical value, such as 63, between these two numbers.

Job analysis   A systematic collection of all information about a job to determine its requirements.

Job classification   A type of job evaluation whereby the total job is evaluated and is then slotted into a pay grade that has been defined. Each job is placed into the grade where the grade description most closely fits this particular job being evaluated.

Job comparison scale   A scale similar to the one in Fig. 5.7 which, when a value is placed on a particular job, allows that job to be compared to the other jobs in that factor.

Job description   A written document to record job content and scope in a standard format; a written description of the requirements of the job.

Job evaluation   A systematic method of appraising the value of each job in relation to all other jobs in an organization.

Job pricing   The establishing of the level of pay in accordance with the procedures for wage administration.

Job questionnaire   *See* Job analysis.

Job specification   A rewrite of the job description listing the requirement of each of the factors rather than listing the duties. The specification is divided into sections paralleling the factors listed in the manual.

Longevity pay   A term used for establishing different levels of pay for the same job. Assignment to a higher level of pay on the same job is based on length of time with the company.

Manual   The finished product of the job evaluation program consisting of the job descriptions, rules for evaluation, factor descriptions (including point scores), the pay grades, and wage structure.

Maximum salary   A set percentage figure above the midpoint of a grade salary range. Usually the maximum salary that an employee may receive for doing good work.

Merit rate   The top level of a wage structure. To receive this rate of pay an employee must receive the recommendation of the supervisor.

Midpoint   The midpoint of the salary range. It may represent the average of an area survey of a particular job, or by some other definition the average pay for all employees in that grade salary range.

Minimum salary   A set percentage figure below the midpoint of a grade salary range, usually the starting salary of a particular job grade.

Non-analytical job evaluation   A method of job evaluation that evaluates the total job and assigns it to a pay grade. Ranking and job classification are such systems.

Non-exempt employees   Those employees eligible to receive overtime pay as designated by the Fair Labor and Standards Act. These include workers paid by the hour.

Overlapping wage structure   Two, three, or more wage levels for the same pay grade. It is possible for an employee in a lower pay grade to earn as much as an employee in a higher pay grade.

Pay grades   In a point system of job evaluation, jobs of similar points are grouped together in a systematic order. The jobs in the same pay grade receive the same rate of pay.

Percentage increase   A wage increase granted on a percentage basis to each pay grade. Example: A six-percent pay increase is granted to all pay grades effective Feb. 1, 1981.

Point rating method   *See* Weighted-in-points method.

Progressive increment   The assignment of weight in such a manner that the differences between numbers increase, such as 10-14-18-22; the increment is increasing by four at each level.

Ranking A method of job evaluation whereby the jobs are placed in a grading hierarchy.

Reclassifying The content of jobs, over a period of time, may change. If so, they should be re-evaluated and, if the change is substantial, be placed—reclassified—into a different pay grade.

Red circle rate A rate of pay determined for a job when the personal rate of the employee, prior to the evaluation program, is higher than the rate determined by the evaluation program. An attempt is made to transfer the employee to a job where he or she will earn the higher rate, or to bring the employee's rate down to the classified rate over a period of several years.

Rules for evaluating Job evaluation manuals last for many years. Consequently, it is necessary to establish ground rules on the evaluation as it was first done, in order that subsequent evaluations can be made in the same manner. These procedures are entitled Rules for Evaluating.

Salary management Keeping the cost of labor in line with company objectives. Keeping records as the number of employees in the various jobs, departments, and the company, as well as each employee's position in the salary range. By using this information managerial decisions can be made on the overall compensation program.

Salary range The establishing of a range of salaries for a pay grade. No set figure is assigned to the pay grade. An employee may receive several salary changes on the same job. Usually the salary range is a set percentage figure above and below the midpoint of the grade. An example is shown in Fig. 18.5.

Scatter diagram A diagram whereby dots, representing individual pay rates, are placed on a graph. These dots pictorially describe the wage rates being paid. A line of regression may be computed or drawn through the data.

Slotting of jobs In a weighted-in-points job evaluation program each job is evaluated against certain factors and receives a point score. After all jobs have been evaluated, they are ranked by their point score. This procedure is known as slotting of the jobs.

Wage administration Establishing the pay scale to the job grades. This involves the original installation of the wage structure as well as the yearly adjustments of the pay scale. It also involves determining whether a program has a single rate or multiple rates in the same pay grade.

Wage curve   The plotting on a graph showing the money values on the vertical axis and the pay grades on the horizontal axis.

Wage structure   An arrangement of wages to be paid in a systematic and logical order, usually called pay grades.

Weighted-in-points method   The point method breaks down the job into several compensable factors, giving each job a numerical score on each of these factors and summing these scores to obtain the total points or value of the job. A carefully worded rating scale is needed for each compensable factor.

Weighting   The measure of relative importance of an item to the other items in the group; a percentage rating of one item to the rest of the group.

Bibliography

American Compensation Association. *Booklets 45, 46, 47, 53, 55, 56, 57, 58.* P.O. Box 1176, Scottsdale, Arizona, 85252, 1978.

Benge, Eugene, S. H. Burk and E. N. Hay. *Manual of Job Evaluation.* New York: Harper and Brothers, 1941.

Benge, Eugene J. *Job Evaluation and Merit Rating.* National Foremen's Institute, New York, 1943.

Berenson, C. and H. D. Ruhnke. *Job Descriptions (How to Write and Use Them,* 8th ed. Santa Monica, Calif.: Personnel Journal, 1976.

Burgess, Leonard. *Wage and Salary Administration in a Dynamic Economy.* New York: Harcourt, Brace, 1968.

Deegan, Arthur X, II, and Roger J. Fritz. *MBO Goes to College.* Boulder, Colo.: University of Colorado, 1975.

Dunn, J. D., and F. M. Rachel. *Wage and Salary Administration.* New York: McGraw-Hill, 1971.

Region One, Education Service Center. *Job Evaluation Manual.* Edinburg, Texas, 78539.

Lytle, C. W. *Job Evaluation Methods.* New York: The Ronald Press Company, 1954.

Management Publication Limited. *Job Evaluation, a Practical Guide for Managers.* 5 Winsley Street, London, WI, England.

Moore, F. C. and T. E. Henrich. *Production Operations Management*, 7th ed. Homewood, Ill.: Richard D. Irwin Co., 1977.

National Electrical Manufacturing Association. *Job Evaluation Manual.* 155 East 44th Street, New York, 10017.

Otis, J. and R. Lenhart. *Job Evaluation, a Basis for Sound Wage Administration*, 2nd ed. Englewood Cliffs, N.J.: Prentice Hall, 1959.

Rush, Carl and R. M. Bellows. *Job Evaluation for a Small Business. Personnel Psychology.* 2(3):301–310, 1949.

Sibson, R. *Compensation.* New York: Amacom, 1974.

Sperling, J. *Job Descriptions In Marketing Management.* New York: American Management Association, Inc., 1969.

U.S. Civil Service Commission. *Job Analysis, Key to Better Management.* 1973.

Zollisch, H. G. and A. Langsner. *Wage and Salary Administration.* Dallas: South-Western Publishing, 1970.

Index

Across-the-board increase, 260, 261
Adjustment to wage structure, 259–267
American Compensation Association, 14, 58, 60, 105–106, 157, 161, 163, 167, 174, 175, 177
Announcing evaluation plans, 86
Area survey, 215–229
  procedures for conducting, 216
  results of, 222–223, 225, 226–227
  samples of, 217–218, 219
Assigning duties to employees, 91–92

Benchmark job, 64–65
Benge, Eugene, 80
Berenson, C., 120
Bias, 78, 185, 324
Box score, 189, 190–191, 192
Budget for wage increase, 276–277
Bureau of Labor Statistics, 216–219

Change in job content, 80
Class, 35–40
  See also Grade
Classification system, 31

advantages of, 40–42
by committee, 31
classification schedule, 33–39
disadvantages of, 42–43
federal government, 35–39
steps for installing, 33–34
wording differentiating between levels, 40–41
Classifying of jobs, 186, 290–291
Clerical, EEOC classification, 117–118
Compensation, 3
Complexity, definition of factor, 156
Confidentiality of work, definition of factor, 171
Consequence of error, definition of factor, 169–170
Consumer Price Index, 261
Control over salaries, 278–279
Cost-of-living adjustment, 260–262
Craft, *See* Trade
Craftsmen, EEOC classification, 118

Definition of grades, 42
Dexterity, definition of factor, 156–157

Differential, 260–295
  computing of, 237
  equal differential, 236
  progressive differential, 236–238
Dual rate structure, 239–240

Education, definition of factor, 167
EEOC occupational classifications,
    117–118
Employee rating form, 302–303
Environment, definition of factor, 176
Evaluating jobs, 85, 184
Executive compensation, 283
Experience, definition of factor, 166
External contacts, definition of factor,
    176–177
Extrinsic rewards, 3

Factor comparison, 55–76
  advantages of, 59–76
  characteristics of, 60
  definition of factor, 61, 63–64
  disadvantages, 59–76
  job comparison scale, 67, 70, 72–74
  listing of factors, 59
  money values, 67
  ranking by factors, 66–67
  ranking money values, 69–71
  use of committee, 71
Factor definitions
  complexity, 156
  confidentiality, 171
  consequence of error, 169–170
  dexterity, 156–157
  education, 167–168
  environment, 176
  experience, 166
  external contacts, 176–177
  hazard, 160–162
  impact of duties on employees and
      students, 177–178
  impact of duties on total university, 180
  initiative and innovation, 172
  interaction with others, 157–158
  job knowledge, 153–154
  level and difficulty of supervision,
      178–179

  management planning, 174
  physical demand, 170–171
  physical effort, 154–155
  practice time, 159
  pressure, 175
  pressure of work, 164–165
  responsibility for directing and coordi-
      nating work of others, 159
  responsibility for equipment, 163–164
  responsibility for funds and property,
      169
  responsibility for processing materials,
      162–163
  specialized training, 168
  supervision and levels and numbers
      supervised, 178–179
  training time, 158
  unusual working conditions, 164–165
  variety and complexity of functions,
      172–173
  work conditions, 151–153
Fair day's work, 185
Fringe benefits, 215
  forms for computing costs, 263–264
Factors, 42, 58, 79
  degrees, 140
  evaluation, 189
  examples, 95
    hourly, 140–141
    managerial, 142
  impasse in grading, 192
  levels of, 183
  naming, 4, 57
  requirements of, 139
  sub factors, 140–142
  See also Job characteristics

General wage increase, 267
Geometric progression, 33
Grade, 3, 5, 42, 61, 79
  See also Class
Grading system, See Classification system
Grievance, 79
Guide rules for evaluating, 183–187

Hazard, definition of factor, 160–162
Hendrich, T. E., 193
Hierarchy of jobs, 15

Impact of duties on employees, definition
    of factor, 177–178
Impact of duties on total university,
    definition of factor, 180
Initiative and innovations, definition of
    factor, 172
Interaction with others, definition of
    factor, 157–158
Interpolation, 80, 184

Job analyses, 6, 93
Job characteristics, 58
    See also Factors
Job comparison scale, 67, 72–74
Job descriptions
    EEOC classifications, 116–118
    examples of, 22–29, 45–54, 131–137
    format for, 115–116, 127–128
    principles for writing descriptions, 119
    terms used on hourly jobs, 121–122
    terms used on salary jobs, 127
    uses of, 120
    writing different levels of skill, 122–125
Job evaluation
    advantages of, 5
    comparison, 4
    custom made, 4
    definition, 4
    methods, 9
    non-analytical, 10, 13, 42, 57
    selection of system, 57
    steps, 10
    supervisor's involvement, 7
Job knowledge, definition of factor,
    153–154
Job specification, 6, 62
    examples of, 196–200
    items appearing on, 194–195
    writing of, 193
Job questionnaire, 90, 93–94
    examples for hourly paid employees,
        96–103
    examples for salaried employees,
        104–111
    supervisor's response, 111–113
    questions used
        for hourly employees, 97, 103
        for salaried employees, 104–106

Key jobs, See Benchmark jobs

Least-squares calculations, 251–254
Letter announcing job evaluation plan,
    86–88
Level and difficulty of supervision,
    definition of factor, 178–179
Level of supervision and numbers super-
    vised, definition of factor, 178–179
Levels within a factor, 150, 193
Longevity increases, 243–246, 271

Management, EEOC classification, 117
Management by objectives
    appraisal of tasks, 312
    description of, 308
    examples of, 308–320
    improvement plan, 313
    instructions for appraising, 310
    suggested readings, 321
    uses of, 308
Management planning, definition of
    factor, 174
Manual, 189
Merit raises, 11, 295
Merit rate
    establishing of, 296–297
    management program, 302–308
Moore, F. C., 193

National Electrical Manufacturing
    Association, 145–146
Non-analytical job evaluation, 10–13,
    42, 55

Occupational, EEOC classification,
    116–117
Office, EEOC classification, 117–118
Operative, EEOC classification, 118
Orientation, 6
Overlapping pay grades, 241

Pay grades
    effect of unionization, 206–207
    establishing of, 203–207, 236
    money differential, 206
    number of jobs in program, 205

Pay schedule, 61, 279
Percentage wage increases, 268–269
Performance appraisal, 299
    percent standing in work force, 299
    using general terms, 300
    using general terms and numbers, 301
    using sentence descriptions, 301
Personal evaluation, 11
Philosophy on wage and salary adminis-
        tration, 231–233
Physical demand, definition of factor,
        170–171
Physical effort, definition of factor,
        154–155
Practice time, definition of factor, 159
Preparing pay grade table, 207–208
Pressure, definition of factor, 175
Pressure of work, definition of factor,
        164–165
Point differential, 203–204
Point values, 203
Points, 58, 78, 151
Professional, EEOC classification, 117
Progression increase, 271
Promotion increases
    permanent, 270
    temporary, 270

Ranking, 13–14
    for medium-size companies, 18
    paired comparison using point values,
        18–19
    paired comparison using X's, 17–18
    steps in installing, 16
    use of index cards, 16–17
Rate of pay, 15
Record-keeping forms
    Affirmative Action classifications, 280
    monthly statistical analysis, 281
Reclassifying an existing job, 289–290
Re-evaluating of job increases, 272–273
Red circle rates, 5, 291–292
Reliability, 297–298
Responsibility for directing and coordi-
        nating others, definition of factor,
        159

Responsibility for equipment, definition
        of factor, 163–164
Responsibility for installing job evalua-
        tion program, 85
Responsibility for funds and property,
        definition of factor, 169
Ruhnke, R. D., 120

Salary management and control, 274–285
Salary range, 265–266
Salary structures, 246–248
Sales, EEOC classification, 117
Scatter diagram—wage line, 233
Sibson, R., 140
Single rate structure, 239–240
Skilled, EEOC classification, 118
Slotting of jobs, 5, 42, 78
Specialized training, definition of factor,
        168
Sperling, Jo Ann, 128
Steps for establishing a job evaluation
        program, 325
Subjective evaluation, 79

Technical, EEOC classification, 117
Trades, 15
Training time, definition of factor, 158
Transfer increases, 271–272

Unusual jobs, 81
Unusual working conditions, definition
        of factor, 164–165
Updating job descriptions, 186
Updating organizational structures, 91
Use of committee, 31, 70, 184

Validity, 297
Variety and complexity of functions,
        definition of factor, 172–173

Wage increase form, 275
Wage regression line, 231
    calculation of, 251–256
Wage scheduling, 248
Wages, 5

Weighted-in-points evaluation plan, 55, 76–83
  advantages of, 78–80
  assigning points, 150
  characteristics, 58
  committee uses, 79
  comparison, 58
  definition, 78
  disadvantages of, 80–81
  examples, 43
  slotting of jobs, 78
  steps in establishing, 82
  weighting of factors, 81, 145–148
Work conditions, definition of factor, 151–153